THE YANKEE INVASION OF TEXAS

NUMBER EIGHT

Canseco-Keck History Series

JERRY THOMPSON, GENERAL EDITOR

The
Yankee Invasion
of Texas

Stephen A. Townsend

TEXAS A&M UNIVERSITY PRESS
College Station, Texas

The paper used in this book meets the minimum requirements
of the American National Standard for Permanence
of Paper for Printed Library Materials, z39.48–1984.
Binding materials have been chosen for durability.

Library of Congress Cataloging-in-Publication Data

Townsend, Stephen A.
  The Yankee invasion of Texas / Stephen A. Townsend
    p. cm. — (Canseco-Keck history series ; no. 8)
  Includes bibliographical references and index.
  ISBN 1-58544-487-1 (cloth : alk. paper)
    1. Texas—History—Civil War, 1861–1865—Campaigns.
    2. United States—History—Civil War, 1861–1865—
  Campaigns.   I. Title.   II. Series.
  E475.4. T69 2005
  973.7′3′09764—dc22

                                        2005021930

This book is dedicated to my son,

Walter Andrew Townsend,

whose history I never got to share.

CONTENTS

ILLUSTRATIONS

PREFACE

$\mathcal{I}$n October 1863 the U.S. Army launched the Rio Grande expedition from New Orleans. The third of four Federal campaigns against Confederate Texas, this expedition was led by Maj. Gen. Nathaniel P. Banks, who had been ordered by Pres. Abraham Lincoln to plant the flag in Texas as a warning to the French in Mexico. Banks was also to stop the export of cotton through Brownsville, Texas. By December, Union forces controlled the Texas coast from Brownsville to the Matagorda Peninsula. By January 1864, however, the expedition had ground to a halt as Banks prepared for the fourth and final attempt to invade Texas—in the Red River campaign.

This book tells the story of the Rio Grande expedition. It examines not only the military activities of Union and Confederate forces but also the fear generated within the civilian population of Texas as Union invaders threatened to overrun the state. It also considers the impact that Federal troops had on events in Mexico, both during and after the war.

$\mathcal{I}$ would like to thank several people who helped in the writing of this book. I want to thank Richard Lowe, my major professor at the University of North Texas, for encouraging me to take my dissertation and publish it as a book. I would also like to thank my family, especially my wife, Jill, whose gentle prodding kept me moving forward. In addition, I extend my thanks to Deborah Reade for drawing two maps that appear here and to Jerry Thompson for contributing a map. Finally, I would like to thank Carol Hoke for her careful editing of the final manuscript.

THE YANKEE INVASION OF TEXAS

To Plant the Flag in Texas

*D*uring the Civil War, the year 1863 marked a turning point for Union armies on the battlefield. The two July victories at Gettysburg and Vicksburg and the crushing Confederate defeat at Chattanooga marked the beginning of the end for the Confederacy. Pres. Abraham Lincoln had waited a long time for such victories to come. Perhaps the Union would be preserved after all.

Despite the major victories of 1863, Lincoln worried about those things that might allow the Confederacy to continue the struggle. Although the Confederacy had been cut in two by the Union victories at Vicksburg and Port Hudson, states west of the Mississippi River still caused grave concern for him. The one state that presented the most problems was Texas.

Despite the best efforts of the Union blockade, Lincoln could not stem the flow of cotton out of the Lone Star State. If one thing could keep the Confederacy alive, it would be its ability to export cotton. This vital commodity allowed the Confederacy to trade for war materials it desperately needed. Lincoln believed he had to stop this activity if he expected to hasten the end of the Civil War. The area where active cotton trading took place was in the lower Rio Grande Valley, and the two principal cities involved in the trade were Brownsville, Texas, and Matamoros, Mexico, directly across the river. Located at the mouth of the river on the Mexican side was the town of Bagdad, the port of entry for goods assigned to northern Mexico. Used as early as 1780 as a port of entry, it never grew large until the Civil War transformed it into a bustling center of commerce. Bagdad offered tolerable anchorage and harbor facilities for the numerous vessels that crowded its waters. Many accounts indicated that a state of lawlessness existed in Bagdad, a characteristic common to many boomtowns. Once goods were unloaded at Bagdad, they were carted thirty miles west over bad roads to Matamoros. Many of these supplies were then ferried across the river to Brownsville. The

Mexican government levied a duty of 12.5 percent on all merchandise destined for export before it was allowed to be ferried to Brownsville. The primary Confederate export, cotton, would return to Bagdad by the same route, with the Mexican government collecting import duties this time. The twin cities of Matamoros and Brownsville were the major centers of the trans-Mississippi cotton trade with Europe.[1]

One aspect of this region's geography posed a difficult problem for Lincoln. Half of the mouth of the Rio Grande was Mexican territorial water and could not legally be blockaded since Mexico was a neutral country. As a result, Matamoros, like Bermuda and Nassau, became a sizable depot for exchanging European goods for cotton.[2] This unique international situation and the commercial opportunities it presented were not lost on a Brownsville business called M. Kenedy and Company. Formed in 1850, this firm had a virtual monopoly on steamboat operations from Brownsville upriver to Rio Grande City by 1861, a distance of about one hundred miles.[3] The company, led by Richard King, Miflin Kenedy, Charles Stillman, James O'Donnell, and Robert Penny, anticipated that the mouth of the Rio Grande would become the back door of the Confederacy, through which large quantities of cotton would flow.

When the war broke out in 1861, the members of the company used their steamboats to aid the Confederate cause. In order for their boats to haul cargo for the Confederacy, the company placed their vessels under Mexican registry. Because of Mexico's neutrality, this meant that Union blockaders could not seize their cargoes. When the Union naval vessel USS *Portsmouth* came to blockade the mouth of the Rio Grande, the steamboats hid behind a front of Mexican ownerships and registry that placed their titles in the names of some of the firm's Mexican friends and business connections in Matamoros. M. Kenedy and Company, with offices in Matamoros, conducted business on both sides of the Rio Grande. Even though the Federal blockaders at the mouth of the Rio Grande were to check on all trade, they would not interfere with vessels flying the flag of a neutral country.[4]

Although M. Kenedy and Company eluded the grasp of Union blockaders, another problem emerged for this firm. The Rio Grande, or "Rio Bravo" as it was sometimes called, proved to be a difficult waterway for steamboat navigation. One foreign visitor made these comments about the river: "Many of the turns were so sharp that the steamer, though of no great length, could not be steered round them, but often had to butt up against the banks, which caused her head to bound off and pushed her round, and by backing and repeating this several times, she succeeded in getting round the corners."[5]

The river, about eighty yards wide, had a depth of seven to nine feet. At the mouth, however, it was only three feet deep. This meant that large ocean-going vessels from Europe could not sail up the Rio Grande to Matamoros without running aground. They thus preferred to stay at the mouth and let the shallow-draft riverboats bring the cotton to them. The roundtrip voyage from Matamoros to Bagdad (roughly sixty-five miles) required about twelve hours to complete.[6]

Although reliable land and water transportation in the lower Rio Grande Valley region was available, getting the cotton to Brownsville from Texas cotton fields became a formidable task in overland transportation. Since there were no railroads leading to the lower Rio Grande Valley, cotton destined for Brownsville and Matamoros had to be carried great distances in wagons drawn by oxen and mules. The distance from Brownsville to San Antonio was 250 miles; to Austin, 300 miles; and to the railhead at Alleyton, nearly 300 miles. Houston, the center of the small Texas railroad network, was another 50 miles southeast of Alleyton. What divided these collection points and Brownsville was 200–400 miles of semiarid terrain. In good weather the cotton wagons made the trip in four to six weeks. From time to time, droughts turned the region into a forbidding desert. Depending on the severity of the drought, the wagon trains might be stopped altogether because there was insufficient water and grass to keep the draft animals alive. Usually after a good, heavy rain, the wagon trains would start moving again.[7]

A number of wagon trails led to the region from the plantations of Arkansas, Louisiana, Texas, and even some states east of the Mississippi. Perhaps the most traveled route stretched from the railroad terminus at Alleyton to Brownsville by way of the King Ranch near Corpus Christi. The teamsters broke the journey into three segments. The first extended from Alleyton to Goliad, about 90 miles. From Goliad, the wagon train traveled another 80 miles to the King Ranch. The last leg of the trip to Brownsville covered a distance of about 100 miles. When the cotton made it to Alleyton or Goliad, Mexican teamsters usually hauled it over the last stretch.[8]

Another wagon trail led from Central Texas through Austin, San Antonio, and then to the King Ranch and Brownsville or to other points on the Mexican border such as Roma, Laredo, or Eagle Pass. A third route went through Gonzalez (east of San Antonio) and then on to Laredo or Eagle Pass. Wagon trails existed on both sides of the Rio Grande from Eagle Pass and Piedras Negras southward to Brownsville and Matamoros. On occasion, cotton was transported from Roma to Matamoros by way of steamboat since the

Rio Grande was navigable up to Roma. By far the most important cotton de-pots were Alleyton, San Antonio, and the King Ranch.[9]

A few wagons made the journey at first, but as the Federal blockade tightened at the end of 1861, these few became an ever-increasing flood of wagons and oxcarts on their way to the Mexican border with cotton to be ex-ported on European ships. They came in such numbers that the Alleyton-to-Brownsville trail was called the Cotton Road.[10] Although exact statistics are few, observers of the Texas cotton trade during the Civil War described one common characteristic: The trade was indeed heavy. One account of this cot-ton traffic came from a British officer, Lt. Col. A. J. L. Fremantle, who visited the settlement of Bagdad at the mouth of the Rio Grande in the spring of 1863. He estimated that seventy vessels were there receiving cotton from two small steamboats. He wrote that, on the banks of the Rio Grande, "for an immense distance endless bales of cotton are to be seen." The celebrated blockade runner William Watson portrayed a similar scene also in the spring of 1863. He noted that at the mouth of the Rio Grande nothing indicated a port or city, but off the coast for a distance of about four miles a fleet of nearly one hundred ships of various sizes were loading and unloading cargo.[11]

Additional accounts from civilian, military, and government officials de-scribed the Brownsville-Matamoros region as a bustling commercial center. A diplomat at the consulate in Matamoros called that city the "great thor-oughfare" to the Southern states. Lookouts aboard Union blockaders at times counted hundreds of ships at the mouth of the river. A Union news-paper writer estimated that, early in 1863, supplies worth four million dol-lars were funneled through Matamoros each month. In June 1864 the city of San Antonio experienced so much wagon traffic that it was forced to levy a tax on each bale carried through its streets to help pay for road repair and for the removal of dead animals abandoned by the wagon trains heading southward.[12]

The last months of the war brought no decrease in the Brownsville-Matamoros cotton trade. Maj. Gen. Lew Wallace, a Union officer on a mis-sion of peace to Texas, described the commercial activity at the mouth of the Rio Grande in a letter to his wife on March 5, 1865: "I find on examination that reports of the extent of trade in progress at Matamoros are not exagger-ated. From the deck of this steamer I can look towards the mouth of the Rio Grande, scarcely nine miles away, and see more vessels than are to be seen any one day in the harbor of Baltimore, all foreign vessels, loading and un-loading cargoes, of which about one-eighth only goes legitimately into Mex-ico. The rest is consigned to Matamoros for the rebel authorities in Texas.

Cotton routes to the Rio Grande. Map by Deborah Reade.

Matamoros is crowded with goods—in fact, skillful judges say there are more in store there than the city of New Orleans. Another evidence of incompetency on our side."[13]

During the four years of the Civil War, Matamoros served primarily as a Confederate port and prospered as a result of this voluminous trade. Cotton sold for fifty cents a pound in gold—about five times its prewar price. In some months, cotton worth four million dollars was exported. The two factors that contributed to the increased cotton trade were the Federal blockade of the Confederate ports and the great shortage of cotton in Europe. The traffic in cotton was so heavy that the area's Mexican population referred to this era as "los algodones"—"the time of the cotton."[14]

The growing magnitude of the commerce in the Brownsville-Matamoros area alarmed the Lincoln administration, which received reports that thousands of bales were being stored in Texas for later export. Disrupting this trade and capturing the stored bales would help the Union cause in two ways, Lincoln realized. First, the Confederacy would be denied this means of sustaining its war effort. Second, the cotton from Texas could be used by textile mills in the North, which desperately needed a reliable and steady supply of the fiber.[15]

Pressure for a military expedition to Texas to gather cotton for the North came from a group called the National War Committee of the Citizens of New York. Its members were prominent Republican merchants who represented New York's economic interests. Texas cotton would revitalize their state's economy. They used the influence of Andrew Jackson Hamilton, a prominent Texas Unionist, to further their goals. Escaping from Texas into Mexico in the summer of 1862, Hamilton achieved hero status when he arrived in New York in September of that year.[16]

A delegation met with Lincoln on October 9, 1862, to discuss the possibility of a military campaign against Texas. The group included members of the New York war committee, A. J. Hamilton, and other Texans. Hamilton informed Lincoln that a Federal force of about five thousand troops would be sufficient to conquer the Lone Star State. Once these soldiers landed at the mouth of the Rio Grande, Texas Unionists would flock to them and join them in restoring Union rule in the state. This force would also disrupt the Confederate exchange of cotton for contraband on the Rio Grande. In addition, the delegation reminded Lincoln that the cotton shortage in the Northeast had prevented military contracts from being filled, thus hurting the Union war effort. Finally, Hamilton informed Lincoln that Union control of the cotton trade in Texas might attract rebels back into the Union by giving them an outlet to sell their cotton.[17]

Although the political union between North and South had been severed, cotton was indeed the fabric that still held it together economically. Even though the Confederacy was at war with the Union, the Confederates continued to trade with the North for war supplies. Merchants in cities under Union control, such as New York and New Orleans, traded actively with the port at Matamoros. Before 1861, a clearance from New York to Matamoros had been given only about once a year, but between August 1861 and March 1864, 152 vessels with an aggregate tonnage of thirty-five thousand and laden with large cargoes had been cleared from New York for that destination. This trade between New York and Matamoros continued throughout the war and in the latter part of 1864 was reputed to be "heavy and profitable." Even Confederate Gen. Hamilton P. Bee, the officer in charge of guarding Brownsville from the Union army in 1863, claimed that pistols and carbines could be bought in New York and shipped to Matamoros to supply the Confederate troops in the Brownsville area.[18] When the Union generals protested to Lincoln about this illicit trade, he related to one general that the war had raised the gold price of cotton to six times its prewar level. This enabled the South to earn as much foreign exchange from the export of one bale through the blockade as it would have earned from six bales in peacetime. Every cotton bale that came into Union lines, even by means of "private interest and pecuniary greed," was one less bale for the South to export. Lincoln then stated, "Better give him guns for it than let him, as now, get both guns and ammunition for it."[19] Occupying the lower Rio Grande Valley offered Lincoln an opportunity not only to disrupt the Confederate export of cotton but also to procure that cotton for the Union cause.

Other factors also prodded Lincoln to action with regard to Texas. When civil war distracted the United States in 1861, Great Britain, Spain, and primarily France moved into Mexico in hopes of establishing a government there that would force that nation to pay off its large foreign debt. Mexico's new leader, Benito Juarez, had suspended payments to all foreign creditors. When Great Britain and Spain discovered that France had visions of setting up an empire in Mexico, they left France alone to operate there. The French leader Napoleon III had dreamed of a second glorious age for the Bonapartes and France. Since the United States was engulfed in its own civil war, it could do nothing to aid Juarez in his resistance to the French invasion of Vera Cruz in 1861.[20]

French control of Mexico would put a European power on the border of Confederate Texas, raising the possibility of European meddling in the Civil War. Secretary of State William H. Seward knew that the best way to prevent a Franco-Confederate alliance would be to occupy Texas, and in March 1862 he urged such a course. The longer the French stayed in Mexico, the greater was the urgency of the dispatches from American diplomats overseas. Charles Francis Adams, U.S. minister to Britain, sent Seward a dispatch on May 1, 1863, that strongly recommended the occupation of Texas. When French armies occupied Mexico City on June 7, 1863, the military occupation of Texas became a national concern.[21]

While Juarez suffered through his most difficult time in Mexico, Lincoln experienced his most victorious summer of the war with the Union successes at Gettysburg, Vicksburg, and Port Hudson. Nonetheless, Lincoln feared that these victories would make the Confederacy more desperate in its pursuit of a foreign alliance. In a letter to Secretary of War Edwin M. Stanton on July 29, 1863, Lincoln conveyed the necessity of occupying Texas. The president asked Stanton, "Can we not renew the effort to organize a force to go to Western Texas? I believe no local object is now more desirable."[22]

On August 5, 1863, Lincoln sent a similar letter to Maj. Gen. Nathaniel P. Banks, commander of the Department of the Gulf at New Orleans.[23] Lincoln congratulated Banks on his victory at Port Hudson but also stated that "recent events in Mexico, I think render early action in Texas more important than ever." Finally, on August 9, 1863, Lincoln sent a dispatch to Maj. Gen. Ulysses S. Grant, commander of the Army of the Tennessee. Grant wanted to follow up his victory at Vicksburg with a campaign against Mobile. Lincoln urgently informed Grant that "in view of recent events in Mexico, I am greatly impressed with the importance of reestablishing the national authority in Western Texas as soon as possible."[24] These letters to Stanton, Banks, and Grant clearly indicate that Lincoln wanted to neutralize the French threat in Mexico by occupying Texas and preventing a possible Franco-Confederate alliance. Too much had been gained in the summer of 1863 to lose it all by allowing foreign intervention on behalf of the Confederacy.

Political pressures also prodded Lincoln to reclaim Texas. When the Lone Star State seceded, not all Texans supported the Confederacy. Hamilton's Texas Unionists, not to mention northeastern capitalists, roamed the corridors of the capitol building in Washington, begging for a Federal army to liberate Texas.[25] Hamilton's first meeting with Lincoln may have been as early as August 1862. A letter from Lincoln to Stanton dated August 4, 1862, mentions "these Texas gentlemen" who wanted an invasion force sent to the Rio Grande to reestablish the national authority there. The chances for a Federal invasion of Texas greatly improved by October 1862. On October 9 a delegation including Hamilton and other groups met with Lincoln. Hamilton urged Lincoln to send a Federal army to the mouth of the Rio Grande. This military expedition to liberate Texas would incite a mass uprising among the state's countless loyal citizens, who would then join the Federal army and help liberate Texas from Confederate rule. The restoration of Texas to the Union would deliver a staggering propaganda blow to the Confederacy. Hamilton talked with Lincoln again on November 8. Hamilton's desire to liberate Texas clearly impressed Lincoln, and by November 14, the president had appointed him military governor of his state with the rank of brigadier general.[26]

While Hamilton lobbied in Washington for a Texas invasion, a small Federal naval force of five ships captured Galveston Island on October 5, 1862.

This small fleet and about three hundred Union infantry held the island for the remainder of 1862. Hamilton's hopes of reestablishing Federal authority in Texas in early 1863 were disappointed when Confederate Brig. Gen. John B. Magruder recaptured Galveston on January 1, 1863. In New Orleans, Hamilton badgered General Banks to send more Union troops to Galveston. These troops, representing the 1st Texas Cavalry (Union), were almost captured by Magruder when they arrived off Galveston on January 4, 1863. The 1st Texas Cavalry quickly sailed back to New Orleans after they discovered that Galveston was in Confederate hands once again.[27]

The loss of Galveston did not decrease Hamilton's desire to reclaim Texas for the Union. Hamilton now urged Banks to undertake the invasion plan Hamilton had long wanted, an assault at the mouth of the Rio Grande. In the spring of 1863, Hamilton returned to Washington for another round of lobbying on behalf of Texas' liberation. Events in the summer of 1863 made an invasion of Texas more urgent than ever. Important Union victories, not to mention the French capture of Mexico City, gave Hamilton the necessary lobbying ammunition to persuade Lincoln himself to begin pushing for a Texas incursion. Letters between high-ranking government and military officials in July and August 1863 clearly indicate that an aggressive entrance into Texas was indeed in the making.[28]

The Union army officer assigned the task of invading and conquering Texas in 1863 was Maj. Gen. Nathaniel P. Banks. Shortly after assuming command of the Department of the Gulf in November 1862, Banks received instructions from General in Chief Henry W. Halleck. At the time of Halleck's appointment, the Union army controlled the Mississippi River north of Vicksburg and the area near New Orleans. Banks's most important objective would be the capture of Vicksburg with the able assistance of Maj. Gen. Ulysses S. Grant. Once Vicksburg was captured, Banks would proceed eastward and attack Mobile, one of the few ports on the Gulf coast capable of handling oceangoing vessels. Banks anticipated sending a force of about twenty-five thousand men against Mobile. After Mobile, Halleck wanted Banks to take Union forces and gain control of the Red River. If Banks was successful on the Red River, Union armies could then move into the eastern part of Texas. Halleck indeed gave Banks sound military advice.[29]

Lincoln modified Union strategy in the Gulf Department in order to show the flag in Texas as a warning to the French. Federal authorities deemed this necessary to discourage any idea that the French might have had of aiding the Confederacy from Mexico. Lincoln wanted Banks to organize a force to go to western Texas, a region referred to today as South Texas, from Austin to the Rio Grande. An attack against Mobile would have to wait. South Texas now became the top priority within the Department of the Gulf.[30]

The planning of a Texas invasion proved to be a strategic dilemma for Banks. Lincoln wanted him to carry out an incursion into Texas to accomplish goals other than military ones. Regrettably, Banks received conflicting information from those above him. General Halleck first suggested a landing on the Texas coast at either Galveston or Indianola. He later recanted this advice to Banks in a dispatch dated August 10, 1863. Although conceding that the army's mission in Texas had become more diplomatic than military, Halleck seized upon a phrase from Secretary of State Seward, stressing that the flag be restored to "some one point in Texas." This gave Halleck the necessary flexibility he sought in issuing orders to Banks. Halleck now stressed a combined army and navy movement up the Red River Valley to Shreveport, culminating eventually in an occupation of northeast Texas.[31]

At this stage of the operation, Banks perceived the difficulty of having a civilian commander in Lincoln and a military commander in Halleck. Since the start of the Civil War, the Lincoln administration had worked diligently to keep European powers from intervening. Diplomatically, U.S. soldiers positioned on the Mexican border would be far more effective in sending a message to the French than would troops stationed in northeast Texas. Lincoln clearly wanted Banks to concentrate on "Western Texas," thus emphasizing the diplomatic nature of an expedition to the state. Lincoln, however, left the military planning of the mission in the hands of Banks and Halleck. Since Banks was a "political" general and not a professional soldier, he was unsure of his own military ability. As a result, he was easily intimidated by professional soldiers such as Halleck.[32]

In the dispatch Halleck sent to Banks on August 10, 1863, he talked of the diplomatic nature of a Texas invasion but stressed the Red River Valley as the best route for Banks to follow to invade Texas. This message mentioned only that the flag should be restored at some point in Texas. Halleck therefore wanted to attack Texas via the Red River Valley through Louisiana. From a military point of view, his plan had some arguments in its favor. First, an invasion up the Red River Valley would not have to depend on a tenuous seaborne supply line. Second, the cotton and granary of East Texas would be a far more valuable prize than the South Texas brush country.

Other arguments could be raised in opposition, however. The strong Confederate forces in the Red River Valley would certainly contest a Union invasion. In addition, an overland campaign would be slow and tedious, and

Steel engraving of Maj. Gen. Nathaniel P. Banks. Property of the author.

since the Red River was nowhere near "Western Texas," an incursion aimed at Shreveport would do little to influence the French in Mexico. Once he stated his opinion for Banks's benefit, Halleck then abdicated responsibility for the conduct of Banks's expedition to Texas. He never ordered Banks to take a specific course of action there. The general in chief would tell Banks his military opinions, but Halleck always left himself a way out by emphasizing that his comments were suggestive in nature and not actual orders. For example, on August 10, 1863, Halleck stated, "I write this simply as a suggestion and not as military instructions." These vaguely worded messages allowed Halleck to take full credit for a military operation if it succeeded or to censure a commander for his failure if he neglected Halleck's advice. In the end Halleck placed the responsibility for any action taken against Texas squarely on General Banks.[33]

By mid-August, Banks had decided on his course of action. His strategy called for an assault against southeast Texas. Banks believed that the rebellion in Louisiana was kept alive by the military support of Texas. The Galveston-Houston area was indeed a major dispersal point for supplies coming in from Europe. Banks's tactic was to call for troops on naval transports to land near Sabine City, Texas, on the Louisiana border. From there they could dash into nearby Galveston and Houston from the north and east. Banks knew that the Confederates were already anticipating this attack but believed his troops could smash through the Texas defenses. The plan to invade southeast Texas did not totally ignore diplomatic issues. Once Galveston was secured, Banks planned to send an expeditionary force of five thousand men to the Rio Grande to establish a Union presence there.[34]

The campaign began in September 1863 with the Union's ill-fated assault against Sabine Pass. On September 4, 1863, five thousand men of the XIX Army Corps under the command of Maj. Gen. William B. Franklin left New Orleans bound for Sabine Pass. The twenty troop transports were escorted by four gunboats (the *Sachem, Arizona, Granite City,* and *Clifton*). The invasion force under Franklin arrived at Sabine Pass on September 6 but did not attack until two days later. The invaders were supposed to disembark about twelve miles below Sabine City. Instead, Franklin decided upon a frontal assault by attacking the lightly defended Fort Griffin, which was guarding Sabine City. The fort was protected by Lt. Richard Dowling and forty-two men of the 1st Texas Artillery Regiment. After losing two Union gunboats and suffering 380 casualties, Franklin broke off the attack. Instead of making a second attempt to land troops, the mentally beaten Franklin ordered the expedition back to New Orleans. Banks's first attempt to invade Texas ended miserably.[35]

After the defeat at Sabine Pass, Banks determined that he would attack Texas by an overland path. Union troops could move into Texas by two routes. They could advance across southern Louisiana toward the lower Sabine River or by way of the Red River into northeastern Texas. General Franklin, who had commanded the assault against Sabine Pass, was given command of this overland expedition. Franklin left New Orleans with an army of about thirty thousand men. Advancing westward across southern Louisiana, Franklin could decide whether he wanted to continue westward toward the Sabine or turn northward and follow the Red River into Texas. By October 10,

1863, Union soldiers occupied Vermilionville (present-day Lafayette) and then continued north toward Opelousas. Several things hampered their movement in this direction. Water levels in many of the major rivers would not allow supply boats to reach Franklin's army. The Confederates who retreated in the path of Franklin's men destroyed all of the available supplies and made logistical support very difficult. By mid-October a Red River advance into Texas seemed impractical.[36]

Once Vermilionville fell, Banks returned to New Orleans and contemplated a two-pronged invasion of Texas. Franklin's advance across Louisiana would draw the majority of the Texas troops toward the Louisiana border and leave most of the Texas coastline lightly defended. One target on the Texas shore that offered multiple objectives for Banks was the city of Brownsville, on the Mexican border. Federal occupation of Brownsville would serve as a warning to the French in Mexico not to attempt an intervention on behalf of the Confederacy. Second, Brownsville funneled large quantities of Southern cotton to Matamoros in exchange for war materiel. Finally, in Brownsville, Texas Unionists would have an opportunity to establish a state government loyal to Washington. On October 22, 1863, Banks informed Lincoln that, while one portion of his army moved across southern Louisiana, he proposed to land troops on the Texas coast between the Sabine River and the Rio Grande.[37]

While Banks planned an attack on the Texas coast, the Union army under General Franklin had stalled near Opelousas and Barre's Landing (modern Port Barre). The last order Banks issued to Franklin on October 11, 1863, essentially told him to hold his position and send out scouting parties to ascertain the best invasion route into Texas. Over the next two weeks Franklin sent dispatches to New Orleans trying to get specific orders from Banks on how his army should proceed. On October 26, 1863, Franklin informed headquarters that he might move his army southward to New Iberia and then attempt a cross-country drive toward Texas through Niblett's Bluff and the lower Sabine valley. While waiting for headquarters to approve this plan, Franklin received news that Banks had embarked on another naval expedition to attempt a landing at the mouth of the Rio Grande. The commander of the expedition would be Maj. Gen. Napoleon J. T. Dana. Upon hearing this news, Franklin decided to retreat to New Iberia in order to have a more dependable supply line. During this withdrawal, a portion of his army became separated from the main body and was attacked by Confederates under Gen. Richard Taylor. This Confederate victory at the battle of Bayou Bourbeau on November 3, 1863, reinforced the idea that the Red River route through Louisiana into Texas might have to be abandoned.[38]

Franklin's movement in Louisiana had put the Confederate forces on alert from Galveston to Shreveport, and, by the time Banks left New Orleans for Texas, the overland expedition had stalled. Brazos Santiago, a small island at the mouth of the Rio Grande, would be the location for Banks's third attempt to penetrate Texas. This invasion would be called the Rio Grande expedition.[39]

All of the Union activity in southern Louisiana ultimately served Banks in his third effort to invade Texas. South Texas was indeed lightly defended. The Confederate commander at Brownsville, Brig. Gen. Hamilton P. Bee, had fewer than two hundred men to hold off a Federal invasion.[40] Even these men, who were part of the 33rd Texas Cavalry Regiment under Col. James Duff, were ordered to Houston on October 26, 1863. Either by design or sheer luck, Franklin's activity in Louisiana had caused Maj. Gen. John B. Magruder, who commanded the Department of Texas, New Mexico, and Arizona, to move adequate Confederate forces to eastern Texas to repel these Union invaders.[41] In doing so, Magruder left Brownsville virtually unprotected.[42]

Banks assigned the Rio Grande expedition to the 2nd Division of the XIII Army Corps under the command of General Dana. The 2nd Division included regiments mainly from three states: Illinois, Iowa, and Maine. Their commander, General Dana, had been promoted to the rank of major general after being severely wounded at the Battle of Antietam. The regiments under his command were well seasoned by combat, and many of them had seen action at Vicksburg and Port Hudson. On paper, the Rio Grande expedition consisted of nearly seven thousand troops, although only about four thousand were present for duty.[43]

The Rio Grande expedition left New Orleans on October 26, 1863. Although various sources gave conflicting numbers, the invasion fleet consisted of at least twenty ships, most of them troop transports, which were escorted by three warships, the *Monongahela*, the *Owasco*, and the *Virginia*. Cmdr. James H. Strong led the naval element, and Banks accompanied the fleet as overall commander. On the day the fleet set sail, Strong received information that French and British warships were stationed off the Rio Grande. This meant that the invading force had to exercise caution when approaching the mouth of the river.[44]

The Federal ships encountered a severe storm on October 30, 1863, off Aransas Pass near Corpus Christi, Texas. Since many of the ships were overloaded with troops and supplies, these vessels had great difficulty navigating the rough waters of the Gulf of Mexico. An account by an Iowa soldier, an officer aboard the *General Banks*, described how they had to lighten the ship in order to keep it from sinking. They threw overboard eleven mules, one battery wagon, and forage for the livestock on board. The next day the *General Banks* had to be towed by another steamer because she almost ran out of fuel. Another account, given by Capt. Edward Gee Miller of the 20th Wisconsin, described how the seas became so rough that one sailor was washed overboard and others became seasick and were eager to make landfall.

The ships arrived at the mouth of the Rio Grande on the morning of November 1, 1863. The welcome cry of "Land ho" was passed along from vessel to vessel. Banks, who sailed on the flagship *McClellan*, described the sea as high and the wind so strong that a landing was not attempted that day. Since the larger vessels could not get too close to shore, an effort was made to lighten them, which included letting the cavalry horses swim to land. One ship, the *George Peabody*, upon which part of the 1st Texas Cavalry traveled, lowered twenty-five horses overboard to allow them to swim to the beach. Only seven of the horses made it safely, however, and it was decided to terminate this method lest the cavalry become infantry. With the arrival of auxiliary vessels, the slow and tedious task of transferring men, equipment, and horses from the troop transports to the landing craft commenced. At noon on November 2, 1863, Union troops of the 19th Iowa Regiment were the first soldiers to land on the island of Brazos Santiago near the river's mouth.[45]

The arrival of the invasion force at the mouth of the Rio Grande was not totally unexpected by the Confederates. A series of fires was lit along the Texas coastline when the Rio Grande expedition was spotted. The *Houston Telegraph* ran the headline "Let the Enemy Come" and encouraged civilians to assist the gray-clad troops in the defense of their state. The article invoked scare tactics by reporting that the enemy planned to garrison captured Texas towns with black soldiers "with a view eventually of colonizing American citizens of African descent—free Negroes—in this State."[46]

Perhaps the most colorful account of the Rio Grande expedition's journey across the Gulf of Mexico came from Pvt. James S. Clark of the 34th Iowa Volunteer Infantry. His regiment traveled on the steamer *Belvedere* with a battalion of the 1st Texas Cavalry. Clark remembered how General Banks ordered the steamers into two parallel columns one-half mile apart. Clark recalled that "the spectacle of this formation of twenty-three steamers moving majestically across the sea, smooth as a lake, with the sun shining and the bands playing, was impressive and inspiring." Although the expedition started with good weather, it soon encountered fierce storms. Clark wrote, "Our fleet is scattered to the four winds. Some of them we fear are lost entirely. The white caps are madly tossed in air, and the furious billows roll mountain high. Our old boat creaks and bends in a frightful manner, and reels and lurches from side to side like a drunken man. There is a great fear lest she will go down with her cargo of life. As a partial relief all the cavalry horse were thrown overboard."[47]

After the intense storms abated, another soldier traveling with Clark composed a short poem about their adventure on the Gulf of Mexico:

> Banks moves in a mysterious way,
> His blunders to perform.
> He puts a fleet upon the sea
> To be scattered by the storm.[48]

The debarkation occurred at the same spot where American soldiers under Gen. Zachary Taylor had gone ashore during the Mexican War. Because of the shallow water, most of the fleet anchored about a mile offshore. The Union troops encountered no Confederate resistance, although two sailors and seven soldiers drowned when boats from the *Owasco* were swamped in the surf. Two regiments of cavalry were sent ashore first as an advance guard—both horses and men were forced to swim to the mainland. The infantry followed shortly, some wading up to their armpits. From the time the expedition left New Orleans until the actual landing at Brazos Santiago, the losses of the invasion fleet had been relatively light. Commander Strong reported losing only three boats, but the crews were rescued.

In a message to Halleck dated November 4, 1863, Banks said, "I have the honor to report that on November 2, at meridian [noon], the flag of the Union was raised on Brazos Island, which is now in our possession." He then related how the recent troop movements in Louisiana had drawn Confederate defenders from the Rio Grande to eastern Texas. Without that activity, the landing at Brazos Santiago might have been strongly contested. Finally, Banks announced his intention to move up the coast toward Galveston as soon as the Rio Grande was secured. He therefore requested that Halleck send reinforcements. Banks still had in mind the eventual capture of Galveston, but instead of attacking from the sea or from the north, Union forces would advance up the Texas coast and take Galveston from the south.[49]

By November 3 all of the Union soldiers had disembarked and were ordered forward to Brownsville. Some of the soldiers landed at Brazos Santiago, others at the mouth of the Rio Grande. Just north of the latter location was a small inlet called Boca Chica, separating Brazos Santiago and the mainland. One Illinois regiment crossed this body of water, but with great difficulty.

Col. Charles Black, commanding the 37th Illinois Regiment, gave a detailed account of the crossing: "It was a most ludicrous sight. Men with kettles, pans, tincups, guns, knapsacks, clothes, accoutrements [sic] etc. dotting the wide ford, some naked, others in drawers and shirts, others in full dress." The colonel also mentioned that most of the men took off their shoes, only to receive severe lacerations to their feet from the sharp oyster shells that covered the bottom of the ford. To ease the crossing of Boca Chica, army engineers built a pontoon bridge composed of two long india-rubber bladders overlaid with cross-timbers. Capable of carrying immense loads, the bridge greatly assisted the invading army.

Their first major target, the city of Brownsville, lay thirty miles inland. On the morning of November 6, 1863, the 94th Illinois Volunteers, under the command of Col. William M. Dye, were the first Union soldiers to enter Brownsville. The troops discovered that the evacuating Confederates had set fire to Fort Brown and destroyed large quantities of property that could not be removed. Part of the fire burned two city blocks and set off four tons of condemned gunpowder, sending debris flying across the river into Mexico. Many Union soldiers commented on the immense quantity of cotton lining the wharf of Matamoros. One of the officers remarked that an estimated 10,000 bales "stood in plain sight on the opposite side," while only 150 bales remained on the north bank. These bundles were quickly confiscated. Colonel Dye then established headquarters at what was left of Fort Brown.[50]

War was no stranger to the lower Rio Grande Valley. If anything, war had promoted the population and economic growth of the region. The principal fort in the area, Fort Brown, had been built by Gen. Zachary Taylor during the Mexican War. Located on the north bank of the Rio Grande just opposite Matamoros, it received its name from Maj. Jacob Brown, who first commanded the post and was killed in a Mexican bombardment on May 9, 1846. Two years later, the city of Brownsville was founded by prominent businessman Charles Stillman, and a new fort was built just a quarter of a mile north of the original. When Texas seceded, Federal troops evacuated Fort Brown on March 20, 1861. Once they left, the Texas militia under Col. John S. Ford occupied the stronghold and began to make repairs.

The fort's future commander, Brig. Gen. Hamilton Bee, made an inspection in October 1861. He described the repairs begun by Colonel Ford as unfinished but noted that in a short time the garrison could be made strong. The facility contained twenty-five cannons of different caliber and three hundred rounds of ammunition for each piece. Bee recognized the importance of defending Brownsville as a port of entry for European goods coming from Matamoros. Ironically, he pointed out that if enemy troops landed in force, a regiment at the fort could not hold them off or save the precious artillery. This invading column could march overland and capture San Antonio within two weeks. Bee thus urged that Brownsville either be strongly defended or given up at once and the cannon removed while there was still time. When Bee arrived to command Fort Brown on January 29, 1863, he commanded not only the fortification but also the western subdistrict of the Department of Texas, which included the entire territory south of San Antonio to Brownsville and from the mouth of the Rio Grande to Laredo. On February 3, 1863, Bee complained that he would need at least five thousand men to defend the line of the Rio Grande from Brownsville to Laredo. All he had at his disposal, however, was one infantry regiment and two batteries of light artillery.[51]

What Bee had predicted two years earlier became a reality on November 1, 1863, when the first U.S. vessels appeared at the mouth of the Rio Grande. He now confronted the biggest dilemma of his military career. In his first telegrams to district headquarters in Houston on November 2, Bee explained the countermeasures he would adopt against the invading Federals. He knew he was about to be overrun; after all, he had only about one hundred men to defend Brownsville. Nevertheless, he stated that he intended to hold the enemy in check as long as possible, retreating upriver and drawing supplies from the Mexican side of the river. Bee then sent a detachment of troops north to inform the cotton wagons headed for Brownsville that the city was under attack. He also planned to take any valuable supplies from Brownsville, leaving nothing of value for the enemy. As any officer in this situation would, he also asked to be reinforced.[52]

Bee had established two points of observation to keep him well informed of Union movements at the mouth of the Rio Grande. Fifteen men of Company A, 33rd Texas Cavalry, under Capt. Richard Taylor, were stationed there. Another fifteen men of Company F were positioned at Point Isabel. Both companies reported on November 2 that they had sighted fifteen vessels off the island of Brazos Santiago. When Bee heard this news, he issued preparatory orders to evacuate Brownsville. The following day a courier informed Bee that Union cavalry, two hundred strong, were pursuing him and that no time should be wasted if he intended to withdraw from the city.[53]

Even before the courier arrived, Bee had already sent a train of forty-five wagons with one million dollars' worth of supplies northward to prevent the enemy from seizing them. Once Bee received word of hostile cavalry moving toward Brownsville, he realized that that column represented the advance movement of a much larger invasion force. Realizing the hopelessness of the situation, Bee ordered the garrison fired and personally supervised the burning of all cotton that might fall into the enemy's hands. During these crucial hours, Bee reported that of the great number of Confederate citizens in Brownsville, only about a dozen turned out to help him and his men in their effort to vacate the city. Col. James Duff of the 33rd Texas Cavalry confirmed the lack of assistance by the citizens of Brownsville. It was not until 5 P.M. on November 3 that Bee and eighty men of the 33rd Texas Cavalry left Brownsville bound for the King Ranch near present-day Kingsville. During his retreat northward, he sent a message to General Magruder in Houston: "The enemy are in force. Brazos Island is covered with tents; twenty-six vessels, some of them very large. I think the expedition is from Fortress Monroe."[54]

As Bee marched northward, he encountered cotton wagons headed for Brownsville. Following orders, he set fire to their cargo. In one instance, he met twenty-five wagons that had come all the way from Arkansas. When Bee's men destroyed the cotton, one of the old teamsters commented that "The loss falls so heavily on so many. They had toiled so hard and so long and they are poor and needy. And to think we were so near our journey's end. I don't know how we can ever go home. To go back empty will be awful and besides, as you see, we have nothing to wear and winter is near and in all our company there is not so much as two dollars. I don't know why General Bee would want to burn our cotton."[55]

What followed in the wake of the Confederate evacuation of Brownsville can be described as pandemonium. Perhaps the best eyewitness account of the fall of the city comes from a cotton teamster named John Warren Hunter, a recent arrival there. On the morning of November 3, a runner arrived at Fort Brown with the shocking news that a Federal fleet was off Brazos Santiago with at least fifty thousand men. Hunter noticed that, shortly after the arrival of the messenger, confusion reigned in the streets. One rumor that emerged early was that ten thousand drunken black troops under noted Unionist Edmund J. Davis were only a few miles from Brownsville and intended to burn the city to the ground. People cried out, "The Yankees are coming!" Hunter then observed heavily loaded wagons pulling out of Fort Brown. His first impression was that General Bee was going out to meet the enemy. A Confederate officer walking by was asked the meaning of all of the commotion. "I don't know. Ask General Bee!" was his curt response.[56]

Hunter also saw a company of artillerymen rolling their guns into the Rio Grande, including a fine 64-pounder. This revealed the true nature of the situation: Fort Brown and the city of Brownsville were to be abandoned to the enemy. A civilian approached the artillery officer in command and asked, "Lieutenant, what does all this mean?" The officer replied, "I am obeying orders." About this time, the citizens noticed dense black smoke coming from the cotton yard: Soldiers had put the torch to the bales stacked on the riverbank so the enemy could not appropriate them. The greatest cotton depot of the South had became a swirling holocaust. At first, some thought the enemy had committed this destruction. No one believed that the Confederate authorities would ruin such a valuable commodity. The panic worsened when the military buildings were also set on fire. Realizing they had to fend for themselves, the civilians now headed for the ferry to seek protection across the river in Matamoros.[57]

Hunter described the terror-stricken citizens hurrying toward the ferry and using wagons, carriages, and even wheelbarrows to transport their household items to the dock. The edge of the Rio Grande became cluttered with personal possessions that many had hoped to save from the invaders. The going price to get across the river was five dollars in gold for each passenger. As a large mass of people gathered at the ferry, eight thousand pounds of condemned gunpowder exploded at Fort Brown, showering fire upon the town. The force of the explosion sent a timber flying across the river and into the Mexican customhouse. When Hunter heard the explosion, he believed that "heaven and earth [had] collided." He also remembered that people on the sidewalk were knocked to the ground by the concussion. A small boy standing at the edge of the river was thrown into the water and drowned. When the fires finally died down, most of Fort Brown had been destroyed, two city blocks were badly damaged, and the massive pile of household items by the ferry was scorched. The gunpowder explosion at Fort Brown created a scene out of Dante's *Inferno.* Unfortunately, the terror had just begun.[58]

After sundown on November 3, with the retreat of Bee's men northward, criminal elements from both sides of the Rio Grande looted Brownsville. Hunter stated that mounted Mexicans rode up and down the streets, shouting in Spanish, "Death to the gringos!" The horsemen then fired their guns at houses, stores, and even terrified citizens standing on the sidewalks. Stores and private homes were plundered. The bandits shot at everyone, for madness unleashed respects neither race nor social standing. By the end of the next day, a home guard under the leadership of Gen. José Maria Cobos, a political refugee from Brownsville, finally restored order to the panic-stricken city.[59]

When Federal troops arrived on November 6, they found a smoldering city guarded by General Cobos, who surrendered the city to them and moved back across the river into Matamoros. Once there, Cobos led an insurrection and deposed the Juarista governor of Tamaulipas, Don Manuel Ruíz. In a communiqué dated November 6, 1863, Banks described Cobos as a political chameleon who was willing to sell his interests to the highest bidder. Banks believed Cobos was pro-French and an enemy of the United States. One of Cobos's followers, Juan N. Cortina, had Cobos killed, however, and as a sign of good faith placed three steamboats on the Mexican side of the river under Union control. Cortina was actually a general serving the Juarista cause in northern Mexico. He had been sent by Juarez to kill Cobos and thus prevent an Imperialist takeover of Matamoros. When Banks reported to Lincoln and Halleck on November 9, 1863, he asserted that Brazos Santiago, Point Isabel, and Brownsville were under Union control and that Governor Cortina was friendly to the United States. So far it appeared that the Rio Grande expedition would be a success, both militarily and diplomatically.[60]

Confederate Texans, on the other hand, braced themselves for what they thought would be the beginning of an all-out invasion of their state. When the 19th Iowa unfurled its regimental colors on Brazos Santiago, the fear of invasion, with all of the horrors Union armies were reportedly bringing to the South, became acute. General Bee, in retreating from Brownsville, suffered a hard blow to his military reputation. Richard Fitzpatrick, a Confederate commercial agent in Matamoros, called Bee's retreat from Brownsville "one of the most cowardly affairs which has happened in any country." Fitzpatrick's comments came roughly two months after the Union repulse at Sabine Pass by a force of fewer than fifty Confederates. Apparently Fitzpatrick assumed that history would repeat itself at Brownsville. He also believed that the fire set by Bee was an effort to cover up extensive corruption in the Confederate cotton trade. Bee responded to this personal attack by pointing out that any attempt to defend Brownsville with the small force under his command would have been suicidal. One other factor must also be considered in Bee's defense. He had orders from Magruder not to allow cotton or military supplies to fall into the enemy's hands. In this regard, most historians believe that Bee followed the orders of a superior officer fairly well. But bruised reputations were a minor concern for Magruder. Texans would soon find that the capture of Brownsville was only the beginning of a major campaign by Union forces to occupy Galveston and the whole state of Texas.[61]

Two

The Finest Campaign of the War

*O*nce Brownsville was under Union control, Maj. Gen. Nathaniel P. Banks continued to advance up the coast, intending to occupy all of the ports and passes between the Rio Grande and the border with Louisiana. Once the Texas coast was secured, his forces would move inland, capture Houston, and destroy rebel authority within the state. Another military option also presented itself to Banks. By cooperating with Union forces under Brig. Gen. James Carleton in New Mexico, Banks contemplated the capture of the Texas border from Brownsville west to El Paso. This move would not only shut down the Texas-Mexico cotton trade but also send a stronger message to the French in Mexico. Whichever option Banks chose, he believed it would be the "finest campaign of the war." He did not want to lose the momentum gained from his successful landing and occupation of the lower Rio Grande Valley.[1]

The Rio Grande expedition had already accomplished some of its goals. It disrupted the cotton trade through Brownsville and established a significant Union presence on the Rio Grande for the French to ponder. Banks, however, received mixed reviews of his actions on the lower Rio Grande. When General in Chief Henry W. Halleck heard about Banks's activities, he was furious. Banks did not have instructions to operate on the Texas coast. Halleck described the Brownsville invasion as another "wild goose chase" in which Banks violated military principles by dividing his forces and leaving New Orleans vulnerable to attack. Secretary of State William H. Seward, on the other hand, congratulated Banks for his successful landing on the Rio Grande, pointing out the important diplomatic impact it would have on "the confusion resulting from civil strife and foreign war in Mexico."[2]

Gilbert D. Kingsbury, a former U.S. postmaster in Brownsville and Union sympathizer, enthusiastically welcomed the Rio Grande expedition. In a letter to his sister Mariah, Kingsbury stated that "On the 6th instant, General Banks and a part of his command arrived here. I crossed to Brownsville for the first time in 22 months. I was made acquainted with the General and his staff, and was nominated a candidate for the madhouse. Indeed I learn that all my friends voted me to be a maniac, but my joy and enthusiasm surprised nobody."[3]

Once the Brownsville garrison was organized, Banks left for Corpus Christi on the morning of November 13, 1863, with about fifteen hundred men aboard nine vessels. He left behind at Fort Brown Maj. Gen. Napoleon Dana, commander of the XIII Army Corps. The attack force was commanded by Brig. Gen. Thomas E. G. Ransom of the 3rd Brigade, 2nd Division of the XIII Army Corps. Ransom, once described by General Grant as "the best man I ever had to send on expeditions," acquired considerable combat experience prior to the Rio Grande campaign. He had fought at Fort Donelson, Shiloh, and Vicksburg and was wounded three times in those battles. At the time of the Rio Grande expedition, he was twenty-six years of age, one of the youngest generals in the Union army. Banks's orders to Ransom, dated November 15, 1863, told him to attack the city through Corpus Christi Pass, which separates Padre and Mustang islands, then land troops on Mustang Island to capture a Confederate artillery battery there. Since the water level at the pass was low, a shallow-draft steamboat, the *Matamoros*, was to land troops on the inner side of Mustang Island. The U.S. gunboats *Monongahela*, *Virginia*, and *McClellan* would provide naval support for the landing.[4]

Union soldiers bound for Corpus Christi began loading their transports on November 15, 1863, at Brazos Santiago and left that evening. The regiments involved in the attack included the 13th and 15th Maine; the 34th, 26th, and 20th Iowa; the 8th Indiana; the 1st Engineers of the Corps d'Afrique; and one battery of artillery. The group arrived at Corpus Christi around 2 P.M. on November 16. Banks hoped to land troops on the inner side of Mustang Island, through Corpus Christi Pass. A sandbar prevented the steamer *Matamoros* from accomplishing this task, however. Banks therefore landed his invasion force on the outer coast of Mustang Island by means of surfboats. The landing, which occurred on the south end of the island, occupied most of the night.[5]

Ransom landed with about 1,200 troops on the south end of Mustang Island; the remainder landed about four miles below Fort Semmes, a Confederate outpost at the northernmost end of the island, commanded by Capt. William N. Maltby of the 8th Texas Infantry. Banks supervised the more northern landings from the *McClellan*. Some of the soldiers who went ashore at this point waded through the surf near present-day Bob Hall Pier. The Confederate position contained an artillery battery with three heavy siege cannons and about 100 men from Company I of the 8th Texas Infantry and a few men from the 3rd Texas (state troops).

Ransom made a forced march of about twenty-two miles to approach Fort Semmes. Enemy skirmishers put up a faint show of resistance about one mile south of the camp on the morning of November 17. At this point, Ransom deployed the 13th and 15th Maine regiments to advance in line of battle against the fort. The gunboat *Monongahela* fired a few shells at the rebel position. The Confederates, not expecting an attack, fought for a brief time but then surrendered unconditionally to General Ransom. The enemy flag was taken down from the fort, and the Stars and Stripes was raised in its place. One soldier of the 15th Maine pointed out that the rebel flag taken from Fort Semmes later hung over the state treasurer's office in the state capitol building at Augusta, Maine. In January 1928, sixty-five years later, Maine returned the captured flag to Texas in a ceremony held in Washington, D.C.[6]

Ransom praised not only the men directly under his command but also the naval support under the command of Capt. L. P. Griffin. Not only did the navy help in landing troops, but it also fired fifteen shells at the enemy garrison. In addition, Captain Griffin served as a naval aide to General Banks, providing valuable advice for landing troops in the rough surf. Contrary to what a noted historian has written, Banks coordinated the army and navy movements against Mustang Island fairly well. Although the spoils of victory were relatively light, the action proved significant in view of the fact that Mustang Island controlled one of the choke points that restricted access to the landward side of the barrier islands along the Texas coastline.[7]

During the battle for Fort Semmes, panic gripped the citizens of Corpus Christi. The sound of gunfire could be heard in the town, and the terror-stricken inhabitants expected invasion momentarily. Weeping wives and parents were distraught with worry over the fate of the local troops serving in Maltby's command on Mustang Island. News of the battle was sent to General Bee, who was in camp on San Fernando Creek near present-day Banquete, west of Corpus Christi, and he began a hurried march to the city. Meanwhile, the Confederate steamer *Cora* had been sent from Fort Esperanza to rescue the men at Fort Semmes but was driven off by Federal fire. When Bee arrived in Corpus Christi, he was of no great help to the frightened people. He did, however, send Lt. Walter Mann, under a flag of truce, to determine the fate of Fort Semmes and the *Cora*. The Federals held Mann prisoner for several days but later released him. By that time, word reached the city that Maltby's men were safe, though prisoners, and that the *Cora* had returned safely to Fort Esperanza.[8]

The next Union target on the Texas coast was Fort Esperanza on the north end of Matagorda Island. The garrison guarded Pass Cavallo, the entrance to Matagorda Bay, formed by Matagorda Island to the south and Matagorda Peninsula to the north. This Confederate post, built in early 1863 by slave labor under the direction of Caleb G. Forshey, had impressive armament. It consisted of one 128-pounder Columbiad, six 24-pounder smoothbores, one 12-pounder mounted on a carriage, and one 32-pounder Parrott. Two thousand Confederates were reportedly defending the stronghold. In fact, only about five hundred men were on duty in November 1863. Most of these soldiers belonged to the 8th Texas Infantry under the command of Col. W. R. Bradfute. Around the fort snaked several hundred yards of trenches. About six miles directly east of the fortification, near the Pass Cavallo lighthouse on the coast, a maze of trenches with redoubts at each end was dug completely across the island. Five miles west of the fort on the interior side of the island was the small settlement of Saluria, a health resort established in the 1850s. A ferry connected Saluria and Fort Esperanza to the mainland. On the mainland side of the ferry, the Confederates had established an artillery battery consisting of two Dahlgren boat howitzers and two rifled Parrotts. These armaments provided protection for a possible evacuation of Matagorda Island.[9]

The Union expedition against Fort Esperanza was commanded by Maj. Gen. Cadwallader C. Washburn. Born in Maine in 1818, Washburn moved to Wisconsin in the 1840s and became a prosperous lawyer and businessman. His brothers Elihu and Israel were prominent in northern politics, and even General Washburn had served three terms in the House of Representatives. In 1862 he was commissioned a colonel of the 2nd Wisconsin Cavalry. Serving primarily in the western theater of the war, Washburn achieved the rank of major general by the time of the 1863 Vicksburg campaign. By November 1863 Washburn commanded an aggregate of various army units within the XIII Army Corps. The major elements under his command included the 1st and 4th Divisions and the 3rd Brigade, 2nd Division. This last unit, under General Ransom, captured Mustang Island. Washburn now replaced Ransom as senior officer on the upper Texas coast.[10]

Fort Esperanza was a tougher obstacle to overcome than the small garrison at Mustang Island. As a result, the Union expedition was reinforced by another thirteen hundred men. On November 21, 1863, Washburn arrived at Mustang Island to take command. On the following day, he received orders from Banks to commence an attack. By this time, Union troops occupied

Saint Joseph Island, just to the south of Matagorda Island. The men were ferried from Mustang Island to Saint Joseph Island. Washburn arrived at Saint
Joseph Island aboard the steamer *Clinton* on the November 22. The next day
he marched his men to the north end of the island, a distance of eighteen
miles.

Washburn had sent ahead General Ransom, commanding the 3rd Brigade,
2nd Division, to see whether a bridge could be built between Saint Joseph and
Matagorda islands, a distance of about 300 yards. When Washburn arrived at
this pass (called Cedar Bayou), he saw that it would be impossible to build a
bridge. As a result, he decided to ferry his men across to Matagorda Island.
He also learned that the element of surprise that had helped the Union forces
at Mustang Island had been lost. An advance Union scouting party on Saint
Joseph, led by the 34th Iowa Infantry, fought a skirmish with a Confederate
scouting party from Fort Esperanza on November 23. A Confederate officer
named Maj. Charles Hill was killed, and one Union soldier of the 15th Maine
was slightly wounded. One account of this incident described how Major
Hill, an artillery officer from Fort Esperanza, marched a small party of soldiers to the south end of Matagorda Island. As he arrived at Cedar Bayou under a flag of truce, Sgt. James Saunders of the 15th Maine swam over to ascertain the party's wishes. Major Hill questioned Saunders as to the purpose
of the expedition and the disposition of the men taken prisoner at Fort
Semmes. When Saunders refused to reveal any information, a struggle ensued, and the rebel major drew his revolver, shooting the Maine sergeant.
Union soldiers from Saint Joseph Island returned fire, killing Major Hill.[11]

Washburn was delayed in crossing from Saint Joseph to Matagorda Island
by a strong winter storm on November 24, but the troops were finally able
to ferry over the next day. On November 26 they trekked twenty miles toward the north end of the island. One veteran described this seaside march
as "among the hardest" his regiment ever made. To make things worse, a rare
snowstorm buffeted the Union soldiers. Some of the men dug holes in the
sand and covered themselves with the hides of wild cattle recently slaugh-
tered. One soldier of the 15th Maine commented that Texas "northers"
"completely throw our New England winter gales into the shade." A "Texas
norther cannot be adequately described; it must be experienced to be fully
appreciated."

Despite the harsh weather, the Union forces were now within ten miles
of Fort Esperanza. Washburn's men finally got a better view of their objective on November 29, when they marched to within 800 yards of the fort.
According to one Union soldier, Esperanza had parapets 10 feet high and

15 feet thick, flanked by water on both sides. It was an awesome sight to the Union infantry that foggy November morning. The inclement weather prevented an immediate attack. While awaiting better conditions, the Federals scouted the enemy's position and moved their artillery into place. The bad weather also prevented the Federal gunboats from offshore shelling. A small skirmish occurred a few days earlier, however, on the morning of November 27, when Confederate pickets were driven into the fort. The Union soldiers started digging trenches and prepared to lay siege.[12]

The battle of Fort Esperanza took place on November 29, 1863. Two Union artillery batteries, the 1st Missouri Light and the 7th Michigan, shelled the fort throughout the day. The Confederate artillery responded, but neither side inflicted much serious damage. At one point during this exchange, troops of the 33rd Illinois Regiment, Vicksburg veterans, taunted the rebel gunners by pretending to catch cannonballs in their hats. One of the few Union casualties in the engagement involved a soldier who, seeing an apparently spent cannonball rolling on the sand, foolishly tried to stop it with his foot. This piece of solid shot ended up breaking his leg.

The Confederate commander, Colonel Bradfute, held a council of war that night and decided that the stronghold would have to be abandoned. Exploding magazines after midnight on November 30 signaled the Confederates' evacuation. The victorious Yankees described the explosion and fire as a "grand exhibition" and "one of the wildest and grandest scenes mortal man ever witnessed." Bradfute also spiked the cannons and took his men to the mainland, realizing that his small garrison could not survive a Union siege or fight off the ever-growing Federal force on Matagorda Island. Both sides suffered light casualties. The Confederates had one man killed and ten taken prisoner. The Federals reported one killed and ten wounded. A few of the Confederate prisoners stated that the governor of Texas wanted to surrender the state and all of the troops he had enlisted. They went on to say that half of the people in Texas supported the Union and there would be little fighting in the state.[13]

Soldiers of the 8th and 18th Indiana regiments were the first to enter the fort. The Hoosiers chased the fleeing Confederates to a ferry used to cross over to the mainland. Before the attack on Fort Esperanza, Union forces had failed to capture the ferry because the shallow water at the entrance of Matagorda Bay prevented ships from entering. By the time the Federal troops arrived, they found only the disabled ferry but seized a cannon used to guard the crossing point. If the Federals had been able to capture the ferry, the whole Esperanza garrison might have been captured. Instead, when Washburn's men entered the fort, they found most of the cannons spiked and one dead soldier left unburied. They also found valuable supplies they desperately needed. During this coastal campaign, Washburn's men endured not only supply shortages but also forced marches and severe weather. Despite his victory at Fort Esperanza, Washburn received no orders to advance.[14]

While some Union regiments advanced up the Texas coast, others stationed at Brownsville launched an expedition up the Rio Grande to capture Fort Ringgold, about ninety miles west of Brownsville, and seize any cotton the Confederates might attempt to move across the river at that location. The fort was named after Maj. David Ringgold, who was killed while leading an attack at the battle of Palo Alto on May 8, 1846. Federal soldiers had abandoned the fort on March 7, 1861, and Confederate forces occupied it off and on throughout the Civil War. Like many settlements on the Rio Grande, the town had a ferry to transport goods into Mexico. A military road along the north bank linked Fort Ringgold with Fort Brown.[15]

Seven companies left Fort Brown aboard the steamer *Mustang*, and three other companies marched toward Fort Ringgold by land. One of the officers with the expedition was Col. John Black, commander of the 37th Illinois Regiment, also known as the "Fremont Rifles." Another officer was the noted Texas Unionist Col. Edmund J. Davis, commander of the 1st Texas Cavalry Regiment. Davis, who had lived in Texas since 1848, fled the state in 1862 to avoid reprisals for his Unionism. In the fall of 1862, he organized the 1st Texas Cavalry (U.S.), composed mostly of Texas Unionists. That unit had seen action in Louisiana with the XIX Army Corps in the summer and fall of 1863. On November 20, 1863 the 1st Texas and the 37th Illinois regiments advanced upriver toward Fort Ringgold, where a force of Confederates was rumored to be stationed. The entire expedition consisted of four hundred men. Capturing the fort would hinder, if not stop, the Confederate trade with Mexico, especially the cotton exchange. Colonel Black, who traveled with his troops aboard the *Mustang*, reported that the steamer made only ten miles a day. Because the river was shallow and tortuous, he ran aground several times on sandbars, making it impossible to keep up with Davis and his cavalry. Colonel Black blamed the boat's slow progress on the captain, who was in the employ of "Mexican owners who still operated under the orders from a staunch Confederate."[16]

While the *Mustang* was being loaded for the journey upriver, Davis and three companies of the 37th Illinois commenced their march toward Rio Grande City. The Illinois soldiers traveled on wagons so as not to impede the cavalry's progress. Davis and the men of the Fremont Rifles arrived at Fort

Ringgold on November 25 without meeting the enemy. An officer with the Illinois troops described the barracks in the fort as "once a fine collection of houses, but the bloody hand had been there and they now stand torn defaced and decapatated [sic]." The officer also observed that there was a 100-foot-high conical mound in the center of the barracks on which a 70-foot flag staff had stood, flying the "ever glorious stars and stripes." Regrettably, "the revengeful secessionists [had] applied the torch and burnt it to the ground."[17]

Immediately upon his arrival at Fort Ringgold, Colonel Davis sent a courier to locate the *Mustang.* The messenger found the vessel about thirty miles downriver. Colonel Black responded on November 26, pointing out that a 100-foot sandbar had stalled his progress upriver. Black also learned that the river above the sandbar was "only knee deep." He informed Davis that he would remain where he was until further notice. He also mentioned that the *Mustang* had full rations for the land detachment. Upon receiving Black's response, Davis instructed him to come if he could; otherwise, Davis would march toward the *Mustang.*[18]

The expedition procured little cotton at Rio Grande City. The bales that were confiscated fell into Union hands quite by accident. A Southern cotton train, unaware of the Federals' presence, rolled into town with eighty-three bales, valued at twelve thousand dollars. The paucity of cotton in the area had to do with the fact that the Confederates were informed of the enemy's campaign against Rio Grande City. As a result, the cotton crossings were moved upriver to Laredo and Eagle Pass.[19]

After confiscating the bales, Davis ordered Black to land the *Mustang.* Once the cotton arrived, Black was to load it on the boat and wait for Davis. The land forces under Davis remained at Fort Ringgold for two days but eventually joined the rest of the expedition on November 29. The three Illinois companies that came with Davis to Rio Grande City rejoined the rest of their regiment aboard the *Mustang.* The return trip for the 37th Illinois began on December 2.[20]

Although the voyage downriver was as tedious as the one to Fort Ringgold, a couple of incidents broke the monotony for a few of the officers and enlisted men. One involved a dozen officers who accepted an invitation to a fandango at "Old Rijenesa" (Old Reynosa) on the Mexican side of the river. The party was held in a shady grove near the town. One soldier described the dance floor as "mother earth made level," surrounded by refreshment tables and chairs. The Federal officers, including Colonel Black, had a great time and stayed until 3:00 A.M. About thirty "ladies, tastefully dressed, modest and gentle looking," attended the festivities. Colonel Black exclaimed: "Oh! such dancers!

Gauze and silk, gold and jewels floated and swam through the night." The Union men left "fully satisfied that a fandango was a big thing."[21]

On the last evening of the journey, the *Mustang* stopped six miles above Brownsville. Many of the men went ashore but were instructed not to shoot any cattle since there were ranches in the vicinity. Although a guard was assigned to prevent the soldiers from leaving the vessel with their rifles, the "boys swarmed ashore with guns and without." Those with guns went after cattle; those without wanted permission to march to Brownsville. The request was denied. Cpl. Andrew L. Swap described how the troops "threw stones at the officers cabin [until] the commanding officer went ashore and gave orders" allowing the men to kill all the beef they wanted. The soldiers, some of them black troops, apparently did pretty well in their search for cattle. Ramijo Garza, who worked on the Latham Ranch near Brownsville, reported that "one hundred and fifty head of horned cattle of the value of six dollars in coin each . . . was [sic] taken from the Frank Latham Ranch in Cameron County, Texas, by the U.S. Army commanded by Genls Banks, Dana, and Herron." Later in the deposition, Garza stated that "negroes from a steamboat [were] under command of Colonel Black who was on said boat at the time, that he called on Colonel Black three times who sent him to commander [sic] in Brownsville, Texas." Garza never received compensation for the cattle because it was discovered that he had supplied the Confederate forces at Fort Brown earlier in the war.[22]

The Fremont Rifles under Colonel Black arrived in Brownsville on December 12, 1863. Although no great quantity of cotton fell into Union hands, the Federal forces showed that their reach extended upriver to Rio Grande City. The campaign also confirmed that Union soldiers could travel by water as far as Rio Grande City. Penetration beyond that point would have to be made by land. Colonel Davis predicted great difficulty in any attempt to occupy the whole river with the small number of troops at Brownsville.[23]

After about a month in Brownsville, Banks's army had confiscated only about 800 bales of cotton. On December 2, 1863, General Dana wrote to his superiors that about 2,500 bales had been transported over the river within the last two weeks. He concluded in a hopeful manner by stating "that trade is about stopped this side of Laredo." To further hinder the cotton exchange, Dana moved outside the realm of military operations. He sanctioned a policy of terrorism on the cotton roads leading to the Rio Grande, and in December he wrote a letter to the U.S. vice consul in Monterrey: "I desire to make the road from San Antonio to Eagle Pass and Laredo so perilous that neither Jew or Gentile will wish to travel it. Please make this known, confidentially only, to good, true and daring men. I wish to kill, burn, and destroy all that cannot be taken and secured."[24]

Not all of the military action in the lower Rio Grande Valley took place along the river. Another prime target, about fifty miles northwest of Brownsville, was El Sal del Rey (the King's Salt), a salt lake in Hidalgo County near present-day Edinburg, Texas. Salt was a valuable commodity for the Confederacy, used primarily in food preservation. When Texas Gov. Francis R. Lubbock visited Pres. Jefferson Davis in Richmond in 1861, he learned that the Confederacy needed an estimated six million bushels of salt per year. The substance was in such high demand that salt and saltworks became military targets, and salt workers were exempted from the draft.[25]

In November 1861 the Texas legislature authorized Lubbock to appoint an agent to take possession of El Sal del Rey and sell the salt at the customary price. The revenue would then go into the state treasury. Lubbock appointed Antonio Salinas of Brownsville as agent in charge of processing the salt. Salinas supervised production for eighteen months until the 1st Texas U.S. Cavalry plundered the works in November 1863, shortly after the capture of Brownsville. Colonel Davis's cavalry destroyed the equipment and halted the salt production.[26]

Another inland target was the King Ranch, an important depot for cotton wagons bound for Brownsville. In a dispatch sent to New Orleans on December 15, 1863, Dana announced his intention to occupy the ranch, and he soon sent a scouting party of eighty men to carry out this objective. He also intended to capture Richard King, owner of the ranch and a loyal Confederate. The raid, led by Capt. James Speed, included soldiers from the 1st and 2nd Texas Cavalry (U.S.).[27] King paid for his loyalty to the Confederacy when the Union cavalry under Captain Speed stormed his ranch on December 23. Three days before the assault, a friend came to the ranch to inform King that the enemy was nearby and an attack was imminent. Not wanting to risk moving his four children and pregnant wife, Henrietta, King believed that if he left the ranch, the ranch hands stood a better chance of being unmolested by the enemy.[28]

At dawn on December 23, Speed and the Federal cavalry attacked King's house. They rode their horses through the hallway and killed one of his men, Francisco Alvarado, whom King had entrusted to protect his family. When the soldiers carried Alvarado's body inside the house, they saw that they had slain the wrong man. After an extensive search for the owner, the soldiers wrecked the interior of the home, terrifying the King family. When the raiders left on December 24, Speed summoned Hiram Chamberlain, King's father-in-law. Speed directed Chamberlain to give King a warning: "You tell King that if one bale of cotton is carried away from here or burned, I will hold him responsible with his life. Colonel Davis will be paying you a visit soon. When they do, you will think all hell has broke loose." Although they failed to capture King, the Union soldiers took some of his cattle back to Brownsville to feed the Federal army. Their departure was hastened by the arrival of Confederate cavalry on the night of December 24. In a letter of January 20, 1864, to Col. A. G. Dickinson, adjutant general at San Antonio, King mocked the Yankee cavalry, stating that they were "worse frightened than the ladies of the house."[29]

As the Union forces out of Brownsville attacked inland targets, the Federal soldiers who had advanced up the Texas coast continued to fortify their positions. Shortly after the raid on the King Ranch, troops under Maj. Gen. Fitz Henry Warren fought the Confederate 33rd Texas Cavalry under Col. James Duff near Port Lavaca, about 185 miles north of Brownsville. On December 26 six regiments of infantry, supported by two companies of cavalry and a field battery, engaged about forty Confederates at Norris Bridge between the towns of Lavaca and Indianola. Both communities were on the coast, six to eight miles apart. The Confederates had established a picket station at Norris Bridge to observe the enemy's activities at Indianola. The Federal soldiers first entered Indianola on December 13, 1863, when a Union regiment arrived aboard the vessel *Alabama.* After a brief skirmish, the Stars and Stripes was raised over the little port. The frightened citizens of Indianola believed that the soldiers were going to destroy the town, a false impression created by Confederate Maj. Gen. John B. Magruder, commander of the District of Texas, New Mexico, and Arizona. When the Federals returned to Fort Esperanza, they not only left the town intact but had also instilled a measure of goodwill among the people.[30]

Forty Confederates under Capt. Richard Taylor slowed the advance of about three thousand Union troops under General Warren at Norris Bridge on December 26, 1863. The Union soldiers were on their way to Lavaca to obtain supplies. Federal artillery lobbed about thirty shells at the Confederates, who retreated in the face of superior numbers and firepower. When Warren and his men came across Norris Bridge, they inquired about the soldiers defending the bridge. Warren commented that they were either very brave or the biggest fools in the whole western hemisphere. Although forced to retreat, the reputation of these forty Confederates did not suffer. "Desperate Engagement," the title of a long account of the battle, appeared in the *San Antonio Herald* and described how the Confederate troops had hurled back the invaders several times before falling back. The article concluded by saying, "The spirit shown by our troops must convince the authorities at Washington of the utter hopelessness of subjugating a proud and haughty people." After the skirmish at Norris Bridge, Warren marched on to Lavaca, procured supplies, and then burned the business district of the town. He then returned to Indianola and on December 29, 1863, officially placed it once again under Federal occupation.[31]

In late December, Union land and naval forces from Fort Esperanza sent out reconnaissance missions on the Matagorda Peninsula not only to ascertain Confederate troop strength but also to probe for weak spots on the Texas coast where Federal troops would be landed. On December 29 two Union scouting parties arrived on the Gulf shore of Matagorda Peninsula. One landing, involving one hundred men of the 13th Maine Infantry Regiment, commanded by Lt. Col. Frank Hesseltine, took place opposite the town of Matagorda, situated at the mouth of the Colorado River on Matagorda Bay. They arrived aboard the gunboat *Granite City*. A second landing, from the gunboat *Sciota*, was made farther up the coast near a Confederate post called Fort Caney. This second scouting party ran into Confederate soldiers from the fort and had to be evacuated. The *Sciota* rescued these men while firing a number of shells at the pursuing Confederates. The *Sciota* then steamed southward to assist in the landing of the 13th Maine.[32]

The 13th Maine landed at 7 A.M. in small boats that battled a rough surf. Shortly after debarkation a south wind came up and cut off all communication with the *Granite City*. Hesseltine sent a detachment to scout northward up the peninsula. When this unit returned, the regiment began a reconnaissance down the peninsula. After marching about seven or eight miles, Hesseltine heard cannon shot exploding behind him. The *Granite City* had begun firing at Confederate cavalry. Hesseltine reported that "By aid of my glass, I was able to discern the head of a body of cavalry moving down the Peninsula under a heavy fire from the gunboat. Their line stretched heavily towards us, and without seeing the last of it, I made out a force from eight hundred to a thousand cavalry." The Confederate 1st Texas Cavalry under Col. August Buchel was advancing rapidly toward the 13th Maine. Buchel, described by Magruder as a "gallant, efficient, and meritorious officer," had been assigned to patrol the Matagorda Peninsula since December 3. Fortunately for Colonel Hesseltine, he located a sand dune and began building a breastwork with the scattered driftwood that had floated ashore.[33]

When the horsemen of the 1st Texas Cavalry approached the improvised position, they hesitated to launch a direct assault against it. Buchel described the breastwork as formidable, and, with only three hundred men, he believed no military advantage could be gained by attacking it. Other factors also prevented Buchel from striking. First, a marsh intervened between him and the enemy. Second, his regiment had been scattered by cannon fire from the *Granite City*. Finally, the Union gunboats *Sciota* and *Granite City* had arrived on December 30 to provide additional naval support. Confederate Pvt. William Kuykendal, Company D, supported his commander's decision not to attack. He described the Union defenses as "a very strong position," and "[with] these natural advantages" and the naval support, it was "not deemed advisable" to attack.[34]

Despite these advantages, Hesseltine was afraid that he would be overrun. Heavy skirmishing ensued for the next two days. He later reported that "I knew my men; they were cool; and determined rather than the rebels should meet the first encouragement of this campaign, that they would die there, with as many of their foes lying about them." Land forces as well as Union and Confederate gunboats got into the act. Union naval commanders were unaware that a Confederate gunboat was on the other side of the peninsula. A heavy fog that morning allowed the *John F. Carr* to sail close to shore. When the fog lifted, the gunboat, under the command of Capt. James Marmion, began shelling Hesseltine's position. The distance from the gunboat to the Union troops was about 1.5 miles and about 2 miles to the Federal gunboats. The shocked commanders of the Union vessels immediately returned fire, and, according to Marmion, "some well-aimed shots [passed] over us and others [fell] short at a distance of about three hundred yards." The naval duel ended at about 3 P.M., but the *John F. Carr*, according to Hesseltine, "made some very good shots."[35]

After the naval exchange, the *Sciota* ordered the *Granite City* back to Fort Esperanza on December 30 for reinforcements. Three Union gunboats (the *Monongahela*, *Estrella*, and *Penobscot*) arrived with reinforcements on December 31, but severe weather kept them from landing any troops. While waiting for the storm to abate, Union naval commanders received orders to evacuate all Federal troops from the peninsula and return to Fort Esperanza. The Union gunboats successfully carried out this order under adverse conditions. Although casualties were light on both sides, Colonel Hesseltine received the Congressional Medal of Honor for heroism and saving the men in his regiment. He did so by marching them out of their original position on the night of December 30. Enduring bitter cold, the regiment moved twenty miles southward and were finally rescued by the *Sciota* on December 31. Hesseltine described how, on that march, "the sick and exhausted soldiers had been nobly aided by their comrades, so that not a man, musket or equipment was left to the enemy." He later commended not only the officers under his command but also the naval officers involved with this reconnaissance mission.[36]

The expedition garnered valuable information. While Union troops were landing on Matagorda Peninsula, the *Sciota* was ordered to observe the coast as far north as the Brazos River. Naval officers, along with General Ransom, reported strong enemy works at the mouths of the Brazos, Caney, and San Bernard rivers. At the Brazos River, the Confederates had built two strongholds, Fort Quintana and Fort Velasco. Together, these two installations mounted thirteen cannons. Fort Caney, built on the Caney River, and Fort Bernard, on the San Bernard River, were also formidable obstacles on the Texas shoreline. The Confederates clearly intended to contest very vigorously any further Union advance up the Texas coast. Despite these powerful fortifications and the repulse of Federal forces on the peninsula, Union scouting missions continued well into 1864.[37]

By the end of 1863, Union forces occupied the Texas coast from Brownsville to Indianola. General Banks boasted at the beginning of December that, if he were furnished with another division, he could capture Houston and Galveston. He intended to march up Matagorda Peninsula to the mouth of the Brazos, capture Forts Velasco and Quintana, and use them as his base of operations for the final assault against Houston and Galveston. General Washburn had similar aspirations. As the end of 1863 approached, however, Union scouts reported that General Magruder had massed a large force of Confederate and state troops on the prairie west of the Brazos to repel the expected Federal invasion of the Texas interior. Confederate soldiers who came into the Union lines also reported that Magruder had six to eight thousand troops in the whole state but that half of them were Union men and would probably not fight. Despite these conflicting reports, Washburn continued to organize the Union forces for an attack up Matagorda Peninsula toward the Brazos. His dispatches throughout December requested additional troops and supplies, but all were slow in coming. Washburn knew that the momentum of victory on the Texas coast should not be allowed to dissipate further. Nevertheless, by the end of December the Union advance had ground to a halt, allowing Magruder valuable time to fortify his positions on the coast.[38]

Other factors also contributed to the Union inactivity on the Texas shore. Throughout the Rio Grande expedition, Generals Banks and Halleck continued to argue over the proper strategy for conquering the Lone Star State. Halleck had never favored the Rio Grande expedition and held unfavorable opinions about amphibious landings in general. In a telegram of December 7, 1863, Halleck berated Banks for the expedition and the subsequent move up the coast. Halleck then stressed the importance of a Union campaign through central Louisiana and into northeast Texas, a strategy that had become almost an obsession with him. Perhaps the most damaging part of the telegram was his statement that "you must not expect any considerable reinforcements from other departments." When it came to a showdown over strategy in the Department of the Gulf, Halleck was determined to prevail.[39]

Climate, terrain, and the persistent shortage of supplies were other problems faced by Union soldiers fighting in South Texas. The winter of 1863–1864 was extremely harsh. Texas was not the land of milk and honey advertised in antebellum literature. A soldier in the 96th Ohio Infantry Regiment stationed on Matagorda Peninsula gave a typical description. He stated that "the rippling waters sighing along either shore gave the location a kind of romantic character, which was counterbalanced by frequent ice-cold winds, that lashed the same shores with angry surges, and sent us to cover, pining for scenes less romantic and more agreeable." Private Clark of the 34th Iowa described the severity of the winter storms by pointing out that, when a norther arrived, it froze water into ice a half-inch thick. To survive, "every soldier would roll himself up in his blankets and lie on his bunk and shiver. I put on all my clothes including mittens and a cap, and rolled myself in my blankets and read Victor Hugo's *Les Misérables,* the most wonderful of all novels. After that I got a copy of Rollin's *Ancient History,* and read that with great interest and profit." In many of their official reports, the Union officers pointed out that the troops endured the brutal weather without major complaints. The Confederates, equally resilient, compared their ordeal during the winter of 1863 to Valley Forge during the American Revolution. One soldier in the 1st Texas Cavalry Regiment, stationed on the Matagorda Peninsula in December 1863, gave a similar account of this frigid winter on the coast. He pointed out that the regiment had a severe shortage of winter gear, and, as a result, "our suffering was necessarily severe."[40]

Shortages of wood and forage plagued the Union army in Texas. Soldiers fighting on the coast often spoke of the scarcity of wood for campfires. Reuben Scott, a soldier in the 67th Indiana Infantry Regiment, gave testimony to the lack of wood. Stationed on Matagorda Island, Scott described the difficulty of keeping warm during the severe winter of 1863. Since no timber grew on the island, the troops burned driftwood that washed up on the beach. They exercised the strictest economy by digging small pits in the sand to cook and warm themselves.

Scott also discussed the severity of the winter storms in Texas. On one occasion he noted that, "This cold, penetrating wind being so unbearable . . . we retreated to our tents and rolled up in our blankets. But we had not long been rolled up when orders came to march immediately; and this was one of the trying times which tested the nerves of the strongest, to crawl out of our warm blankets into this death chilling wind." Lack of forage for the animals also hampered the Federals. In a dispatch dated December 13, 1863, General Washburn stated that on Matagorda Island eight to ten animals a day were dying of starvation. He informed headquarters at New Orleans that they need not send any more animals to the coast because they would eventually meet the same fate. General Dana at Brownsville also mentioned the insufficient feed for his cavalry horses and recommended a move north to Corpus Christi as a base of operations, where the Nueces River Valley would furnish abundant water and grass.[41]

While the Union generals awaited Banks's orders to advance, they busied themselves by fortifying the positions they were holding. At Brownsville, soldiers had begun making repairs to Fort Brown, headquarters for the commanders in the region. The men dug trenches around the garrison, built a large breastwork on the sod embankment, and placed fifteen 12-pounders and five 20-pounder Parrotts on the works. They then constructed a camp about 1.5 miles upstream at the first bend in the river above Fort Brown. Their officers believed that a garrison of 500 men could hold off an attack by 5,000 good troops.[42]

Another body of Union soldiers, under Col. Justin Hodge, was stationed at Point Isabel. It consisted of the 1st and 2nd Engineers, Corps d'Afrique, and the 16th Infantry, Corps d'Afrique. These men dug an extensive maze of rifle pits from the Point Isabel lighthouse to a point 1,000 yards north on the bay. They also constructed two redoubts at points along the rifle pits to accommodate artillery. Fortifications sprang up on Brazos Santiago in early 1864, including a military road connecting Boca Chica to the mouth of the river. Brazos Santiago became a principal commissary depot for troops serving on the lower Texas coast.[43]

No other region of Texas was as heavily fortified as Matagorda Island and the surrounding areas. Seven thousand Federal soldiers camped there shortly after the battle of Fort Esperanza and established three principal fronts. The main fortification was Fort Esperanza. Shortly after the capture of the stronghold, General Ransom set up a fortified battery on the other side of Pass Cavallo on the southern end of Matagorda Peninsula, known as DeCrow's Point. Soldiers from the 1st and 4th Divisions of the XIII Army Corps garrisoned this position. In addition to fortifying the entrance to Matagorda

Bay, the XIII Army Corps also stationed men in Indianola and built a series of forts and trenches. They occupied the city for several weeks and built five strongholds capable of mounting fifteen heavy guns. Union troops also fortified the township of Saluria, a short distance inland from Fort Esperanza.[44]

By year's end, at least ten thousand Federal soldiers were encamped on the Texas coast from Brownsville to the Matagorda Peninsula. The Union commands had also undergone some shuffling. On December 24, 1863, General Banks ordered Maj. Gen. Francis J. Herron to take command of the 2nd Division, XIII Army Corps, at Fort Brown. Dana, who commanded the XIII Army Corps, would assume command of Fort Esperanza. Banks gave Herron specific instructions concerning the Brownsville command. Herron must defend the present holdings, maintain cordial relations with those in power in Matamoros, and recruit local citizens for service in the Union army. To this end, Col. Edmund J. Davis and Lt. Col. John L. Haynes recruited Unionists, Mexicans, and Confederate deserters into the 1st and 2nd Texas Cavalry Regiments. Finally, Herron was expected to link up with other forces that might later be aimed at the capture of Galveston. By New Year's Day, the only important coastal positions still under Confederate control were Forts Quintana and Velasco (at the mouth of the Brazos), Galveston, and Sabine Pass.[45]

The Rio Grande expedition achieved some of its objectives in the first two months of the campaign. Diplomatically, Banks established a Union presence on the Rio Grande as President Lincoln had desired. Economically, the export of Confederate cotton, although not severely crippled, was slowed. Prior to the campaign Banks had predicted that the Federals could procure 50,000–100,000 bales of cotton in Texas. After little more than a month, they had secured only about 800 bales, hardly a brilliant reward for a large military expedition. A Brownsville merchant and Union supporter, Gilbert D. Kingsbury, credited the Union occupation with reducing the amount of cotton crossing the Rio Grande by half. He realized, though, that the Confederates diverted their cotton to Eagle Pass and Laredo, creating greater difficulties for the Federal soldiers on the Rio Grande. Kingsbury astutely observed that it would be impossible for the Union forces to occupy the Rio Grande from Brownsville to Eagle Pass. He believed that General Dana should concentrate on occupying San Antonio or Austin, thus blocking the major cotton routes from the interior of Texas.[46]

The Rio Grande expedition also had a political mission, one that was centered on A. J. Hamilton, military governor of Texas. Hamilton had been authorized to "reestablish the authority of the Federal government in the State of Texas and to provide the means of maintaining the peace and security to the loyal inhabitants of that State until they shall be able to establish a civil government." Much discretion was left to Hamilton in carrying out the assignment, and he was promised the support of the Lincoln administration in whatever he did. Hamilton patiently waited in New Orleans for Banks to occupy some portion of Texas. When Banks readied his troops for the Rio Grande expedition, Hamilton wanted to join them. Banks, however, believed that if Hamilton joined the mission and it failed, it would serve only to magnify the loss. Banks thus insisted that Hamilton stay in New Orleans until he heard of the success of the invading force, and Hamilton acceded to his request.[47]

Upon hearing of the capture of Brownsville, Hamilton left New Orleans, arriving in Brownsville on December 1, 1863. In a telegram to Secretary of War Edwin M. Stanton, Hamilton described how hundreds of Texas citizens had migrated from the interior of the state to Brownsville. The morale of these refugees was low. From talking to them, Hamilton formed the impression that the rebellion in Texas was about to collapse. Rebel commanders had abandoned any idea of defending the country west of the Colorado River. Twenty-five thousand men could seal the fate of Texas in two months. Hamilton also wanted to establish a Federal court at Brownsville to "help settle questions arising under the act of Congress providing for the confiscations of property of persons engaged in the rebellion."[48]

Concerning the proposed court, Hamilton ran into opposition from General Dana. Hamilton had extradited a suspect from Matamoros to be tried for murder. In a telegram dated December 15, 1863, Dana pointed out to Hamilton that, in an extradition treaty of 1861, when the civil authority in a state is suspended, "the chief military officer in command of such state" shall conduct the extradition of criminals. Dana qualified his statement to Hamilton by observing that even he was not sure whether he could extradite criminal suspects from Mexico or whether that power resided with General Banks. In the end, Dana concluded that he wanted no clash of authority, but he asked Hamilton to write the War Department about the military governor's authority with regard to Mexico.[49]

A far more serious problem concerning Mexico emerged when Hamilton, at a reception in Matamoros, promised American aid to Benito Juarez, the resistance leader fighting the French occupation of Mexico. This assurance angered President Lincoln and Secretary of State Seward. The Lincoln administration had worked diligently to avoid anything that might offend France. General Banks, who received authority from Seward and Stanton to suspend Hamilton, wrote the Texan a friendly note reminding him of the delicate diplomatic situation in Mexico while assuring him of his continued support.[50]

The friction between Dana and Hamilton ended when Dana received orders to command Fort Esperanza in late December and was replaced by General Herron. Despite the decline of military activity in Texas by the end of 1863, Hamilton continued to issue ineffective proclamations and appointed a few civil officers in the Brownsville area. He also made speeches supporting emancipation and the Union. In one address, given on January 1, 1864, Hamilton made an appeal "to the people of Texas." He remarked that they had been deceived by their leaders in the South over issues such as secession and slavery. He described the plight of the Union men in Texas, defending their actions since the day the Lone Star State had seceded. Despite his effort for the cause of the Union in Texas, Hamilton probably realized during his brief stay in Brownsville that his political power in the state depended greatly upon the military conquest of Texas.[51]

Although Hamilton's political power extended to only those areas controlled by Federal troops, his presence had a demoralizing effect on people living on the Texas coast. In March 1864, the inhabitants of Corpus Christi learned that he intended to establish a Federal court in their city. The first session was expected to be held sometime in May. Corpus Christians believed their city was chosen because of an anticipated Federal invasion of the interior emanating from Corpus Christi that spring. Neither the court nor the spring invasion ever materialized. They were only rumors, ever present in wartime. However, these stories undoubtedly created a sense of foreboding in the hearts of many loyal Confederates, not only in Corpus Christi, but along the lower Texas coast as well.[52]

The Rio Grande expedition, which controlled a large section of the Texas coastline by December 1863, stalled when it failed to penetrate the interior of the state. That failure can be blamed partly on the differences of opinion over grand strategy between President Lincoln and the military men who controlled the fate of the Department of the Gulf. Lincoln wanted the Union forces in Texas to perform primarily a diplomatic function. Halleck, the military purist, wanted to close with the Confederate forces in northwest Louisiana and northeast Texas and give battle. Banks believed that the Rio Grande expedition, if properly supported, could accomplish both its military and diplomatic missions. Unfortunately, this assistance never came. By January 1864 Halleck had already recruited Major Generals Ulysses S. Grant, William T. Sherman, and Frederick Steele in support of a campaign up the

Red River. Banks, who as late as December 30 wanted to continue the Texas operations, informed Halleck on January 23, 1864 that he supported the Red River route. With so much military savvy massed against him, Banks's transformation of attitude can easily be understood. It also meant that, if the Red River campaign failed, others besides Banks could share the blame for its collapse.[53]

At the end of the year, the Federal soldiers on the Rio Grande expedition, which stretched from the mouth of the Rio Grande to the Matagorda Peninsula, went into winter quarters. Encamped at Brownsville was the 2nd Division; on Matagorda Island was the 1st Division; and on Matagorda Peninsula were elements of the 1st and 4th Divisions—all from the XIII Army Corps. Although the Union soldiers at first suffered from the harsh winter of 1863–1864, they later established comfortable cold-weather accommodations. The 20th Iowa built small houses on Mustang Island from lumber that had been torn from deserted homes on the mainland. One soldier stated that these shelters had "all the comforts of home." Four companies of the 33rd Illinois at Indianola occupied "splendid winter quarters" in a vacated two-story office building. Men of the 21st Iowa set up shop in the Indianola courthouse, and the 19th Iowa at Brownsville took up residence in an abandoned warehouse. It appeared on the surface that the Federals were not planning to leave Texas any time soon.[54]

Despite its confinement to the Texas coast, the Rio Grande expedition caused grave concern for those charged with the defense of the state. The loss of Brownsville, which absorbed the initial brunt of the assault, sent a shock wave throughout Texas as Federal regiments crept up the coast. Confederate authorities adopted countermeasures not only to repel the Union invaders but also to protect the precious cotton trade with Mexico.[55]

Three

Fall Back and Save the Cotton

*O*n July 13, 1863, the commander of the Confederate Trans-Mississippi Department, Lt. Gen. Edmund Kirby Smith, issued an invitation to the civilian leaders of the four states within his region.[1] Prompted by the fall of Vicksburg and Port Hudson, Smith asked these leaders to attend a conference in Marshall, Texas, sometime in the middle of August. The loss of the Mississippi had severed ties with Richmond; consequently, Smith realized the Trans-Mississippi "must be self-sustaining and self-reliant in every respect." He also wanted to allay the public's despondency by providing convincing proof of the loyalty and unanimous determination of the Trans-Mississippi's leading men to fight on to ultimate victory. Smith also hoped to relieve people's fears of army despotism by arranging an exhibition of the civil government's supremacy over the military. Ironically, the calling together of civilian leaders by a Confederate general seemed to be an assertion more of military power than civilian.[2]

On August 15, 1863, civilian representatives from Texas, Louisiana, Arkansas, and Missouri met at Marshall to discuss the future of the Trans-Mississippi Department. Texas sent Gov. Francis R. Lubbock, governor-elect Pendleton Murrah, Maj. Guy M. Bryan, and Confederate senator W. S. Oldham. The participants examined topics such as Smith's authority, foreign affairs, and the department's resources. They discussed the problem of securing and disposing of cotton without stirring up opposition. The delegates stated that "cotton is the only safe and reliable means for carrying on efficient military operations for the defense of the country west of the Mississippi." As a result, Smith was advised to take charge of all of the cotton in his department except what was required to meet the people's needs.[3]

Although the Marshall conference had no legal standing, it reaffirmed what Smith already knew: The department had to export cotton in order to obtain war supplies. Prior to the meeting, Smith had established the Cotton Bureau and sixteen other executive and military agencies. The representatives at Marshall gave Smith a vote of confidence to assume extraordinary powers during this crisis. The officials who attended also expressed the determination of the Trans-Mississippi Confederacy to fight on to the bitter end.[4]

In August 1863 Smith established the Cotton Bureau, which centralized control over the cotton trade in the Trans-Mississippi Department. He appointed Lt. Col. W. A. Broadwell to head the bureau, which would have its main headquarters in Shreveport, Louisiana. Since Texas provided the only viable means of exporting large amounts of cotton through the Brownsville-Matamoros region, the Confederate Trans-Mississippi Department established a Texas Cotton Office in Houston. This branch was designated as the purchasing agent of all supplies through the medium of cotton and had direct authority over all of the Confederate agents engaged in the purchase of cotton in Texas.[5]

Cotton was vital to the Confederate war effort west of the Mississippi River. A list of purchases made by the Texas Cotton Bureau in December 1864 impressively illustrates its purchasing power. More than one million dollars' worth of ordnance stores was bought, including 23,000 rifles, 10,000 percussion caps, 200,000 pounds of gunpowder, 200,000 pounds of niter, and a varied assortment of cannons, swords, and pistols.[6]

When the first U.S. vessels appeared near the mouth of the Rio Grande on November 1, 1863, panic enveloped Texas. The first dispatches sent from Brig. Gen. Hamilton Bee, commander at Fort Brown, clearly illustrated what he considered to be a top military priority. On November 2 he said, "I have sent out a detachment to turn back all cotton wagons en route for this place." On November 3, Bee destroyed six hundred bales of cotton that would have fallen into the enemy's hands. That same day his scouts informed him that Union troops were advancing on Brownsville. Later that day Bee and eighty men of the 33rd Texas Cavalry left Brownsville, heading for the King Ranch, about one hundred miles to the north. On November 5, Bee sent a dispatch to Maj. Gen. John B. Magruder, commander of the District of Texas, New Mexico, and Arizona, informing Magruder that he had destroyed, as ordered, all of the cotton at Brownsville and removed one million dollars' worth of supplies. Clearly, Magruder wanted nothing of value, especially cotton, to be appropriated by the enemy. By stopping at a major cotton depot such as the King Ranch, Bee hoped to divert the cotton wagons bound for Brownsville to a point farther up the Rio Grande to prevent their capture.[7]

Unfortunately, the idea of rerouting the cotton wagons to upriver cross-ings dawned slowly on Bee during this chaotic time. While at the King Ranch, he ordered the burning of twenty-five wagons of cotton recently ar-rived from Arkansas. John Warren Hunter, a sixteen-year-old teamster, ar-rived in time to view what he recorded as a "pathetic incident" but also one of the "rarest spectacles" he had ever witnessed: "[T]he air was yet laden with the odor of burning cotton and the pall of smoke that hung over the landscape. The dismantled wagons, and the half-consumed, yet burning cot-ton bales, the forlorn and woeful look of the teamsters—all these gave mute evidence of the fearful ravages under the thin guise of expediency. The old men were sitting around as if in a stupor, while the boys wandered aimlessly about, silent, morose, as if trying to comprehend the enormity of the ca-lamity that had engulfed them in general ruin."[8]

The fall of Brownsville did not come as a complete surprise to Magruder. On November 2, 1863, he wrote a letter to Governor Murrah and informed him that an expedition bound for the Texas coast had already set sail. Ma-gruder considered this expedition to be a diversion; the real attack, he be-lieved, would come by way of the Red River Valley. Prudence, however, de-manded that the state prepare itself for any possible assault. Magruder went on to state that the scarcity of arms in Texas was one of the greatest imped-iments to organizing an effective army. Accordingly, he asked Murrah to promote the production of war materiel within the state. The department commander then requested the cooperation of state troops and an additional two thousand men to fill a prior requisition submitted to former governor Lubbock. Magruder realized that, in order to repel an invasion of Texas, the energies of the state and the Confederate authorities had to be combined. This letter to Murrah also described the great fear that the Rio Grande ex-pedition had generated throughout the state.[9]

Kirby Smith learned of the fall of Brownsville on November 13. Although unable to send reinforcements to Magruder, he directed him to order Bee to remain between the Federals and the river crossings at Laredo and Eagle Pass. Bee was also to protect the southern approaches to San Antonio with whatever cavalry he could spare. Like Magruder, Smith believed that the Rio Grande expedition was a ruse; the real attack would instead come by way of Louisiana. As a result, Smith sent no reinforcements to Texas. Magruder, re-alizing that additional troops were not forthcoming, took evasive measures against the Union assault. He wanted nothing of value to fall into the hands of the enemy. He ordered army patrols to drive all of the livestock north of the Nueces River. These same troops would also move any slaves from areas that might end up under Federal control. Finally, transportation facilities were to be destroyed. The tracks of the San Antonio and Mexican Gulf Railroad, which connected Victoria and Port Lavaca, were smashed. Port facilities at Aransas Bay, Corpus Christi Bay, and Matagorda Bay had to be demolished as well. Much of this destruction was done against the protests of prominent citizens living along the coast.[10]

In a letter to Pres. Jefferson Davis on November 13, Smith defended Magruder's actions. He explained that, with the limited number of troops at Magruder's disposal, it would have been impossible to prevent the Federal occupation of Brownsville. Smith also pointed out that, even if Magruder had additional forces, the remoteness of Brownsville and the difficult terrain between that city and Houston would have made supplying those soldiers a very difficult task indeed.[11]

Magruder also worked to strengthen the morale of the Confederate Texans. He realized that the Union invasion of Texas could sap the civilian population's fighting spirit. Therefore, he ordered Confederate regiments below the Nueces River to make themselves very visible to inspire the confidence of the residents. These same forces were also ordered to prevent potential recruits from escaping into Mexico or, worse yet, joining the Union army. In addition, Magruder circulated a rumor that Confederate troops from East Texas were on their way to San Antonio.[12]

Raising additional manpower was Magruder's biggest challenge in repelling the Yankee invaders. At the time of the Rio Grande expedition, he had only about nine thousand men to defend the state. To raise additional troops, he adopted every possible expedient. Home guards and invalid reserve companies from as far away as Houston were armed and charged with relieving the regular garrison troops for field service. Magruder then asked Governor Murrah to call up every able-bodied white male between the ages of sixteen and seventy. Murrah, however, failed to act upon this request because state law prevented him from raising additional forces. Magruder then instructed post commanders in the invasion areas to enlist anyone who seemed fit enough to hold a rifle. Even men who were detailed as cotton teamsters were ordered to report to their regiments immediately or be listed as deserters. Even with all of these measures in place, Magruder still failed to produce the necessary troops to stop the Union advance.[13]

The loss of Brownsville meant that cotton would have to be crossed further upriver at Eagle Pass and Laredo. The Confederate officers who were charged with the defense of South Texas knew this situation all too well. On November 8, 1863, General Bee, the most prominent among them, sent a lengthy telegram to headquarters in Houston. The message, sent from Bee's temporary command center at the King Ranch, stated that no cotton should be crossed below Eagle Pass and a determined effort should be made to hold that position. He then issued orders that all cotton wagons bound for Brownsville be rerouted to Eagle Pass. He requested that Magruder publish this order in the Houston newspapers. Bee then asked for one thousand cavalry to protect the cotton wagons and to prevent Laredo and Eagle Pass from falling into Union hands.[14]

The following day, Bee sent a dispatch to Maj. Santos Benavides, who was commanding about 120 men of the 33rd Texas Cavalry. Benavides, a prominent Laredo citizen, played a crucial role in defending the upriver crossings at Laredo and Eagle Pass. Born in Laredo on November 1, 1823, he had served as both mayor and chief justice of Webb County. At the time of the fall of Brownsville, Benavides had achieved the rank of major in the 33rd Texas Cavalry. His two brothers, Refugio and Cristobal, also served in the same regiment. The telegram of November 9, 1863, informed Benavides that cotton wagons were now being sent to Laredo and Eagle Pass. Bee clearly wanted an officer who was familiar with the region now that Laredo would become a major cotton crossing. Bee pointed out to Benavides that "there must be an active officer at Laredo to expedite the passage of the cotton across the river, and make the necessary arrangements with the Mexican authorities for its safety after it crosses."[15]

That same day Bee also sent a message to J. A. Quintero, a Confederate representative living in Monterrey, Mexico, since the fall of 1861. Quintero had established friendly relations with Santiago Vidaurri, who controlled the Mexican border states of Nuevo Leon and Coahuila. Quintero's residence in Monterrey, the capital of Nuevo Leon, placed him in a crucial position to protect the Confederate cotton trade. Bee asked Quintero to use all of his influence with Governor Vidaurri to allow the safe passage of cotton across the Rio Grande from Laredo and Eagle Pass. Bee reminded Quintero that the economic benefits to Nuevo Leon and Coahuila would be immense and that Vidaurri should therefore do everything in his power to protect this vital trade.[16]

On November 10, General Magruder acknowledged Bee's telegram announcing the fall of Brownsville. He reported that two companies of state troops, an artillery battery, and the 33rd Texas Cavalry under Col. James Duff were being sent to Bee to protect his wagon train. Magruder then indicated that, if the enemy landed in force at Corpus Christi, Bee must burn all of the cotton and other valuable supplies that could not be carried off. He also recommended that Bee then fall back to Goliad, about sixty miles north of Corpus Christi, to await further orders. Magruder clearly did not want the enemy to obtain anything of value.[17]

The next day Bee informed headquarters in Houston that 12,000 Federals occupied Brownsville and threatened the territory as far west as Rio Grande City. Anarchy reigned in both Brownsville and Matamoros. Bee knew that this chaotic situation would hold the Federals in place for some time, allowing him an opportunity to regroup. He then summarized a message from Major Benavides. Benavides and the 120 men he commanded defended Fort Ringgold, near Rio Grande City. When Benavides offered his men the option of a discharge if they chose not to fight, the men replied, "Viva la confederación! Viva Major Benavides!" When Bee learned of the loyalty of those soldiers, he ordered all of the cotton wagons to Laredo, realizing that Benavides had considerable influence in that Texas border town.[18]

Benavides proved to be a valuable military asset. On November 12 he wrote Bee that a considerable number of cotton bales (twenty-six hundred) had accumulated at Rio Grande City. Benavides made arrangements with a man named Don Rafael Lopez in Camargo (opposite Rio Grande City) to receive the cotton and pay the duties on it. The cotton would then be transported to Matamoros. Benavides also sent some of the cotton to Laredo to await later shipment. Like Bee, Benavides planned to move any valuable military stores to either Laredo or San Antonio. In addition, he made arrangements with Juan Cortina, governor of the Mexican state of Tamaulipas, to allow the cotton to be transported safely to Matamoros. Benavides eventually withdrew from Rio Grande City in late November. As the Union troops moved up the coast, Bee was held in check and could not reinforce the outnumbered Benavides. Col. Edmund J. Davis's Federal cavalry expedition against Rio Grande City failed to capture him, however.[19]

Another prominent South Texan, Richard King, was gravely concerned about the Federals' presence in Brownsville. Since March 1862 his ranch, about 120 miles north of Brownsville, had been designated by the Military Board of Texas as an official receiving, storage, and shipping point for Confederate cotton. Thousands of bales, both private and government, arrived at his ranch bound for the Mexican border. When Bee showed up at his ranch on November 8, King feared that South Texas would be given up without a fight. On November 12 King sent an urgent letter to Houston, pleading for help: "We hope to God this section of the Country [will] not be abandoned without a struggle or at least without giving the people notice that it is to be entirely abandoned, so that we can at least send our families to a place of safety. We think from 2 to 3,000 Cavalry can protect this section against any-thing the enemy can bring—if [we] cannot get this number, let us have 500 good determined Texans, from whom a good account will be given, and this Country saved from utter destruction—do not abandon us for God Sake!"[20]

As the northern invasion continued to move up the Texas coast, Ma-gruder ordered Bee to remove any cotton from threatened areas. By mid-November, Corpus Christi had become the most vulnerable coastal city. Magruder also wanted Bee to reinforce San Antonio and Eagle Pass to pro-tect the cotton trade. Bee, already short of men, decided to strengthen only Eagle Pass. He ordered his aide at the western subdistrict headquarters in San Antonio, Maj. A. G. Dickinson, to send a company of soldiers to Eagle Pass. Bee realized that, in reducing the troop strength at San Antonio, he was defying Magruder's wishes, but he had no other choice. Bee realized that the troops on the border would not only protect the border crossings but bolster the confidence of the people as well.[21]

Kirby Smith urged Magruder to keep the Federals bottled up at Browns-ville and not to allow them to make any raids in the direction of San Anto-nio. The cotton routes from San Antonio to Laredo and Eagle Pass had to be protected. Magruder's men in the field (Bee and Benavides) had already im-plemented measures to protect the cotton trade. What these officers wanted to hear from headquarters was an order to attack the Yankees. Bee realized that constant retreat hurt the morale of his men. He sent Magruder an out-line of the measures he proposed to take in stopping the invasion of South Texas. With his temporary headquarters at Corpus Christi, Bee proposed three lines of defense. The first one stretched from Corpus Christi to Laredo. If Corpus Christi fell, the second line would be from Saluria on the coast to Eagle Pass. The last line of defense would be the Colorado River, extending from Austin to the township of Matagorda, at the mouth of the Colorado. Bee of course needed additional soldiers to make any kind of stand succeed. He requested the 1st Texas Cavalry under Col. August Buchel and the 32nd Texas Cavalry under Col. P. C. Woods. Bee confidentially stated that with more men he could "annihilate Banks on the edge of this desert."[22]

Bold talk, however, could not allay the worries of the civilian population in the Lone Star State. Civilian leaders as far north as San Antonio feared that the Rio Grande expedition would quickly overrun their city. In a letter to Major Dickinson on November 16, leading citizens of San Antonio ex-pressed not only their loyalty to the Confederate cause but also their concern for the safety of their families. The letter stated that "the landing of the Yankees at Brownsville and the depredations along the Rio Grande admonish us that every man should now enter the service. However, a request is made in order that we may, as far as possible, remove our families and dependencies to a place of greater security, or within the lines of the army." Dickinson, charged with the defense of San Antonio, was asked to forward the letter to Magruder to apprise him of the grave concern these civic leaders had for the safety of their city and their families.[23]

One of those prominent San Antonio figures was Mary Maverick, who had four sons in the Confederate army, one of whom was Capt. Lewis Maverick of the 32nd Texas Cavalry Regiment. In a letter to Lewis, Mary remarked that "The Yankees took Brownsville on the 4th. The Federal force is believed to be 12,000. Our knowing men here suppose they are intended to break up our trade with Mexico, or maybe to make a demonstration against French rule in Mexico. I suppose Magruder will hurry troops out West or is it true that he declared San Antonio outside his line of defense? Some here censure Duff and Bee for not fighting, but how could they with only 150 men? Possibly these Feds will make raids up this way, if we are not strengthened soon." In another letter, Mary informed Lewis that "if the Yankees advance from the coast, Magruder will meet them and our Texas boys will give them a hostile reception."[24]

Civilians in Austin also expressed similar concern for the safety of their city. They believed that the natural object of the Federal invasion was the state capital, where they lived. With feelings running high, Austin's leaders called a meeting of Travis County residents. The assembly condemned the Federals for forcing "a war of the races" upon them because the invading Union army included black troops. These Austinites also exhorted every man and boy capable of holding a rifle to help repel the enemy. A few days after the meeting, seventy-three Austin and Travis County residents who had been exempted from military service enlisted in a cavalry company to defend the capital. Throughout November, as the Union invaders continued to move up the coast, panic gripped the city. "Their purpose is evidently to overrun Texas, and the occupation of the Capital will be their first object," asserted an Austin newspaper. General Magruder had similar apprehensions. He ordered that Austin be fortified, appealing to the people of Travis and nearby counties to send half of their adult male slaves to the capital to strengthen its defenses.[25]

In mid-December, Maj. Getulius Kellersberger, a Confederate engineer, rode into Austin with five hundred slaves to begin work on earthen fortifications. "People stared at us very curiously and our arrival caused a great deal of anxiety," he recounted later. Slaves continued to arrive in town for the next several days, and the construction of defense works on the Austin perimeter continued into early 1864. The proximity of the Union forces compelled Travis County's provost marshal to impose new restrictions under martial law. All civilians and soldiers arriving in or leaving Austin had to carry passports issued by the provost marshal, even if traveling only a short distance. When a prominent Unionist named George Paschal refused to carry a passport, he was arrested and taken to military headquarters in Houston.[26]

An interesting account of Paschal's arrest and the general anxiety created by the presence of Federal troops in Texas came from Laura P. DuVal, the wife of federal judge and prominent Unionist Thomas H. DuVal. In a letter to her husband, she said, "Nobody can leave the country on any business of whatever character without being suspected and I hope you will stay in Mexico until things are a little more settled. I want to see you terribly as you may well imagine but I am glad you are not at home now and hope you will not come until I advise you to do so. Do not let your anxiety on our account hurry you back. We are doing as well as can be expected and I am sure Mexico is a much pleasanter place to be in than Texas." Later in the letter, Mrs. DuVal's concern for her husband became more emphatic: "For God's sake don't come back until the fighting is over in Texas. Your health is not robust enough to stand the fatigue of war and if you could stand [it], I could not the yankee bullets. Don't come home *I charge you* until the matter is settled!"[27]

Laura DuVal also gave a detailed account of George Paschal's arrest. Apparently, Paschal had allowed himself to be taken into custody in order to test the legality of the passport requirement for travel outside the city. When he asked to be allowed to go home for a change of clothes, he was escorted there in a wagon—under armed guard. Laura DuVal described the moment: "A scene that we little expected to see in our once happy country, his little Betty screaming and begging them not to hang her papa, and cousin Marcia alternately shrieking and begging them to tell her where they were going to carry him, which they refused doing." Paschal was sent to Houston but was released by General Magruder a week later. This incident clearly reflected the increased tension created by the enemy forces in Texas, especially with regard to suspicions of treason and disloyalty.[28]

Prominent newspapers in Texas contributed to the uneasiness created by the presence of Federal soldiers on the Texas coast. In Austin, the *State Gazette* gave a detailed account of the fall of Brownsville and General Bee's retreat. In one edition, the paper reported that "Banks is in command of the Federal force, which is near 12,000 strong. In landing, he lost all his artillery, horses as well as many stores, and is by this means too much shattered to attempt to move soon. His expedition is doubtless the one which was planned in Washington, and has probably more reference to Mexican affairs, than those on this side of the river. However matters turn out, it is clear that our trade with Mexico, via Brownsville, is at an end." To punctuate the fear, Kirby Smith made an urgent appeal to the people within the Trans-Mississippi Department: "Your homes are now in peril, vigorous efforts on your part can alone save portions of your State from invasion. You should contest the advance of the enemy at every thicket, gully and stream; harass his rear and cut off his supplies. Thus you will prove important auxiliaries in my attempts to reach him in front and drive him from our soil. Determination and energy only, can prevent his destruction of your homes. By a vigorous and united effort you preserve your property, you secure independence for yourselves and children, all that renders life desirable. Time is now our best friend. Endure a while longer, victory and peace must crown our efforts." [29]

Later accounts of the Federals' drive up the coast were provided by the *Houston Tri-Weekly Telegraph*. One article informed readers that "The Yankees are advancing to this direction, and have effected a foothold at Aransas Pass. On the night of the 16th they landed a force supposed to be 3,000 strong in the lower end of Mustang Island, and marched on the fort at the Pass. These troops were conveyed in five sailing vessels (transports). On the morning of the 17th they made the attack, with this force and five steamers from the sea cooperating. The engagement lasted two hours and twenty-five minutes, when our troops surrendered, being overwhelmed with numbers. The plan of the enemy appears to be to take such points as he can up the coast, with the view of getting a base near his proposed field of operations. There can be no doubt that he meditates the conquest of the State." [30]

In a later edition of the *Houston Tri-Weekly Telegraph*, the fall of Fort Esperanza on Matagorda Island also received considerable coverage. Although the attack on the stronghold came as no surprise, the writer of the article was clearly displeased at the meager resistance shown by the Esperanza garrison: "We have anticipated an attack on Fort Esperanza, at Saluria, with satisfaction, from the fact that we were led to believe that the Fort was prepared to make a satisfactory resistance to the progress of the enemy. Whether it has made all the resistance it could, we are not prepared to say, but that it has yielded sooner than we anticipated we candidly confess." In portraying the civilian response to the attack, the article claimed that "the people were preparing to leave Lavaca for the interior. The whole country has become thoroughly aroused, and a determined spirit of resistance everywhere prevails." [31]

A few days later, the *Houston Tri-Weekly Telegraph* published more critical articles about the fall of Fort Esperanza. One of them addressed the level of provisions in the fort, pointing out that "according to reports of the Commissary General, [there were] enough to have lasted the garrison thirty days. Other reports make them equal to a 15-day siege. Be that as it may, there were provisions enough there to have kept the garrison until a force from the mainland could have raised the siege. It was not for the want of provisions that the fort was evacuated." The same edition also considered the number of soldiers in the fort as well as their leadership. The *Telegraph* asserted that it was not "a lack of men to have defended it against the assault. It is believed that the fort could have withstood assaults for a month or even longer, as it was well constructed for that purpose." Concerning the command of the fort itself, the newspaper reported "charges of incompetency against the commanding officer, of which it is not our duty to take cognissance [*sic*], further than to hope, for his own credit, as well as that of the service, he will at once demand an official investigation into this affair." The *Telegraph* believed an inquiry into the loss of Fort Esperanza was necessary because of the demoralizing impact it had made on civilian morale. The newspaper maintained that "the loss of the fort, which our people had been led to believe was capable of withstanding a siege, and would arrest the progress of the invasion, has made the public mind painfully sensitive to the causes of the evacuation. Whatever they are should be set forth officially at the earliest possible moment, since, in the present uncertainty, the popular imagination will inevitably assign the worst reasons, and these, if not denied, can but do injury to the cause dearest to all, both soldier and citizen."[32]

A few days later, the *Telegraph* changed direction and actually applauded the efforts of the Confederate officers in the field. Colonel W. R. Bradfute, the ridiculed commander at Fort Esperanza, received praise for his actions during the battle. The paper mentioned that "seeing that he was at any moment to be surrounded and cut off from retreat, [he] evacuated the fort. We consider his foresight in this matter, and his successful evacuation as a great military movement, and consider the gallant Colonel entitled to much credit." The *Telegraph* also commended General Bee, the Brownsville commander: "General Bee is spoken of as an able officer, and his late skillful movements have established his fame as a military leader—we honor this gallant officer. He does not forget how to be a gentlemen, although he is a general. He is loved by his troops and the people of Western Texas have unbounded confidence in him. Thousands are flocking to the standard of General Bee." These statements clearly indicate that the *Telegraph* wanted to express to its readers the newspaper's continued belief in the leadership of the Confederate forces in Texas.[33]

Although the *Telegraph* tried to instill faith in the citizens of the Lone Star State, the harsh reality of war sometimes crept into its articles. One journalist stated that "We and the entire country [are] in great excitement. The majority of planters have removed their negroes towards the interior, and many families have left them all behind, in fleeing from the perils of invasion. We see families flying in every direction from the coast. The people feel they have nothing to hope for that the scenes of outrage perpetrated in Louisiana will not be re-enacted in Texas."[34]

As the Rio Grande expedition continued its progress up the coast, the journalists for the *Telegraph* realized that Houston might be under enemy attack by the end of the year. As a result, their appeals to all Texans, but especially Houstonians, became more aggressive. One article made this patriotic statement: "Our people now see the Yankee invasion upon their shores. It is advancing upon the heart of the country. Are they ready to meet it? Let the free people flock to the point of danger. The people of Houston are arousing and organizing for the fray. They understand that their city is the tempting bait that is luring the enemy on. In attacking successively Brownsville, Aransas, Esperanza, and Velasco, he is but attacking the outposts of Houston. These were the picket stations. The pickets have fallen back from one after another. The battlefield will take place near the citadel. Houston today is the heart of the Trans-Mississippi Department. It must be defended at all hazards. Every man in the army or out of it must throw himself into the breach. The more volunteers added to our force, the further from the citadel will the decisive battle be fought."[35]

These appeals continued to appear in the *Telegraph.* Another example is an entreaty to the people of Houston by Maj. W. Hyllested, who was commanding Houston while Magruder was in the field:

> The enemy are advancing upon the soil of Texas—his footsteps are desecrating your land. He is within a few hours travel of your firesides and homes of your families.
>
> The major general commanding is in the field—the men of Texas are rallying to his standard, and he is determined to not only chastise the enemy, but to drive him from the State by compelling him to return to his ships, or submit to ignominious capture.
>
> To do this, it is necessary that every well armed and drilled man should be in the field. I have a company of troops doing Provost

Marshall guard duty in this city. I wish to send them to the Major General at the scene of action. I can only do so by having a company of Citizens, who will organize for local defense and tender their services during the present emergency to act in this County. Such Company can relieve the present guard, that they may go and meet the enemy.

Will not the exempts in this city organise [*sic*] and tender their service at once! Every man who does so will enable me to send a good soldier to the front. The advance of the enemy for a few days would put him in your city. Will you not assist in his discomfiture before he reaches your homes? I feel confident that you only wish to know that you can thus serve the cause, to ensure your prompt action.

While you are reading this, your neighbors between this and the coast are abandoning their homes, sending their wives, children and servants to the interior, and going themselves to join the army in front of the foe. Will you stand idly by and wait until it is too late, or will you act at once!

All good citizens are requested to assist in this matter. The Commandant of the Post will furnish ammunition, arms, and equipment as soon as the company has organised [*sic*] by the election of officers.
W. Hyllested
Major, Commanding Post[36]

The increased Confederate military activity, especially in the Austin–San Antonio area, was confirmed by refugees arriving in Brownsville. Thomas DuVal corroborated this when he wrote in his diary that "Men occasionally drop in here from the interior. One a German has arrived from Houston via San Antonio leaving the latter place 8 or 9 days ago. Reports that many of the soldiers were frozen near Houston in the late cold spell. They are fortifying San Antonio and Austin, and that from 16 to 50 are being forced into the ranks. No doubt there is a degree of military despotism existing beyond all that has gone before."[37]

Although friction certainly existed between the state government and General Magruder, in general the state officials supported the war effort and the defense of their state. When outgoing governor Francis R. Lubbock addressed the Tenth Legislature on November 4, he told the representatives that there was "no reason to despond or falter" but admitted that the war had "assumed gigantic proportions, demanding sacrifices on the part of all."

With Union forces in Louisiana, Lubbock realized that another invasion of Texas was indeed possible. He closed his address by asking the legislature to do its part to defend the state by making Texas "the grave, not the inheritance, of the invader."[38]

Even Governor Murrah, who had initially defied Magruder, began to make concessions as the enemy continued to march up the Texas coast. On December 16, Murrah signed a bill that extended the enlistment of the state troops for another six months. The terms of service of many of these militiamen were originally to expire on December 31, 1863. This act thus gave Magruder additional manpower through the spring of 1864. The Texas Senate also expressed a defiant tone to the Yankee invaders. On December 16 it adopted a resolution that declared the following: "Now that our presumptuous enemy treads our soil in heavy number and menacing attitude, we bid him a proud and scornful defiance. We here record our full confidence in the patriotism and ability of President Davis. We would not exchange him for any citizen of the Confederacy, as the pilot to carry us through the present stormy struggle for liberty as a people, and for independence as a nation."[39]

While Austin and other cities prepared for the worst, San Antonio tried to improve its defenses. Dickinson, the Confederate commander charged with the city's protection, understood San Antonio's importance for the cotton bound for the Rio Grande. With only 129 men, not to mention the additional responsibility of Eagle Pass, Dickinson asked Magruder for additional troops and supplies. Fort Duncan, near Eagle Pass, had only 25 men to defend that border crossing. Magruder, however, had to do some considerable juggling of men and supplies during this chaotic period. Bee, Dickinson, and even Kirby Smith made demands on Magruder for men and equipment, yet Magruder had nothing to spare. Becoming insistent, Smith told Magruder to take the rifles out of the hands of his men and send the arms to Shreveport if necessary. These were indeed desperate times for Magruder. As a vital link in the cotton trade, San Antonio had to be held. By November 17, Magruder, like Bee, determined that the last line of defense would be the Colorado River. If Bee continued to retreat, troops would be massed at Columbus, about sixty miles west of Houston. Finally, Magruder asked Smith to come to Texas not only to help him direct the defense of the state but also to boost the citizens' spirits.[40]

As the Federals moved up the Texas coast, Magruder continued to receive reports of the declining morale of the citizens and the soldiers in the threatened areas. Bee, attempting to rally his meager forces near Corpus Christi, confirmed the gloomy mood. He reported that state troops near Corpus

Christi could not be relied upon to defend the state because these men had families there and would not leave them at the mercy of the Yankee invaders. The fall of Mustang Island sparked this concern since the city was vulnerable to Union raids from the island. Chaos reigned in Corpus Christi. The local government broke down, and the county's records were hidden for safekeeping. News of the fall of Fort Esperanza further intensified the fear of invasion, resulting in a mass exodus from the town. The local newspaper, the *Corpus Christi Ranchero*, ceased publication and moved to San Patricio. Reporting that an attack by Union forces threatened the whole Nueces Strip, the *Ranchero* concluded pessimistically, "We are in the hands of God." Bee had to contend with not only the enemy troops but the fear they generated as well.[41]

Closer to headquarters in Houston, Magruder received disturbing reports from Col. A. T. Rainey, who had taken command of the garrison at Galveston on November 24. Four days later Rainey sent Magruder a status report of the conditions on the island. His biggest complaint had to do with the shortage of fuel for heating purposes. He said, "I would respectfully call your attention to the great scarcity of fuel at this point. I have just received complaints from almost every command on the Island in reference to this subject. The destruction of private property, which has already commenced, will be most fearful unless the troops are supplied with a sufficiency of fuel. I would therefore respectfully ask the quartermaster at Houston to send thirty days supply of fuel." Rainey also expressed concern over the current military situation on the Texas coast: "If Galveston is to stand a siege in the event of the fall of Houston, which I am informed is the policy of the commanding general, it then becomes highly important that the Garrison be supplied in advance with several months supplies of fuel and subsistence stores."[42]

The last week of November saw no letup in the flurry of dispatches between Magruder, Bee, Kirby Smith, and Texas governor Murrah. On November 23 Magruder warned Murrah of the possibility of Federal cavalry raids on San Antonio and Austin and then sent slaves to both cities to help strengthen their defenses. The following day he informed Kirby Smith of the countermeasures he wanted Bee to adopt on the Texas coast. At this time Magruder also received news from Colonel W. R. Bradfute, who was commanding Fort Esperanza on Matagorda Island. Bradfute reported that the enemy was within striking distance of Saluria, the small town located nearby. In response, Magruder sent gunboats to the fort, but if they did not arrive in time, Bradfute was to link up with Bee at Victoria. Magruder also sent the 32nd Texas Cavalry to Victoria to reinforce Bee. If Victoria fell, Bee would fall back to San Antonio. If that city surrendered, Bee would retreat toward Houston to Columbus, where the final stand would be taken. Magruder instructed Bee to assure his men and the citizenry west of the Colorado River that Magruder fully intended to defend that territory.[43]

Fort Esperanza fell on November 30, but the Confederates succeeded in rerouting the cotton into Mexico. The loss of Brownsville and its environs forced cotton traders to cross their cargoes upriver at Laredo and Eagle Pass. Laredo was about 235 miles from Brownsville, and Eagle Pass another 90 miles upriver from Laredo. When Bee fell back from Brownsville, he intercepted many cotton wagons and directed them to Laredo and Eagle Pass. These westerly crossings doubled the distance the wagons had traveled before the loss of Brownsville and added 50 percent to the cost of shipping the cotton. Customs officers on the Mexican side of the Rio Grande demanded one bale of cotton for every bale landed. Many of those who were engaged in the cotton trade complained of the difficulty of making a profit because of the added time and expense caused by the Federals' control of Brownsville.[44]

Testimony from those involved in the trade vividly described the immense quantities of cotton that continued to cross into Mexico despite the loss of Brownsville. Jesse Sumpter, a customs inspector at Eagle Pass, noted in the spring of 1864 that "there was scarcely a day that hundreds of bales were not unloaded and crossed over as fast as possible." A founding citizen of Eagle Pass gave a similar account. He commented that "the whole river bottom from the bank of the river to the edge of town was covered with cotton."[45]

Although the cotton trade continued to be quite heavy at Eagle Pass and Laredo, the distance over which the trade items traveled added greatly to their cost. Kirby Smith wrote a gloomy letter to his wife describing the difficulty of obtaining certain commodities. He warned her that she "must carefully keep [account] of our stock of goods for it now really amounts to a stock, you must not be too liberal in disposing of them—the Rio Grande is in possession of the enemy, the blockade is closed, everything will be dearer and will increase rapidly in value." Colonel P. C. Woods of the 32nd Texas Cavalry wrote a similar letter to his wife. Camped with his men on the Brazos River, Woods cautioned her that she would have to manage everything at home, for "the Yanks are determined to invade us this winter." He also instructed her to safeguard their supply of salt and to store enough to last for a year.[46]

December was Magruder's busiest month. The ever-changing situation along the coast forced him to repeatedly shift Confederate units to endangered areas. When the Federals captured Matagorda Island on December 1,

Magruder had troops march from Houston to repel them. He also changed his last line of defense to the Brazos River just southwest of Houston and gathered nearly five thousand men in that region. Confederate units along the Brazos included the 2nd Texas Infantry, commanded by Col. Ashbel Smith; the 1st Texas Cavalry, under Col. Augustus Buchel; and the 3rd Texas Infantry, led by Col. Philip Luckett.[47]

On December 7 Magruder moved his headquarters to the plantation home of John C. McNeel, near the mouth of the Brazos River. Francis R. Lubbock, former Texas governor and now assistant adjutant to Magruder, indicated that Magruder spent most of December in the saddle, inspecting the deployment of his men from Victoria to Velasco. The general expected the enemy either to march inland from Matagorda Bay or to advance up the Matagorda Peninsula toward Galveston. When Union soldiers landed on the south end of Matagorda Peninsula on December 7, Magruder ordered Bee (at Victoria) to fall back toward Columbia on the Brazos River. During the retreat, Bee was to destroy the railroad leading from Indianola to Victoria. Since the evacuation of Brownsville, Bee had continued to implement Magruder's scorched-earth policy, leaving nothing behind for the enemy.[48]

As the loss of Texas loomed on the horizon, Magruder sent out desperate pleas for reinforcements. Throughout December he asked Texas governor Pendleton Murrah to use his authority to raise additional men. In one letter to the governor, Magruder greatly overestimated the Union strength (actually about 10,000 men) on the coast. He believed that "the enemy's force on the coast is from 15,000 to 20,000 men, of which 15,000 are at Decrow's Point and Saluria."[49]

Magruder also requested reinforcements from Kirby Smith. Smith, who had to contend with more numerous Federal forces in Louisiana, did not believe the situation in Texas was as desperate as Magruder pictured it. On December 15 he informed Magruder that "General Banks, in person, had returned to New Orleans." This seemed to indicate that the Union invasion had stalled. Smith also mentioned that, according to his sources, "no more than 6,000 troops had left Louisiana for the coast of Texas" and that no further reinforcements would be sent to Magruder.[50]

During these hectic times Magruder employed every military tool at his disposal, including the Texas Marine Department, which was assigned the task of defending 385 miles of Texas coastline. By October 1863 the Marine Department included eight small vessels, most of which served as transports, although some were commissioned as gunboats. The latter, called "cottonclads," used bales of cotton as armor rather than conventional iron plates. Tiers of cotton lashed to the decks of the vessels absorbed the Union shot. Small openings left between the bales allowed the Rebel gunners to fire their weapons.[51]

At the time of the Rio Grande expedition, Cdre. Leon Smith commanded the Marine Department. In December 1863 the task of defending Matagorda Bay fell to Capt. James Marmion, commander of the Marine District of Matagorda. Commodore Smith's sphere of responsibility included the coastline from Corpus Christi to the mouth of the Brazos River, a distance of 120 miles. When his appointment came in December, his jurisdiction had shrunk to only Matagorda Bay because of Union victories along the coast. His command consisted of the gunboats *John F. Carr* and *Cora*, the armed schooners *Buckhardt* and *Dale*, the steamer *Mary Hill*, and a few transports. In addition, he had small companies of soldiers detached for service as marines and artillerymen.[52]

The shortages of men, boats, and artillery severely hindered Marmion's defense of Matagorda Bay. One natural advantage worked in his favor, however—the relatively shallow waters of Matagorda Bay, including Pass Cavallo, the entrance to the inlet. This kept larger Federal warships from entering that body of water and destroying the smaller Confederate gunboats. It also kept Union blockaders from seizing the shallow-draft boats that continued to trade along the coast. On the other hand, the shallow waters of the bay also worked against the Confederates. Union gunboats could stand off safely in the Gulf of Mexico and fire into the bay at their smaller, overmatched adversaries.[53]

During the winter of 1863 the men of the Texas Marine Department performed many valuable services for Magruder. Their boats helped transport men and supplies to threatened areas. They also served as scouts, reporting the location and strength of the Union forces on the Texas coast. In addition, they provided naval support to the Confederate land forces. In one such engagement, the *John F. Carr* assisted the 1st Texas Cavalry in repulsing a Federal scouting party in late December 1863 on Matagorda Peninsula.[54]

Federal landings and raids along the Gulf Coast and up the Rio Grande resulted in sagging morale during the winter of 1863. Nothing depicts the ebbing spirits better than the letters written home by soldiers serving on the shore. In a missive to his wife, Jeff Morgan of the 35th Texas Cavalry mentioned that the regiment was ordered to leave Houston to fight along the beach. He also wrote that the future looked gloomy and he would not be home for the winter.[55]

Writing home in late December, Rudolf Coreth of the 32nd Texas Cavalry described the depressed mood of his regiment: "Confidence in this war has

Middle Texas coast. Map by Deborah Reade.

now sunken very much. I talked yesterday with several and they were all in accord with one another that they would rather have mules than Negroes and Confederate money." Colonel P. C. Woods, who commanded the regiment, wrote to his wife on November 26. He conveyed to her "how much I appreciate home and things at home. There is much to lament in this horrid war. I hope it will close soon, but I see little prospect."[56]

The city of Corpus Christi is an interesting example of the anxiety an invading army generates. As the fear of the impending arrival of Federal soldiers increased, desertions and disunity became more evident. Local residents who were lukewarm to the Southern cause now began to aid and abet the enemy. Maj. William G. Thompson of the 20th Iowa, commander of the Union garrison on Mustang Island, reported that he had obtained information "from a reliable man, direct from Corpus Christi," that hundreds of rebel deserters were hiding near the city awaiting the coming of the Federal troops. Some of the Corpus Christians captured on Mustang Island went over to the enemy. Thompson also remarked that "Some of my prisoners volunteered to go out and help capture two schooners in the bay. They piloted our men straight as a string and seemed tickled as much as the rest of the men over the capture."[57]

There were accounts, however, that differed somewhat from the happy, converted Confederates depicted by Major Thompson. One such case involved Capt. John Anderson, a Corpus Christian, who helped the Union forces. According to Anderson's son, the elder Anderson was forced into the role after his boat was blown ashore on Mustang Island. Nevertheless, Captain Anderson became a pilot for Major Thompson and for a time commanded the steamer *Planter*, which brought three black regiments from New Orleans to the Corpus Christi area for occupation duty.[58]

The first Union soldiers, members of a scouting party, entered the town on Christmas Day of 1863. The following day, an elated Major Thompson wrote to his wife that "Many were pleased to see us come, but a few cut dirt and run [sic]. There are many good Union men in the place and they send me much valuable information, every word of which would hang them if the Rebel leaders knew it. All complain of the barbarities committed by the leading Rebels. The Rebels have left the place."[59]

Disunity had taken firm root in Corpus Christi. Some of the residents who provided Thompson with information were doubtless local opportunists who saw Federal occupation as a means of bettering their own positions. Others may have been from the city's rather large immigrant population, which had maintained a silent loyalty since the secession crisis. (Other immigrants, members of European nobility, such as Charles G. Lovinskiold and Felix Blucher, maintained their allegiance to the Confederacy throughout the war.) Although some of the defections may have been for reasons of sentiment, the terrible winter of 1863–1864, described by one local rancher as the "bad times," may also have been a factor in the growing discord. Food shortages emerged as a serious problem. The people in town subsisted on fish or other foodstuffs obtained by trading their valuables to local Unionists or Federal troops. For whatever reasons, the presence of Thompson's men on Mustang Island gave courage to the local Unionists.[60]

Major Thompson, although serving in enemy territory, could not ignore the suffering of the families still living in the town. He frequently sent food to the starving residents, regardless of their loyalty. He pitied them and wrote his wife that he had dispatched provisions to several families "whose names I had as being in destitute circumstances and many more have sent me piteous letters and appeals for help and I cannot refuse to let them have something to eat, notwithstanding I know that a part of their people are in the Rebel army, but I cannot see women and children starve while I can divide."[61]

Despite his compassion for the townspeople, Major Thompson continued to take into custody Confederate civilians pointed out to him by Union sympathizers or opportunists. One such incident involved the arrest of three citizens identified by a local informant: George Robertson, a druggist who owned a drugstore; a man named John Riggs; and another unnamed resident. Attempting to detain the three men, U.S. soldiers chased them to the home of a Mrs. Swift, who hid Robertson in a closet and pushed a wardrobe in front of the door. This was fortunate for the druggist, for he eluded capture. The other two hid under a bed, but they were not so lucky. Because Riggs had such long legs that they were not entirely concealed, Federal troopers found the two men. Robertson was apprehended later, and all three prisoners were taken to Mustang Island. Robertson's luck still held, however, as he managed to escape again a short time after his capture.[62]

Although one area rancher recorded in his diary that the "Yankees made great time in Corpus and that the Union soldiers committed a great many depreations [sic]," the Federals appear to have behaved rather well. There are no available records of actual plundering by Union soldiers, other than the taking of furniture and lumber from the homes of civilians who had fled from the city. In addition, there was apparently no physical mistreatment of the citizens, although the Union troopers continued to arrest prominent Confederate civilians when they returned to Corpus Christi to visit relatives. Major Thompson maintained this policy well into the spring of 1864.[63]

Civilians in the path of the military forces along the Rio Grande also suffered. These deprivations came to light with the establishment of the Southern Claims Commission, formed in 1871 by an act of Congress. This agency allowed loyal Southerners to submit claims to the government for compensation for losses they incurred as a result of the wartime activities of Union soldiers. Petitions were usually barred or disallowed if the claimant's loyalty was not adequately proved. More than 22,000 claims were made nationwide, but only 7,092 were actually approved.[64]

Three barred claims from Cameron County showed that civilians in Brownsville and the surrounding region experienced property loss at the hands of the Federal troops. The three petitioners were Pauline V. Butler, Nicholas Champion, and Francisco Solis. All three claimants asserted that they owned property in Point Isabel (present-day Port Isabel) that was used by Union forces stationed on Brazos Santiago. They all claimed damages in excess of three thousand dollars. Since there were few permanent dwellings on Brazos Santiago, the soldiers allegedly took building materials such as lumber, bricks, and other items. Francisco Solis, who owned a hotel in Point Isabel, asserted that his entire dwelling had been torn down and taken by Federal soldiers to Brazos Santiago. His petition stated that "All of said buildings, fence and bricks were taken down by the Army of the United States and carried by said Army from Point Isabel to Brazos Santiago for Quarters and warehouses for said Army under the command of N. P. Banks." Nicholas Champion reinforced Solis's claim by stating that the U.S. Army had used his fifty-eight-foot schooner, *Square Nose,* to move supplies from Point Isabel to Brazos Santiago. When the vessel ran aground, it was torn apart by Union troops to build shelters and other structures. All three petitions concluded with consistent statements of loyalty to the United States. The claimants knew each other because each one had appeared as a witness on the other two claims. For example, Nicholas Champion's name appears as a witness on the petition of Francisco Solis, which is proof of collaboration.[65]

Claims for damages were also made by people from invaded areas farther up the coast. Maj. William Thompson, commander of the Union garrison on Mustang Island, made many visits to Corpus Christi, and his name appears in a petition made by Alvin C. Priest, who lived in the town of Flour Bluff on Corpus Christi Bay. Priest asked for three thousand dollars in damages for the destruction of building materials and livestock. Priest had a good memory, for the details he related more than ten years later were fairly accurate. His deposition states that "The aforesaid property was furnished to and taken by Major Thompson commanding the United States troops then stationed on Mustang Island. Petitioner believes it to have been the Twentieth Regiment of Iowa troops, and that the said property so taken, was removed from said Flour Bluff to said Mustang Island and used for the support and benefit of the United States troops stationed there." Although claiming that he was too poor to send witnesses to Washington to speak on his behalf, he included in his deposition the names of several people who vouched for his loyalty to the United States and for his good character.[66]

Not all of the cases that came before the Southern Claims Commission were disallowed. One such claim involved Louisa Steinberg of Indianola, Texas, in Calhoun County. Her petition concerned the loss of her home to the Federal troops stationed in Indianola during the Rio Grande expedition. Many Southerners who submitted petitions usually lost because they could not prove their loyalty to the Union during the war. However, Steinberg's husband, William, took a loyalty oath to the Union during the Federal occupation. Fortunately, she kept that document and presented it along with other materials to bolster her claim. Although Steinberg started the paperwork for her petition in 1872, she did not obtain recompense until 1878. Her claim was for $600, but she received only $100.[67]

Although general histories of the Civil War sometimes imply that the Lone Star State was untouched by the war of the 1860s, civilians along the Gulf Coast and up the Rio Grande Valley experienced some of the same hardships suffered by families in other parts of the Confederacy. Armies, friendly or not, exerted extraordinary stresses on the surrounding civilian society. It was only too clear to the people along the coast and in the valley that the Civil War had indeed reached Texas.

Four

The Red River Beckons

$\mathcal{B}$y the end of 1863, the Rio Grande expedition had achieved few significant results for Maj. Gen. Nathaniel P. Banks. Galveston, Houston, and Sabine Pass (on the border with Louisiana) still remained in Confederate hands. When Ulysses S. Grant became general in chief of all U.S. armies in March 1864, he ordered the abandonment of the entire Texas coast except for the Brownsville area. By that time, even Banks had to admit that the opportunities in Texas did not seem "as large as when we started."[1]

Yet as late as December 30, Banks spoke of his desire to continue military operations in Texas. In a letter to then General in Chief Henry W. Halleck, Banks continued to object to the Red River Valley as the best route by which to invade Texas. In a dispatch dated January 23, 1864, however, Banks conveyed to Halleck his change in position on the Red River approach, which resulted from the fact that Generals William T. Sherman and Frederick Steele would cooperate in a Red River expedition. Banks now stated that "the Red River is the shortest and best line of defense for Louisiana and Arkansas. I shall most cordially cooperate with them in executing your orders." A Union soldier serving with the 15th Maine Regiment on the Matagorda Peninsula offered a somewhat different commentary on General Banks's support for the Red River campaign. It was well known that Banks wanted to capture Galveston, he wrote, but "the government was unable to furnish the additional troops deemed requisite" for the attack on that port city. The soldier went on to comment that, "like a good soldier, the commander of the Gulf Department could only obey orders, though entertaining very grave apprehensions as to the wisdom of the plan and its probable outcome."[2]

Politics and cotton also played a role in Banks's change of mind concerning the Red River campaign. In late January 1864 Banks received news of large quantities of cotton in the Red River Valley. The procurement of thousands of bales of cotton for the northern textile mills would greatly benefit the economy of his home state, not to mention Banks's own political standing. Politically, Lincoln placed pressure on Banks to restore Louisiana to its proper place in the Union under the terms of the Ten Percent Plan, which had been announced in December 1863. In January 1864 Lincoln informed Banks that he was "master of all" political arrangements in Louisiana. If Banks could capitalize on the military, economic, and political opportunities that Louisiana presented, he would receive a boost in a run for the presidency in 1864. Staying in Louisiana certainly offered Banks an opportunity to advance his political career.[3]

Mother Nature, however, prevented an immediate drive into northwestern Louisiana. Banks, who began making preparations for the campaign in January, realized that the water level of the Red River would not support Federal gunboats until March. As a result, he intended to continue operations on the Texas coast until at least the end of March. By that time, the water level would be high enough for him to begin the trek toward Shreveport. Maintaining Federal troops on the Texas coast would hold in place the already nervous Confederate Maj. Gen. John B. Magruder, who still expected an enemy drive on Houston in the spring of 1864. Banks also realized that a rapid withdrawal from Texas would send a clear signal to the Confederates of a new campaign in Louisiana. The Rio Grande expedition now became a diversionary strategy for the Red River campaign, one that would hold the Confederates on the coast and prevent their transfer to Louisiana.[4]

Banks made no secret of his intention to move up the Matagorda Peninsula in the fall of 1863. Throughout January 1864 Federal gunboats shelled Confederate positions between the San Bernard and Caney rivers (on current maps of Texas, these rivers are actually shown as creeks) at the northernmost end of the Matagorda Peninsula, preparatory to a possible landing. General Magruder ordered Col. Ashbel Smith of the 2nd Texas Infantry to garrison Fort Caney, at the mouth of the Caney River. Magruder wanted a veteran regiment to command the fort in case the enemy launched an invasion in that region. Brig. Gen. Hamilton Bee called Fort Caney "the Post of Honor" and said, "It appropriately belongs to the 2nd Texas." Kirby Smith and Magruder had considered abandoning Matagorda Peninsula, but Ashbel Smith talked them out of it.[5]

Another veteran regiment also played a crucial role in defending the Texas coast from a Federal invasion: the 1st Texas Cavalry under Col. Augustus Buchel, whose regiment patrolled the Texas coast between the San Bernard and Caney rivers. In early January 1864 Magruder ordered Bee to prevent, under any circumstances, the enemy from landing in that region. Magruder also instructed him to dismount all of his cavalry except the 1st Texas. These men, along with the regular infantry, held the line against the Federal forces that occasionally ventured forth from DeCrow's Point on Matagorda Peninsula. While the infantry manned the forts, the 1st Texas Cavalry, the only mounted cavalry regiment in the area, patrolled the coast and scouted the beaches for enemy landings. Bee also issued directives to ensure that "not less than 100 men remained in the forts at all times."[6]

The USS *Aroostook* commenced shelling Confederate positions on January 7, firing on Fort Bernard at the mouth of the San Bernard River. Confederate engineer Lt. Edward Sandcliffe reported that the *Aroostook* disrupted the fortifying of Fort Bernard: "I am so much annoyed by gunboats that I can only work in the nighttime. Our work this morning [January 8] [was] literally strewn with fragments of shells, grape, and canister."[7]

On January 8 the *Aroostook* fired at Fort Caney, and Pvt. William Behrends of the 1st Texas Cavalry was killed. Colonel Buchel reported that the *Aroostook* lay at anchor all night. The following day the same vessel "commenced shelling them again" at "first light" and fired about forty rounds into the fort, disrupting the fortification work and silencing one of the stronghold's guns. The Confederates who were guarding Forts Caney and Bernard believed that the shelling could mean only one thing: A Union assault was fast approaching.[8]

As the invasion tension mounted, the 1st Texas Cavalry remained on constant patrol. But as Federal activity on the coast continued, regimental returns for the 1st Texas indicated a major reduction in personnel between December 1863 and the end of January 1864. The soldiers listed as present for duty dropped from 1,273 to 703. Desertion, casualties, disease, or some combination of these factors led to this decline. William Kuykendall, a private in the 1st Texas Cavalry, regretted that the combination of fatigue and cold weather led to the loss of many of the men in the regiment. One diary entry by Kuykendall points out that the men were "Tired and wet after this adventure [Matagorda fray]. I was prostrate[d] by a severe attack of typhoid pneumonia from which I only recovered after many weeks of suffering in the hospital." He also wrote that "about this time measles broke out in the camp, resulting in many deaths."[9]

The shelling by the Federal gunboats during this period had the desired impact on Confederate morale. An account given by Edward Pye, a physician who served with the 4th Texas Infantry (state troops) near the San Bernard and Caney rivers, describes the anxiety created by the enemy's offshore

shelling. In a letter to his wife, Pye addressed his children about making resolutions for the New Year. He told them that they should "begin the *New
Year* with good resolutions and actions—these are times such as one sees
only once—When we are all dead and gone many lifetimes hence—they will
be spoken of as the *'bloody age'*—the time of horror—of famine—misery—
wretchedness. Think children of the *thousands in camps* all over the land—
many badly provided without clothing—without tents. Thousands in bad
health not fit for service and the sick in hospitals—dying hourly—many for
the want of comforts such even as you possess—Think of all this—and *resolve* never to *complain* of the little difficulties and troubles that come your
way." [10]

In another letter to his wife that December, Pye noted that the shelling
had dampened the spirits of those who served with him, although he continued to doubt the possibility of a Federal invasion. He spoke skeptically of
the continued rumors of invasion, instructing his wife to "give them no
credit. From all appearances it will be a bloodless campaign—But we have
heard the big guns firing all day within 12 Miles of us. I have two men in the
hospital who were at the Mouth of the Bernard when the Yankees shelled us.
They say there was a considerable *scattering* among the men." Pye also described the despondency and war weariness created by the shelling: "[T]he
poor fellows are mighty gloomy and out of spirits—the most of them abuse
old *Magruder and the war*—each one considering himself the worst off of
any man in *The Confederacy*. I try to put them in good humor with themselves as well as I can—and we discourse of home, children, and our wives." [11]

The fairly constant bombardment by the Union gunboats during this period also resulted in some amusing anecdotes. Ralph Smith, a soldier in the
2nd Texas Infantry Regiment serving inside Fort Caney, described how a
Spanish sailing vessel ran aground during one of the January shellings. The
soldiers confiscated the cargo of the ship, which included, among other
things, "soothing syrup." As to its effects on the men, Smith wrote, "Meanwhile the boys had tested the various brands of soothing syrup which they
found to be exhilarating in its effects. However, after continual sampling
they discovered it to be overpoweringly intoxicating. In fact, by twelve
o'clock at night the whole command was stretched out on the beach helplessly drunk, except for Major Fly, Sargeant [sic] Bill, and myself." [12]

The Federal gunboats continued to harass the Confederate positions
above Matagorda Bay throughout January. Toward the end of the month,
the Union soldiers stationed at DeCrow's Point at the south end of the
Matagorda Peninsula embarked upon another scouting mission up the peninsula. Brig. Gen. Thomas E. Ransom commanded the expedition, which

was made up of troops from the 1st Brigade, 4th Division, and the 3rd Brigade, 2nd Division. Ransom began the march northward on January 21 with the soldiers from the 4th Division. Meanwhile, the USS *Sciota* landed two hundred soldiers of the 13th Maine about ten miles below Fort Caney. For the 13th Maine, this was familiar territory. About one month before, they had tangled with the 1st Texas Cavalry in the same area. The two Federal units linked up on the afternoon of January 22. Ransom then sent ahead some mounted men beyond the head of the peninsula and determined that no more information could be gained short of attacking the enemy on the Caney River.[13]

As a result, Ransom boarded the *Sciota* in order to make a closer observation of the enemy works on the Caney River. He reported three thousand cavalry, one thousand infantry, and a few pieces of field artillery. One body of cavalry (probably the 1st Texas) was seen advancing down the peninsula to drive off Ransom's men. This compelled Ransom to return to his troops on the peninsula and to march them southward. They returned to Decrow's Point on January 24 after completing their scouting assignment. Although Ransom described the expedition as successful, Maj. Gen. Napoleon Dana, commanding the XIII Army Corps at Fort Esperanza, had a somewhat different opinion. Realizing he faced strong enemy works at the head of the peninsula, he requested that two regiments of cavalry be sent to the Texas coast. Frustrated, Dana closed his report by observing that "chances are being thrown away, which are seriously to be regretted."[14]

During Ransom's scouting mission up the peninsula, General Dana received quite a scare at Fort Esperanza. A rumor developed that a large Confederate force had landed on the south end of Matagorda Island and was intent upon attacking and recapturing the garrison. Dana sent word to the soldiers stationed at Decrow's Point to help defend the stronghold against this enemy assault. Troops were ferried across by steamer to Fort Esperanza. One of these regiments, the 15th Maine, was sent out to scout the entire island. During their reconnaissance, no rebels were found. The Maine men returned to the fort tired and footsore although glad to report that the story was only "a very great scare." The garrison remained on high alert for the next week, but by January 25, the tension had subsided, and the Union reinforcements returned to Decrow's Point.[15]

Although most of the military activities on the coast were generated by Union land and naval forces, the Confederates were preparing a major offensive to drive the Federals out of Texas. On December 22, 1863, Col. John S. ("Rip") Ford began preparations in San Antonio for the Confederate Rio Grande expedition. Ford ordered two companies of his newly formed

"Cavalry of the West" to the Nueces River near Corpus Christi to protect that exposed region. Capt. James A. Ware commanded the forces near San Patricio, and Maj. Mat Nolan was placed in charge of the troops near Banquete. Ford instructed Ware to take into custody any deserters or Union sympathizers in the area. In late December, Ware and his men visited Corpus Christi and arrested a man described as a "traitor and communicating with the Yankees."[16]

Maj. William G. Thompson of the 20th Iowa Infantry Regiment, garrison commander on Mustang Island, promptly received news of Ware's visit to Corpus Christi. He also learned the disquieting report that Major Nolan's wife had shown to her neighbors two U.S. flags and a sword that her husband had taken at the battles of Sabine Pass and Galveston. The flags were seized from the USS *Morning Light,* which Company G of the 2nd Texas Mounted Rifles under Nolan's command had helped capture. The sword came from the *Sachem,* a ship captured by the Confederates at Sabine Pass. Although Thompson had shown considerable mercy toward the people of Corpus Christi, he could not tolerate an insult to the Stars and Stripes. As a result, he led what may be termed the first Union invasion of Corpus Christi. On the night of January 21, 1864, three ships and seventy-five men landed at the city's wharves. The rebels had left the city, so Thompson put out pickets and went to bed. The next morning he visited the Nolan home, where he found Mrs. Nolan, her mother, and her sister. At his request, the sword and flags were handed to him immediately and are currently in an Iowa museum. The Iowans remained in the city for a couple of days but then returned to Mustang Island.[17]

The naval bombardment of the upper Texas coast continued throughout early February. From February 6 to February 9, Union gunboats shelled the Confederate positions at the head of the Matagorda Peninsula near the San Bernard and Caney rivers. An intense firefight took place on February 6, when the *Aroostook* lobbed some sixty shells at Fort Caney. Rebel gunners returned fire from the fort, inflicting minor damage on the *Aroostook.* Several muster rolls from the 2nd Texas Infantry confirm the severity of the February 6 shelling. One states that Fort Caney had been "engaged by a Yankee vessel for two hours. Heavy shelling all the time." Other phrases such as "pretty severely shelled" and "gunboats shelled us several times, once very heavy" also appear on these muster rolls. On February 9 the *Sciota* and the *Aroostook* engaged in a rather fierce, five-hour artillery duel with the Confederate batteries near the mouth of the Brazos River. The *Aroostook* took two hits, and three Confederate soldiers were killed, while several were wounded.[18]

Despite constant harassment by the U.S. Navy throughout February, the Confederates along the coast continued to build fortifications, often at night. Colonel Smith, who commanded the 2nd Texas Infantry, worked diligently to strengthen Fort Caney. Under strict orders not to allow an enemy landing on this portion of the Texas shoreline, Smith submitted plans to improve the defenses on the Caney River. His proposals were approved, and construction was carried out under his close supervision. When completed, Fort Caney was renamed Fort Ashbel Smith in his honor. To man the improved fortifications, additional soldiers—Waul's Legion and the 32nd Texas Cavalry regiment—arrived at the mouth of the Caney.[19]

General Dana also worked to demoralize the civilian population of Texas. On February 7 the USS *Queen*, under Cmdr. Robert Tarr, sailed to within ten miles of Fort Caney. He sent ashore a small landing party to post proclamations from President Lincoln and Gov. Andrew J. Hamilton. These public statements spoke of granting conditional amnesty to residents of the middle coast of Texas. Dana wanted to give the impression that Texas was about to be invaded and occupied very shortly. When Iowa troops attacked Lamar, near Corpus Christi, on February 11, a citizen inquired about the intention of the Federal forces on the Texas coast. An officer who was leading the raid informed this citizen that Texas would fall in a few months, that all of Corpus Christi had come over to the Union side, and that General Banks, with twenty-five thousand troops, was about to invade Texas by way of the Red River, a force so large that "Texas would be overrun in less than three months." Two weeks after the Lamar raid, Dana issued general order #14 on February 24. The directive extended conditional amnesty for residents of the middle coast of Texas. The authorization, however, would go into effect only if Federal forces actually controlled the state. Banks and Dana clearly wanted to win not only a military victory in Texas but a psychological one as well.[20]

The presence of the Federal army on the Texas shoreline in the winter of 1863–1864 coincided with Lincoln's amnesty proclamation announced in December of 1863. The declaration created quite a stir in the Lone Star State. Ever since the Rio Grande expedition had landed in Brownsville in November, some Texans had renewed their allegiance to the Union. The announcement also led to false accusations of disloyalty. The most famous of these charges involved Richard King, whose ranch had served as a cotton depot since 1862. In two January letters King emphatically denied that he had taken a loyalty oath to the Union. King suspected that his accusers were jealous men involved in the cotton trade. He also pointed out that his ranch and all of his property were always at the disposal of the Confederacy and that the

Yankees had attacked his property in late December 1863. Although King had been cleared of any disloyalty by February 1864, the presence of the enemy on the coast would always arouse suspicions of treason among the civilian population.[21]

The last engagement of late winter took place on February 13, when Federal forces from the 21st Iowa Infantry skirmished with Confederates from the 33rd Texas Cavalry near Indianola. Although the Union soldiers stationed in Indianola stayed close to town most of the time, they occasionally made excursions into the countryside to determine the enemy's strength and to secure fresh beef. Thirty-five mounted Iowans were rounding up some cattle about eight miles from town when they came upon an enemy camp. Instead of falling back, they amused themselves by attacking the pickets guarding the encampment. Suddenly they were surrounded by fifty-five well-armed Confederate cavalrymen. In the ensuing fight fourteen of the Union soldiers fell from their horses, partly because their horses had not been trained to work amid gunfire. The Confederates quickly surrounded the Federals and took them prisoner. They were later sent to a prison camp in Tyler, Texas. When Brig. Gen. Fitz Henry Warren reported this incident to General Dana at Fort Esperanza, Dana exploded. He told Warren that "such scrapes are very much to be regretted and ought to be carefully avoided, as in addition to the losses and mortification they lay on us, they give great encouragement to the enemy."[22]

The presence of Confederate cavalry near Indianola made General Warren and his men wary of an enemy attack. One soldier of the 22nd Iowa Infantry, Jacob C. Switzer, wrote that the regiment was several times called into line around three o'clock in the morning to repel an enemy assault. Switzer also related an amusing incident that happened to him while on picket duty. One night he heard rustling in some nearby bushes. Believing it to be enemy soldiers, he reached for his cap box to put a percussion cap on his rifle but suddenly realized that he had left the cap box back at Indianola. Unable to fire his rifle, he decided that he would at least try to take the enemy prisoner. He got on his stomach and approached the noise, only to discover that "my invader was nothing but a cow browsing around in the brush, taking a very early morning meal. You may be sure that I never reported the incident in camp because I did not intend they should learn that I had left my ammunition in camp."[23]

As Banks began his campaign up the Red River toward Shreveport in March 1864, the Confederate regiments serving on the Texas coast noticed a redeployment of Federal soldiers there. Banks wanted to give the impression that an invasion of Texas was also imminent along the shoreline to hold the Confederate forces in place there. A Confederate scout who was sent down the Matagorda Peninsula reported in late February that enemy strength on the peninsula had greatly diminished. People living there also noticed that the enemy apparently intended to abandon the peninsula because the Federals were moving all of their stores south to Fort Esperanza on Matagorda Island. Rumors circulated about the purpose of this move. One was that the troops were bound for New Orleans to join Banks. Another was that a Union invasion of Texas from Indianola was afoot to support Banks's drive up the Red River. Magruder believed the latter story and readied his men for a possible Union thrust from Port Lavaca into the Texas interior.[24]

Magruder's fears, however, lessened somewhat upon receiving reconnaissance reports of troop strength near Indianola. He received these accounts from Col. James Duff of the 33rd Texas Cavalry, which had set up camp near Texana, less than fifty miles from Port Lavaca. On March 18, Duff stated that "The U.S. forces evacuated Indianola on the 15th instant and, as the citizens report, have gone to Saluria." Toward the end of March, Duff reported the beginnings of a Federal withdrawal from the Texas coast. After visiting Indianola on March 28, Duff told his superiors that "The impression left on the minds of the citizens from conversations overheard was that the main part of the command was destined for Louisiana, and the invasion of Texas would be from that direction." Duff also said that "On the 25th, there were five steamers inside the bar and one outside, twelve sails inside and four outside. This looks as if they intend removing at least a portion of the forces there."[25]

Despite the beginnings of a Union withdrawal from the Texas coast in March 1864, heavy skirmishing between Union and Confederate forces continued near Corpus Christi. Most of this fighting was related to the Confederate Rio Grande expedition, organized in San Antonio under Colonel Ford. The combined forces in the first of these encounters totaled about 160 men. On March 13, 1864, 62 Confederate troopers under Maj. Mat Nolan charged into about one hundred Union cavalrymen, forcing Capt. Cecilio Balerio's horsemen to retreat after a desperate fight. After the shooting ended, Nolan found five enemy soldiers killed but estimated from the blood trails that a dozen more had died. The Confederates lost three killed and five wounded. Nolan did not pursue because Balerio, in his hasty retreat, left behind some papers indicating that he was about to be reinforced. As a result, Nolan requested that Colonel Ford send him reinforcements to secure the coastal region near Corpus Christi.[26]

Three days after the Balerio incident, Major Nolan learned that Federal soldiers from Mustang Island had landed on the outskirts of Corpus Christi to procure some confiscated Confederate cotton. Nolan, accompanied by seventy of his men, rode to the home of W. S. Gregory, where he discovered a slave and two Texans loading wagons with bales that were to be delivered to Major Thompson's forces on Mustang Island. One of the Texans informed Nolan that ninety-three U.S. soldiers arrested Gregory and took him, along with sixty-seven bales of cotton, to Corpus Christi. Nolan sent a courier to Capt. James Ware, who commanded a company of men on San Fernando Creek, to aid him in attacking the Yankees at Corpus Christi. Meanwhile, Nolan proceeded with his men toward Corpus Christi, spotting the enemy pickets around noon. By this time, Nolan's courier had returned with the distressing news that no immediate backup should be expected.[27]

As Nolan and his men approached the outskirts of the city, they noticed that the main body of Iowa troops was stationed along the wharf on present-day Water Street. At dusk, three U.S. vessels approached the wharves and discharged about seventy-five Union sailors while the Confederates watched from their place of concealment. Outnumbered almost two to one, Nolan decided not to attack the main force. Instead, a little before noon on the following day, he led a charge of nine men on the Union pickets. As with any Civil War fight, two different versions of what happened next were told by the principal officers in charge. Nolan reported that his men drove the pickets into the city. The Confederates killed one picket and wounded another, and Nolan's force suffered only one wounded. Nolan's counterpart, Major Thompson, who was not present during the skirmish, stated that his sentries held off twenty charging Rangers, his appellation of Nolan's troopers. When the shooting started, the Federal soldiers rushed to the pickets' aid and drove the rebels away from the city. Thompson, in his official account, stated that one Confederate was killed and three were wounded but that "Not one of my men got a scratch."[28]

In any case, the Confederates were driven back into the brush surrounding the city and helplessly watched the loading of southern cotton aboard Federal ships. Major Nolan must have had an excellent watch, for he reported that the entire Union force left the city at "exactly" 10:00 A.M. and took with them the families of several city residents who had joined the enemy. The list of residents who left included John R. Peterson (former sheriff of Nueces County), E. Fitzsimmons (listed as a deserter from the 8th Texas Infantry and serving Thompson's forces as a sutler), F. Pettle, Chris Dunn, Melinda Rankin, and Frank Edwards, to name a few. Nolan must have been wary of an enemy ambush of some kind because he and about twenty of his men did not emerge from their cover until the following day. Residents told him that Union soldiers had searched his home and those of others. The angry Nolan was also informed that the enemy had mistakenly arrested his sister-in-law, believing that she was Nolan's wife. She was released shortly thereafter when the Federals realized their error. Recognizing he could accomplish nothing further in the city, Nolan ordered his forces to return to Banquete that evening.[29]

Nolan and Thompson continued their game of cat and mouse. At his headquarters on Mustang Island, Thompson received two men from Nolan's command on May 3. They gave Thompson a note stating that the Confederates could not provide supplies for the people of Corpus Christi. Therefore, the undiplomatic Nolan gave Thompson "permission" to send food to the city without any hindrance from his soldiers. Thompson, who was generous by nature, was extremely irritated by Nolan's suggestion that he needed permission from the "Rebels" for anything. In a letter to his wife, Thompson conveyed to her that "a not very modest proposition when I have went [sic] to Corpus whenever I pleased in spite of them and sent them word that I intended to do as I had done. Supply friends without asking their permission to do so. And that I would hold them as enemies whenever I found them armed against the government and should treat them accordingly."[30]

While the Texans and the remnants of Banks's invading army skirmished in February and March, home-front civilians suffered greatly. Harvey C. Medford, a private who was stationed near Galveston, wrote a detailed diary account of the hardships endured by both soldiers and citizens near Galveston. In one entry of mid-February 1864, Medford's anger and sarcasm about army life is vivid. He first attacked the scarcity and poor quality of the rations the army received. To remedy this, the citizens of Galveston had to turn over a tenth of all they made to help feed the soldiers. Despite this tax, the shortage of rations continued, and Medford suspected mismanagement. He remarked that "I am afraid our country will never prosper where there is so much fraud and perfidy practiced upon the private soldier by the functionaries of the government. I am the last one to [mutiny] or desert; but if there are any justifiable causes for such things, it is here in our army." In his entry for March 10, Medford stated that nearly two hundred families in Galveston were drawing rations from the government. The quantity of provisions that Galveston citizens received must also have been scanty because Medford mentioned that "small children frequently come to our camps and beg for something to eat; and take away every scrap that we throw away."[31]

In late March a Union blockader fired seven times at Fort Velasco on the Brazos River. Confederate batteries lobbed fifteen shells in return, but neither side inflicted any damage. This gunfire created the illusion of a possible Federal landing near the Brazos. Naval bombardment held in place some of the Confederate units on the Texas coast that might have been transferred to Louisiana to Banks's Red River campaign.[32]

The final military expedition on the Texas coast took place in mid-April 1864. Two Federal vessels, the *Estrella* and the *Zephyr*, were sent up Matagorda Bay, formed by the Matagorda Peninsula running up the coast from Port Lavaca to the township of Matagorda. The ships were to obtain information about two rebel gunboats, the *Carr* and the *Buckhardt*. On April 12 these four ships exchanged a few shots but caused no damage. The Union gunboats sailed on to Indianola, where they captured three vessels and burned another. The expedition then landed at Port Lavaca, about twenty miles west of Indianola. Going ashore to obtain lumber, the Federal troops encountered enemy pickets and killed one of them. As the Union soldiers prepared to leave, a fire accidentally broke out in the town. Ordered ashore, the Federals fought bravely to put the fire out. Lt. S. C. Jones of the 22nd Iowa Infantry boasted that "The soldiers labored manfully to put it out, for which they gained the thanks and admiration of the citizens, though they were mostly our enemies."[33]

The Federal probes along the Texas coast served only to heighten the anxiety of General Magruder. As late as May 20—in the final days of the Red River campaign—Magruder warned Shreveport "that the troops left in the State of Texas are totally inadequate to its defense in case General Banks should move upon our coast as I believe he will do." Magruder also warned that it would take more than a month for Texas units to return to the Lone Star State. At the time, he had only about two hundred men posted between Matagorda Bay and San Antonio. Yet, despite the shelling and the raids on the coast, no Federal invasion force ever landed.[34]

By early May, Union troop strength had dramatically declined. Before the Red River campaign, 10,000 Federals were stationed in Texas from Brownsville to Matagorda Bay. This number dropped to a little more than 4,000 by May 1864. Col. George W. Bailey of the 99th Illinois submitted a report on June 15, describing the withdrawal from Matagorda Bay. All valuables, including the heavy guns captured at Fort Esperanza, were removed. Bailey then ordered the fort to be blown up. The following day Capt. James Marmion, who commanded a small fleet of gunboats that patrolled Matagorda Bay, dispatched the *John F. Carr* to take possession of Saluria, the small town just west of the fort. By July, Matagorda Bay and its environs were under Confederate control. The only position still held by the Federals in Texas was Brownsville, occupied by about 3,000 men.[35]

One can only speculate about the possibilities associated with the Rio Grande expedition. Some of the Union generals associated with the campaign believed that golden opportunities were lost and that Texas would have fallen in 1864. General Dana, who assumed command of the XIII Army Corps in January 1864, supported more offensive action in Texas. On February 9, 1864, he stated that "the inactive policy which has prevailed in Texas since its occupation, both here and on the Rio Grande, has resulted in the loss of good opportunities, and tended, in some degree, to impair the impetuosity of this fine body of troops, and has decidedly increased the morale and confidence of the rebels."[36]

Texas Unionist Gilbert D. Kingsbury of Brownsville also became frustrated at the lack of offensive action undertaken by the Federal forces on the coast. In a lengthy letter to the editor of the *New York Herald*, Kingsbury stated that "Some of our Loyal Texans feel disheartened that the Army does not occupy the interior this winter. It is known that if a force was to be thrown into San Antonio or Austin from Indianola or Saluria, and either of those places held and the line from the coast to the place thus occupied be kept open, nearly the whole of the people of Western Texas would take the stand of loyalty which they have desired to do for months." Later in the same letter, Kingsbury became more emphatic: "Great God if we could occupy a place in the interior like San Antonio-Austin or any other place where would our spoils of returning loyalty end? From Indianola or Saluria, both in our possession, the distance is 150 miles. That is of course the point from which the State should be pierced. Now a line of our Army from Indianola or Saluria to Austin or San Antonio, this 150 miles of rich country would restore all Western and Northern Texas."[37]

Another prominent Texas Unionist, Thomas H. DuVal, a former federal judge from Austin, also became demoralized at the lack of offensive action. Living in Brownsville with other Texas refugees, DuVal wrote that "I am heartsick and weary. There is no sign of advance into the interior. On the contrary 4 regiments have been taken to Louisiana from Indianola and one has gone from here North on furlough. Texas is evidently abandoned for months to come, except for a point or two on the Coast. To divert sad thoughts, I am deep in the mysteries of *Les Misérables*." About a week later, DuVal became even more dejected: "I am suffering, mentally, the torments of the damned, and feel that death would be welcome in spite of all darkness and mystery beyond it. How gladly I would take my place with a force marching towards Austin, and fight to get back home."[38]

Dana, fearing that the rebels might take the offensive, believed Union inactivity had allowed the Confederates to fortify the middle Texas coast. As a result, the Federal positions on the shoreline needed to be strengthened. Dana also mentioned that, as a matter of honor, the Union points on the coast should be held because a number of Texans in the occupied areas had taken the oath of allegiance to the United States. To abandon these people would place their lives in peril. When the Federals pulled out of Indianola in March 1864, General Warren announced to the citizens of that town that, if they sought the protection of the Federal government, they would need to leave with the evacuating troops.[39]

Dana's concern for the declining fighting spirit of his men was indeed well founded. Many of the regiments serving in the Rio Grande expedition had fought in some of the major campaigns of the war. The recent idleness and inactivity had led to two notable incidents. One, which took place at Fort Esperanza on Matagorda Island, involved the 14th Rhode Island Regiment of the Corps d'Afrique. On March 30, 1864, the 22nd Iowa was ordered to guard the 14th Rhode Island because it had threatened to mutiny. The main cause of its discontent was that the black troops were paid seven dollars a month compared to thirteen dollars for white soldiers. Another reason for the unrest had to do with the long stretches that soldiers went without pay. One Iowa soldier stationed at Fort Esperanza noted that it was not until March that he had finally received four months' worth of back pay. Although most of the 14th Rhode Island returned to duty, fifty to sixty of them were court-martialed and sentenced to short jail terms at Fort Jefferson in the Tortuga Islands off the southern tip of Florida. Thirteen of the ringleaders were hanged at Fort Esperanza on June 5, 1864.[40]

Another incident occurred at Fort Brown in Brownsville and involved desertion by a Federal soldier, Pedro Garcia, who was part of the 1st Texas Cavalry Regiment. Since their arrival in the fall of 1863, the cavalry regiments had suffered from a lack of discipline, but the 2nd Texas Cavalry especially was the talk of the Union army at Brownsville. The creator of the regiment, Col. John L. Haynes, a Brownsville resident, had recruited most of the men from Mexico. They were Mexican Texans who had fled across the river because of the Confederate occupation of Brownsville. An estimated 958 Mexican Texans fought for the Union, most of them serving in the 2nd Texas Cavalry.[41]

In the first half of 1864 about two hundred men deserted from the 2nd Texas Cavalry. Several problems explain the high desertion rate: the lack of supplies, especially uniforms; months of inactivity; and rumors that Texas cavalry regiments were to be sent to Louisiana. In addition, many of the soldiers served close to home and wanted to visit their families.[42]

Some believed that the court-martial of Private Garcia would curtail the desertion problem. On May 10, 1864, Garcia, while on sentry duty, left his post before being properly relieved. Another incident, which occurred on May 26, reported Garcia as deserting "from Scout" while part of the Independent Company, Partisan Rangers, attached to the 1st Texas Cavalry. As a result, he was arrested and charged with desertion. The presiding officer of the court-martial, Capt. Edward G. Miller of the 20th Wisconsin, stated that, because of "the great number of desertions from the Texas Cavalry Volunteers and the large amount of government property lost," an example should be made of Garcia. Found guilty of desertion, he was sentenced to be "shot to death with musketry." The date of the execution was set for June 27, 1864.[43]

Descriptive accounts of the execution were given by Captain Miller of the 20th Wisconsin and Lt. Benjamin F. McIntyre of the 19th Iowa Infantry Regiments. Miller, who presided over the court-martial, stated that "The ceremony was well-conducted and impressive. The man met death like a soldier—deserter that he was. I believe that it is characteristic of the Mexican people that when death is inevitable, they meet it with unconcern." McIntyre gave a less noble description of the punishment: "The word was given. Make ready. Aim. A dozen rifles were aimed at his breast. It was a moment of painful suspense and was felt by the vast throng—a moment and a human life would be ended. Each one who gazed upon the spectacle I doubt not felt the cold blood curdling in his veins and would prefer never again to witness an alike exhibition." The troops at Fort Brown were ordered to march by and view the body. Pvt. Warner Dewhurst of the 38th Iowa Infantry Regiment reflected after viewing the corpse that "It was a sight no man delights in seeing."[44]

Perhaps the most unusual case of desertion from the Union army involved a former Confederate soldier named Adrian Vidal. In the fall of 1863, Vidal commanded a Confederate unit called Vidal's Partisan Rangers, serving under General Bee in the lower Rio Grande Valley. Bee ordered Vidal's men to sentry duty at the mouth of the Rio Grande and later sent two men to order them back to Fort Brown. Only one of these soldiers returned, reporting to Bee that Vidal and his men had mutinied. When Bee heard this, he feared that Vidal and the sixty men he led would plunder Brownsville. Bee waited for three days, but an attack never materialized. Vidal instead bypassed Brownsville, plundering ranches further up the Rio Grande. By October 29, 1863, Vidal and his Rangers had killed ten people.[45]

While waiting in Brownsville for Vidal's attack, Bee sent couriers out on October 26 to recall three companies of the 33rd Texas Cavalry. When they arrived on October 29, Bee ordered them to pursue Vidal, who, however, had already crossed into Mexico. It was believed that Vidal had joined with the infamous Mexican bandit Juan Cortina. Cortina, though, under orders from Tamaulipas governor Manuel Ruiz, had captured twenty of Vidal's men, but Vidal himself eluded capture.[46]

Vidal's mutiny occurred for several reasons. Since the summer of 1863, Vidal had requested various supplies for his men but never received them. In addition, he had formed some sort of alliance with Texas Unionists in Matamoros and perhaps tried to seize Brownsville in anticipation of the landing of the Union Rio Grande expedition. Finally, some historians argue that Vidal wanted only to plunder the nearly one million dollars in supplies at Fort Brown, knowing that the garrison had only about nineteen men. Whatever his motives, they were frustrated by the return of the 33rd Texas Cavalry. Thus ended the Confederate phase of Vidal's military career.[47]

Three weeks after the Federal occupation of Brownsville, Vidal joined the ranks of the U.S. Army with the rank of captain. His men, about ninety in all, were now called Vidal's Independent Partisan Rangers and were attached to the 2nd Texas Cavalry. On May 30, 1864, Vidal resigned from the army. He was not bothered by life in the cavalry but by the constant paperwork associated with the job of being a company commander. Not being able to speak or read English, furthermore, made that part of his assignment nearly impossible. Colonel Haynes, commander of the 2nd Texas Cavalry, recommended that Maj. Gen. Francis Herron, commander at Fort Brown, accept Vidal's resignation. On July 9 the department headquarters in New Orleans approved Vidal's notification. Before Vidal received news of his honorable discharge, however, he deserted to Mexico with sixty men on June 19. As a result, the army revoked his honorable discharge.[48]

Of the 90 men serving with Vidal, only 23 stayed for the remainder of the war. A shoot-on-sight order was issued for Vidal, who joined the Juaristas while hiding in Mexico. The Imperialists finally captured, court-martialed, and executed the young captain. Because of the civil wars in both the United States and Mexico, Vidal came into contact with four armies, compiling one of the most unusual military records in the annals of the Civil War.[49]

Although supply shortages and low pay contributed to desertions, mutiny, and low morale in general, news from the battlefront also affected the soldiers' fighting spirit. One soldier in the 23rd Iowa Infantry Regiment, Silas A. Shearer, received discouraging news from home while stationed at Fort

Esperanza. In a letter to his wife, he discussed his concern for his three brothers, who were fighting with General Grant in Tennessee: "I expect that Elias and Barty was in that fight that General Grant had. The news is here that a part of the fifth Iowa was taken Prisioners [sic] and they were all in one Division. If you know how they got threw [sic] or anything about the fifth I want you to let me know." About a week later, Shearer wrote another letter to his wife, in which he conveyed to her a family tragedy: "I received a letter from Elias today and it was Sorrowful news to me. It announced the death of Barty and George M. Shearer. It appears as though my brothers has [sic] bad luck. He has fought the Rebs at a great many places and was wounded once. From all accounts he was a brave soldier there. Devis made a charge and was repulsed by a flank movement. The Rebs masked the forces on the right and the right fell back. Then when the two boys was killed Lias said they had to fall back to the support or be gobbled. Enough on this subject for it nearly brakes [sic] my heart to think of it."[50]

The collapse of the Red River campaign in Louisiana also had a notable impact. One Union soldier in Brownsville made this analysis on May 21, 1864: "Since the retreat of General Banks's army to Alexandria, and the reported retreat of General Steele's forces toward Little Rock, the rebel traders here, have taken new life, and are sending enormous quantities of goods to Texas through Eagle Pass and Laredo. Goods find their way into Texas by the upper river crossings as they formerly did through Brownsville." Following this depressing news came uplifting rumors on May 29 that Gen. Ulysses S. Grant had captured Richmond and taken nearly three thousand Confederates prisoner. This latter report was typical of the false tales that appear in wartime. Finally, the Federals in Brownsville received news that Lincoln had been nominated for a second term as president. One Wisconsin soldier, greatly encouraged by this report, wrote in his diary the word "Bueno."[51]

Lincoln's faith in the expedition's mission on the lower Rio Grande was reinforced by a proclamation ending the Union blockade of Brownsville. Announced on February 18, 1864, it did not reach Brownsville until April 2. Lincoln named Charles Worthington as collector of customs for the port of Brownsville. Two days later Maj. Gen. John A. McClernand, the new commander of the XIII Army Corps, stopped in Brownsville on an inspection tour of the Union forces on the Texas coast. McClernand spoke to the men of 2nd Division in Brownsville, relating that he "felt proud of so noble a body of men and so gallant a line of officers." The actions of both Lincoln and McClernand seemed to give the Federals on the Rio Grande a sense of permanence in their expedition.[52]

Despite this sense of stability, the Rio Grande expedition, at least the military portion of it, became anticlimactic after January 1, 1864. Union soldiers controlled the Texas coast from the mouth of the Rio Grande to the Matagorda Peninsula. Although they did not have to worry about ducking minié balls, they occupied themselves with soldier-related activities: gathering wood for shelters, building a railroad from Brownsville to the coast, helping Unionist refugees, and distributing pamphlets that offered amnesty to repentant Rebels. On at least one occasion, a detachment of the 20th Wisconsin crossed the Rio Grande into Matamoros to protect the U.S. Consulate from warring Mexican factions.[53]

Since the occupation of Brownsville, hundreds of Texas refugees, including Texas Unionists, made their way to the Rio Grande. As previously mentioned, A. J. Hamilton established a provisional government in Brownsville. In addition, Judge J. B. McFarland set up a provisional court, which convened at the Episcopal Church. Other refugees, such as federal district judge Thomas H. DuVal and well-known legislator John Hancock, recruited troops for the Federal army and prodded Union authorities to launch an invasion of the Texas interior. The refugees also created a chapter of the Loyal League, an offshoot of the Republican Party, which met every Saturday at Brownsville's Market Hall. At its meeting on February 11, the members predicted the founding of a loyal state government under Lincoln's Ten Percent Plan. They also endorsed the appointment of A. J. Hamilton as military governor of Texas.[54]

The Union soldiers performed other duties as well. They cleaned their rifles, drilled, stood guard, repaired their uniforms, policed their camps, and went on scouting expeditions. Many of them enjoyed—some for the first time—the leisure activities associated with living close to the ocean. Pvt. James Clark of the 34th Iowa Regiment, stationed near Fort Esperanza on Matagorda Island, spoke of how he took his "company to the beach near by and made a charge on the surf. Bathing in the sea is very delightful. The salt water is more buoyant than fresh water, more cleansing, and a greater tonic to blood and nerves." Clark also loved "to ride up and down the beach on horseback on the hard, smooth beach. The sand packed hard and smooth by the beating of the surf makes a perfect course for riding." Two Ohio regiments spent much of their free time, like tourists today, collecting seashells and fishing for "mysterious looking animals from the brimy [sic] deep."[55]

The men who served with the Rio Grande expedition occupied themselves with fairly typical vices as well as more spiritual activities. The proximity to water actually encouraged a religious revival among many of the regiments. W. H. Bentley of the 77th Illinois Infantry Regiment wrote that "It is a great mistake to suppose that soldiers, as a rule, have no respect for religion or religious teachers. On the contrary, a conscientious, God-fearing, faithful chaplain, is regarded by saint and sinner alike, as a great acquisition to any regiment." Bentley also discussed the activities of Rev. L. S. Chittenden of the 67th Indiana Infantry Regiment, who became the spiritual leader of the soldiers in the Matagorda Bay region. The chaplain held a series of revival meetings that "resulted in the conversion of about five hundred." Bentley then described the baptism of twenty-five Illinois soldiers in Matagorda Bay. "With the Chaplain at their head," he wrote, "the candidates joined hands and marched into the gently deepening water, perhaps a hundred yards from the shore, and there, while thousands of spectators sang an old familiar hymn, the rite of baptism was performed, after which the company rejoined hands and came singing to the shore."[56]

Other soldiers spent their free time in less spiritual pursuits. Men of the 48th Ohio took advantage of their quartermaster's ingenuity and drank home-made whiskey. Soldiers of the 20th Iowa, stationed at Brownsville, often went to Matamoros, where they met enemy soldiers "who seemed to congregate there for the purpose of gambling." Most of the Union soldiers "imitated their example in this, and the monte tables were nightly surrounded by eager crowds of Federal, Confederate, and Mexican soldiers, who staked, lost, won, drank, quarreled and sometimes fought all night, parting in the morning after losing all their ready money."[57]

In addition to these moral and occasionally amoral activities, the men of the XIII Army Corps published newspapers, a common practice among many Civil War units. At least two papers were printed by Union soldiers of the Rio Grande expedition. The first one appeared in Indianola in December 1863, when Federal forces took over the town. Called the *Horn Extra*, the paper was published by E. M. Berry of the 33rd Illinois Infantry Regiment after his unit discovered an abandoned printing press. A two-page paper that survived for at least four printings in late 1863 and early 1864, it was, according to Berry, "published semi-occasionally on the first full moon before hog-killing time." The paper's comical tone emerged through its presentation of camp news and reports of hardships in Confederate Texas. Other features included the regiment's roster, an invitation to a temperance meeting, and information on where readers could get good cigars and edible fruit.[58]

The second paper, the *Loyal National Union Journal*, resembled the *Horn Extra* in many ways, except that it had a four-page format and a longer lifespan—twelve issues, of which at least eight have survived. Three men contributed to its publication. G. G. Carman's name appeared as editor on every issue, but E. F. Clewell and Theodore Steever also helped to produce what they mistakenly claimed to be "the first loyal paper in Texas." Of the three men, only Clewell, who served with the 19th Iowa, appears on any roster of regiments occupying Texas. It is not clear whether these men were printers in civilian life, but the *Union Journal* certainly exhibited high journalistic standards. The printing supplies probably came from General Herron, commander at Fort Brown. An aide to the general sent his wife a New Year's card "struck off by our boys on the General's press." Published weekly, the paper cost five cents a copy, and group rates were available for regiments that bought at least one hundred copies.[59]

The items that appeared in the *Union Journal* reflect the desires and concerns of soldiers who had time on their hands and little to fear from battle. From the very first sentence in the first issue, the editors showed their determination to publish "a paper which shall be devoted to the interests of the army, the people and the election of ABRAHAM LINCOLN to the next Presidency of our noble Republic." Within the parameters of this bold motto emerged three themes. First, the paper recognized the soldiers' contributions, defined their role in the war, and promoted their interests. Second, it had a political agenda that reflected the pro-Lincoln, pro-war, and antislavery sentiment of its readers. Finally, the newspaper entertained the troops with funny stories about women, Southerners, and other topics such as the weather, the people, and the usual camp gossip.[60]

The first issue promised to offer such "official news and notices as will be permitted by the Major General commanding" as well as war news from more active areas such as Tennessee, Virginia, and New Orleans. The editors copied many of the war reports from newspapers that arrived at the Fort Brown headquarters. The actions of General Grant, both militarily and socially, were closely covered. Soldierly conduct, both good and bad, also received the publishers' attention. The editors complimented the "good work" of a young soldier who was serving as health officer for the Fort Brown garrison. Favorable comments were also made about Rev. F. B. Wolf, who distributed Bibles to the soldiers, thus encouraging the "deep religious feeling that pervades every regiment." An important story that appeared in April mentioned the escape of seven soldiers of the 19th Iowa from a Confederate prison in Tyler, Texas.[61]

One aspect of the military scene that the troops loved to read was bad news concerning the Confederacy. In the first issue, stories appeared that reported refugees fleeing from besieged Charleston and soldiers deserting from Lee's Army of Northern Virginia. Nearly five hundred Confederate prisoners "acknowledged the rebel cause hopelessly lost." The following week the *Union Journal* mentioned the rumors that Jefferson Davis and his family were so destitute that they were forced to eat leather. The article concluded by pointing out that the Confederate president "has become drunken and desperate." An article that appeared in a May issue continued to report the deteriorating Confederate war effort. Refugees and deserters from Texas stated that "every man and boy capable of doing any kind of duty in the army" had been impressed into the military and that "the soldiers are sadly disheartened." The article concluded by stating that "the last dollar and the last man have nearly come."[62]

The editors of the *Union Journal* wanted to represent the soldiers' interests in ways that were more meaningful than just passing on war news. G. G. Carman waxed philosophic when he described history as a metaphorical structure built of human bricks. The Civil War offered the opportunity for Union soldiers to be "bricks—and corner-stones; key-stones, frontices and arches . . . in the new temple of free government—a house made with noble hands and loyal hearts, imperishable as truth and right." Important work needed to be done: "We can thank God that our souls and bodies are alive now. To live now is to have lived forever. To be true now is to have been a peer of the nobles of all ages. To be false now is worse than never to have been born."[63]

The men in the Union armies were, of course, the foundation of the war effort. The *Union Journal* remarked that "the common soldier defended the great principles of government, and maintained the conditions on which all law and order is based." They protected freedom of religion and ensured that "the children shall be taught—the people educated." Federal troops suffered "cold and hunger and disease and death" in order that everyone in the United States "may be secure and happy." For this, the nation owed the common soldier a "debt of honor" that included treating the soldiers and their families, especially the widows and orphans, with respect and generosity.[64]

The *Union Journal* regularly reported the pride the men maintained in themselves, despite the fact that they were the Union's most distant and isolated fighting force. On March 19 the newspaper ran an emotion-filled article that described a flag-raising ceremony that occurred during the dedication of a soldiers' cemetery at Brownsville. Brigade commander John McNulta of the 94th Illinois exclaimed, "Thus floats aloft the flag of our country, emblem of civilization and liberty. Protected by the blessings of Heaven and the stout hearts and strong arms of freemen, thus it shall ever float oe'r [sic] the bones of America's Heroes!" During "peal after peal" of an artillery salute, "stern, silent and immovable, but with the lighting of enthusiasm sparkling like fire in their eyes, stood the brave old veterans." The troops then gave three cheers for the "stars and stripes" and three more for General Herron, their commanding officer. "This was all of it," proclaimed the *Journal.* "Every man returned more loyal and patriotic." Although civilian spectators were also at the ceremony, the article emphasized, in exaggerated terms, the deeper meaning the ceremony held for the soldiers. They were a distinct breed of men who deserved more respect than even the most patriotic citizens.[65]

The *Union Journal* promoted the political ideals of the Lincoln administration, especially with regard to emancipation. The fact that black troops served with the Rio Grande expedition and received praise from some of the men was mentioned in several reports. The rhetoric in these articles about black soldiers was aimed at convincing the readers of the justice and inevitability of freeing the slaves.[66]

The paper also mentioned that this most controversial war was making progress in the North and even in occupied Louisiana—"the entire Union has undergone the process of inoculation" to the principles of emancipation and "negro equality." In two March articles, the *Union Journal* took a bold step, identifying with the newly freed slaves. In an article titled "Utopian," the writer explained that if he could be "transmuted from an editor to any other animal, all things considered," he "should choose a contraband." It would be, he reasoned, "commensurate with having the world cast at your feet in undisputed ownership," the "monarch of hidden possibilities which human prescience has never surveyed." The newspaper viewed the recent emancipation of the slaves as a rebirth for "a whole race of full grown men, women and children" who had been "born in a single day." With regard to the delights of their new freedom and their fresh start in life, "who can think of all these things being new and fresh to his mind, without envying the Freedmen?"[67]

Northerners who did not support the war effort, such as "copperheads" and speculators, received considerable criticism in the *Union Journal.* One article stated that "The coppers are an accidental growth from some stray mental guano. Five years from now they will be as scarce as Egyptian mummies, and about as respectable." The last surviving issue of the paper attacked Northern speculators in Mexico who were illegally trading for cotton with the enemy. These men "stand without excuse before the bar of public opinion of the world. Oblivious to the dictates of law, honor, and patriotism; acting upon the pretext that if they did not sustain the rebellion by supplying its commercial necessities somebody else would, they have bought from and sold to traitors as if they were loyal men." Such men ought to be punished; "they have bartered . . . they have sold their principles, which to a well constituted mind, are beyond all money price, for lucre."[68]

The *Union Journal* also criticized those Texas natives who joined the Federal troops in Brownsville to escape service in the Confederate army, persecution by Confederate authorities, or the worsening conditions on the Confederate home front. Some of these refugees were quite prominent, and hundreds of Texans—white and Mexican—joined the 1st and 2nd Texas Cavalry Regiments. Although this latter activity seemed loyal and patriotic, soldiers who read the *Union Journal* regarded these refugees as Southerners first and as allies second. One correspondent for the *Journal* stated that "the best and meanest of mankind are in Brownsville. Here is the sneak in the most profound perfection, who deserted the rebels, and, of whom, he was the most blatant and persistent, now cringing and willing to take any oath. Everybody is a refugee, or, as they more properly say, renegade. Some have fled from the Southern Confederacy, some from their wives, some from their husbands, many from justice and all from a better country." An editorial on April 9 derided the Confederate deserters in Mexico who "continue to try to talk in favor of the rebellion" but were really looking to make a quick dollar in the cotton trade. These deserters and refugees were accused of creating fabrications such as military success of the Southern states or European recognition of the Confederacy. Overall, the paper believed that those who fled into the Union lines did so only for ulterior motives.[69]

The *Loyal National Union Journal* was indeed a soldiers' paper. The only civilians mentioned were the copperheads, refugees, Mexicans, and women, none of whom were making any significant contributions to the Northern war effort. In contrast were the actions of the paper's soldier audience, who had fought and died for the ideals of emancipation and the Union. In order to solidify the soldiers' separate identity, the *Union Journal* attacked their enemies, from Northern traitors (copperheads) to the Confederate soldiers in the field. It also supported the soldiers' best friend, President Lincoln. The humor that appeared in the paper centered around life in camp and former battles, which indicated that only soldiers could poke fun at themselves; everyone else had to respect and honor their contributions.[70]

Not everyone welcomed the publication of this newspaper, however. One loyal Texas Unionist commented on "The first No. of a paper, 6 to 10, called the 'Loyal National Union Journal' with G. G. Carman's name at its head. Who he is, or whence he came, I know not. But of all wretched and impotent attempts, in the form of a newspaper, that ever I saw, it takes the lead. It is to be hoped that this first No. will never reach the interior of the State. It is calculated to make loyal men desperate. It will give them the most erroneous impressions about the good sense and intelligence of the officers and soldiers composing the U.S. forces at this point. We must unite in a memorial to General Herron to suppress Carman, and put somebody else forward as his exponents of public sentiment and sense in Brownsville." [71]

By June 1864 the XIII Army Corps had ceased to exist. Regiments of that corps were dispersed, mostly throughout the XIX Army Corps. The failed Red River campaign had diminished the prestige of the XIII Army Corps as it participated in the fourth and final attempted invasion of Texas. After that drive, Banks still commanded the Department of the Gulf, but military operations were now under the jurisdiction of Maj. Gen. E. R. S. Canby, who headed the new Union Trans-Mississippi Department, which covered Texas, Arkansas, and Louisiana. Banks handled only civil functions. [72]

The appointment of Canby came as a relief to some loyal Texans. Thomas H. DuVal expressed relief at Banks's dismissal: "I went down there [Brownsville] with the most confident expectation of soon being home again. But instead of the invasion being made from that quarter, General Banks thought proper to employ all the forces he had in the late ill advised expedition up the Red River. Its disastrous consequences are well known to you. I was gratified to find that General Canby has been appointed to the supreme military command west of the Mississippi. With this I am satisfied, and so will the Union men of Texas be, for General Canby is well and favorably known to them as a gallant soldier and gentleman. I feel every confidence that success will attend him." [73]

In March 1864, the Confederates in Texas sent an expedition to the lower Rio Grande Valley to drive the enemy from their state. The momentum of the war in Texas now turned in favor of the Confederates.

Five

The Cavalry of the West

*O*n December 22, 1863, Maj. Gen. John B. Magruder wrote a letter to the conscript officer in Austin, Col. John S. ("Rip") Ford. In it he suggested that Ford undertake a secret campaign to drive the Federals out of Brownsville and restore the cotton trade through that city. Magruder wanted Ford to make a feint toward the coast, thus creating confusion among the enemy as to his true objective, Brownsville. Ford and Magruder had both received appeals from Brownsville citizens to come to their rescue. With this public pressure weighing on him, Magruder relieved Ford of conscript duty and ordered him to San Antonio to begin organizing the "Cavalry of the West."[1]

Ford had, in the words of a biographer, "a brilliant though erratic career." He arrived in Texas in 1836, shortly after the Texas Revolution. For the next thirty years he served as a doctor, lawyer, journalist, surveyor, leader of the Texas annexation movement, adjutant in the Mexican War, Texas Ranger captain, and colonel in the Confederate cavalry. During the Mexican War, Ford acquired his nickname, "Rip," while serving as a surgeon for a Texas Ranger regiment under Col. John C. Hays. During the campaign against Mexico City, he signed death certificates, putting "Rest in Peace" after the deceased soldier's name. As the number of dead increased, he shortened the phrase to "R.I.P." From then on Ford was called "Rip."[2]

The public pressure that was placed upon Magruder is clear in an article that appeared in an Austin newspaper. The *Austin State Gazette* stated that "The paper learns from a gentleman who left Laredo last Saturday that things are quiet in that vicinity. Roma was sacked by Mexican robbers and not by Abolition soldiers. Laredo is considered safe, and large quantities of cotton are being crossed there. Benavides is in good spirits, determined to defend Laredo at all hazards; but is extremely anxious to be re-inforced. It is the prevailing wish on the Rio Grande that Col. Ford should be sent there;

his presence, it is said, would infuse confidence and new life into soldiers and civilians."[3]

By late December 1863, Magruder still thought the Federals remained committed to the offensive in Texas. The enemy's inactivity possibly meant that it was waiting for the arrival of reinforcements. Fearing a possible spring assault, Magruder boldly decided that he himself would take the offensive. He needed an officer with battlefield experience, organizational skills, and knowledge of South Texas. Ford, who accepted the surrender of Fort Brown in 1861, seemed the logical choice. On December 27, Ford received orders from Magruder to organize the Confederate Rio Grande expedition to drive the enemy out of Brownsville. When Ford arrived in San Antonio, he began recruiting from among conscript-exempt Texans. To ensure that Ford would have sufficient men for the campaign, Magruder gave him command of all of the troops at San Antonio, including those to the south and west of that city.[4]

Ford immediately made an announcement to the people of Texas, imploring them to come to the front and aid in expelling the enemy from Texas soil:

Persons desiring to go into service will report to me at San Antonio, without delay, where they will be subsisted and their horses foraged. Those not belonging to companies will be organized here. Companies already organized are requested to report for duty immediately.

It is highly important that the expedition be organized and placed in the field at once.

The people of the West are invited to turn out. They will be defending their own homes. Shall it be said that a mongrel force of abolitionists, negroes, plundering Mexicans, and perfidious renegades have been allowed to murder and rob us with impunity? Shall the pages of history record the disgraceful fact, that Texans have tamely and basely submitted to these outrages, and suffered the brand of dishonor to be inflicted upon an unresisting people? For the honor of the state, for the sake of the glorious memories of the past, the hopes of the future, you are called upon to rally to the standard and to wash out the stains of invasion by the blood of your ruthless enemies.
John S. Ford
Colonel, Commanding[5]

Ford believed the force that would rally to him would make him the Confederate David who would march into the Rio Grande Valley to slay the Union Goliath. Men quickly responded to his proclamation, and his army grew daily. Even women grew enthusiastic over the upcoming military expedition. Citizen groups in San Antonio gathered supplies to give to the chief quartermaster of the campaign, Capt. C. H. Merritt. Ford's assistant, Maj. A. G. Dickinson, went to nearby towns to gather arms and ammunition. In Austin, contributions were collected to help fund the drive. An article in an Austin newspaper was titled "Contributions towards Col. Ford's expedition."[6]

Besides the volunteers that responded to his call to arms, Ford also had under his command two ranger battalions from Blanco County, Col. S. B. Baird's 4th Texas Cavalry, Arizona Brigade. Despite its name, most of the men from this regiment were from Texas. Once the expedition got under way, Ford would be joined by two companies near Corpus Christi. Maj. Mat Nolan of the 2nd Texas Cavalry and Capt. A. J. Ware of San Patricio would meet Ford as he moved southward. Once Ford reached the Rio Grande, soldiers under Capt. George H. Giddings at Eagle Pass and Col. Santos Benavides at Laredo would also join him.[7]

Despite the help from regular Confederate units in the field, the bulk of Ford's command came from men who were exempt from conscription. These citizens enlisted for short terms with the understanding that they would not be ordered to serve outside the state. In enrolling men for his campaign, the colonel stated that he would sign up any man he could without violating "law and propriety." His view of both narrowed as enthusiasm for the campaign began to wear off. One officer sarcastically stated, "Fifty-seven children have joined my battalions." Ford set the lower age of recruitment at fifteen but did not question good-sized youngsters about their age. In thirty days, the Cavalry of the West had in its ranks some thirteen hundred men and boys. Ford wrote Magruder that he anticipated another thousand to join before he took the field.[8]

Until mid-March 1864, Ford immersed himself in the concurrent tasks of supply procurement, staff organization, and operations of the units under his command already in the field. He sent orders to Colonel Benavides at Laredo to limit his activities to defensive operations and create the impression that the forces gathering at San Antonio were to be sent to Indianola on the coast. Benavides was then directed to gather supplies at Fort Merrill (on the Nueces River) or farther south near El Sal del Rey, a salt lake about fifty miles northwest of Brownsville. Benavides responded that he had no specie with which to buy supplies but that, if Ford sent his chief commissary officer with funds, he could easily procure the provisions in Mexico.[9]

Benavides reported two serious obstacles: supply shortages and insufficient funds to purchase them. He complained that not only were his horses starving but his men had also not been paid in eighteen months. The starvation was due to the severe drought that hit Texas in 1863. Richard King, whose ranch near Corpus Christi became a center of miliary activity, informed Ford that he would supply the Rio Grande expedition with all of the beef it needed. King also pointed out that "The grass is as bad as it gets here. We Western people are, in fact, in a starving condition." [10]

As the winter of 1863 became the spring of 1864, the initial enthusiasm for the enterprise waned. As supplies dwindled, many recruits deserted. Despite these losses, Ford remained optimistic. He continued to urge the people to have faith and support them "in the name of patriotism, of liberty, and all that is dear to man." He then offered fifty dollars apiece to any men who would enlist to "defend their homes and property, their wives and their little ones against the brutal assaults of an enemy who respects neither age, sex or condition, who plunder the homestead." Ford stemmed the desertion problem and by mid-March had nearly thirteen hundred poorly armed troops ready to march south. "With the help of God," he hoped to drive the Yankees into the Gulf. [11]

Ford recounted the difficulties he encountered in taking to the field sooner: "I regret not having been able to take to the field. I have had serious obstacles to surmount. Exhausted resources, a population almost drained of men subject to military duty, oppositions from rivalry, and the nameless disagreeable retardations incident to an undertaking of this character are all well known to the major general commanding." The rivalry Ford referred to involved Col. S. B. Baird of the 4th Arizona Cavalry. This regiment was assigned to the Cavalry of the West, but Baird, who held a regular commission in the Confederate army, believed he outranked Ford and refused to serve under him. Baird eased the situation by obtaining a transfer, and command of the unit fell to Lt. Col. Daniel Showalter. [12]

On March 17, 1864, the men and boys of the Cavalry of the West mounted their horses and rode through the dusty plaza directly in front of the Alamo. "Old Rip" was in the lead, adorned with a black hat and sword sash on his uniform. When it became public knowledge that most of the thirteen hundred cavalrymen were draft exempts—old men and young boys—a newspaper reported that "Old Abe will find that he has undertaken an almost endless task to exterminate the seeds of the rebellion. As fast as he kills one rebel, a dozen spring from his ashes." [13]

A descriptive account of the anxious months prior to the start of the Confederate Rio Grande expedition can be found in the letters of a San Antonio resident named Mary Maverick. Mary had four sons serving in the Confederate army, but many of her letters were addressed to one of them,

Capt. Lewis Maverick of the 32nd Texas Cavalry Regiment. In one missive she mentioned that "Col. Ford is still here, expecting to get off every day. We hear nothing from the Rio Grande below except that they expect an attack and are fortifying very strongly. The Yankees beat us with the pick and spade, don't they? Col. Ford told me that he had never positively ascertained whether the enemy were 2 or 5000 strong at Brownsville, accounts so conflict." [14]

Although Mary's early letters were a bit lighthearted in nature, they gradually became more serious in tone. In February she stated that "Our town was thrown into great excitement by an express from Benavides to the effect that 1800 cavalry of the enemy had left Brownsville, probably for this place. Meetings were called and it was determined to barricade the streets, and money was raised to defend the city, but nothing has yet been done, and the enemy must have gone elsewhere. It may be towards Victoria or only to steal beef. Which way do you think the Yankees intend to move? They have caught 8 deserters and two were taken to Goliad." [15]

A couple of weeks before the Cavalry of the West left San Antonio, the secrecy of their mission was exposed by some San Antonio residents. B. F. Dye, a friend of Lewis Maverick, remarked in a letter that "Judge Stribling, Fisk, and Peyton Smith left this place three or four weeks since pretending to have business in Mexico but last evening a gentleman received a letter from Matamoros stating that Stribling and others had joined the federals at Brownsville and that Stribling told the Yankees that Ford was in San Antonio with four or five hundred men and also gave them other information in regard to our expected movements." Mary Maverick confirmed Dye's account of Stribling's activities in Brownsville: "Stribbling [sic] has been heard of in Brownsville advising the enemy to take this place, and that they would not have over 400 men to fight and that many of our troops would desert to join them upon their advance into this country. Benevides sent an express 2 days ago to say that 2500 of the enemy were advancing up the Rio Grande for Eagle Pass." A week later, Mary described additional traitorous activities: "Stribbling [sic] has gone to New Orleans, [I] suppose to insist on the authorities sending a force to take this place, and this western country." [16]

Despite the lack of secrecy, Ford's men were still in high spirits. As they marched south, the Confederate cavalry began singing "The Yellow Rose of Texas." As they moved into the drought-ridden Texas countryside, dust from the column choked away the melody. Fortunately for the Texans, Ford's chief of staff was Maj. Felix Blucher, grandnephew of Field Marshal Blucher of Waterloo fame. Ford had requested Blucher's service because "He has been surveyor for many years in the country between the Nueces and the Rio Grande, and is thoroughly acquainted with the geography and topography of that section." With these qualifications and remarkable skills, Blucher found the scarce grass and water of South Texas and became a valuable asset to the expeditionary force.[17]

The Confederates' line of march carried them to a point near Pleasanton, about 40 miles south of San Antonio. The soldiers then moved on to the meandering Atascosa River to its confluence with the Frio and the Nueces. After a week of marching, Ford arrived at Camp San Fernando on the Nueces, about 140 miles south of San Antonio, near Corpus Christi. Maj. Mat Nolan of the 2nd Texas Cavalry commanded this camp. While Ford's men moved south, cotton had been stored along the route at different points for the purpose of financing the campaign. The crop could be sold for cash, and cash could buy the Confederates what they needed to fight a long campaign.[18]

While at Camp San Fernando, Ford received a courier from Colonel Benavides at Laredo, which served as a vital trade link with Mexico at this time, especially for the export of cotton. The courier reported a Federal raid on Laredo on March 19 by elements of the 1st and 2nd Texas Cavalry (Union) Regiments.[19]

Although Benavides had patrols around Laredo, the approach of two hundred enemy cavalry on March 19 clearly surprised him. The Federals caught them unawares by crossing into Mexico, then recrossing the Rio Grande just a few miles south of Laredo. As a result of this maneuver, they eluded Benavides's scouts. Alerting Laredo to the presence of the enemy was an excited cowboy named Cayetano de la Garza. Known as the "Paul Revere of Laredo," de la Garza told Benavides that a Union cavalry force numbering one thousand was approaching Laredo from downriver. Benavides, who was ill at the time, doubted the accuracy of the report but sounded the alarm anyway. The battle of Laredo was about to commence.[20]

The Laredo colonel had only 72 men to defend the city. Of these, 42 were in two companies under the commands of Captains Cristobal Benavides and Refugio Benavides, brothers of Santos Benavides. On the eastern side of the city, they waited behind a large corral that provided both cover and a clear field of fire for the Confederates. The other 30 men, mostly state militia, would defend the interior of the town. Colonel Benavides gave strict orders to his brother Cristobal: "There are five thousand bales of cotton in the plaza. It belongs to the Confederacy. If the day goes against us, fire it. Be sure to do the work properly so that not a bale of it shall fall into the hands of the Yankees. Then you will set my new house on fire, so that nothing of mine will pass to the enemy. Let their victory be a barren one."[21]

The battle began at about three o'clock in the afternoon and lasted for nearly three hours. The Federals made three heavy assaults but were repulsed each time. The Confederates suffered no deaths and sent a scouting party to inspect the Federal camp the next day. There they found many bloodstains and blood-soaked rags. Clearly the Union horsemen had suffered some casualties, although no exact number has been determined. Later reports on March 21 confirmed that the Federals were still retreating downriver.[22]

The Federal cavalry retreated from Laredo because, on March 20, Colonel Benavides received reinforcements, notably 150 men of the "Giddings Battalion" from Eagle Pass under the command of Lt. Col. George H. Giddings. The citizens of Laredo rejoiced with "the ringing of church bells and the blowing of trumpets." Despite driving the Yankees from the city, Benavides believed that the enemy might be falling back to regroup and launch another attack. To prevent this, he urged Ford to move his cavalry to the Rio Grande and attack the Union rear. This would put the Yankee invaders in "a bad fix." Ford, although anxious to help Benavides, had to wait for additional men and supplies from San Antonio. Moreover, the country between the Nueces and the Rio Grande was not conducive to a fast march. The drought of 1863 made the region a virtual wasteland with very little water or grass. Ford relayed to Benavides that, for the time being, Laredo must be protected without the help of the Cavalry of the West.[23]

Despite Ford's inability to march immediately toward Laredo, he praised the efforts of Benavides and his men. Outnumbered nearly three to one, the handful of recruits behaved like veterans during that hazardous period. The Unionists went away without plunder, without cotton, and without success. After the battle Benavides collapsed from fatigue, saying that he could rise from bed only "at the hazard of his life." Ford, upon hearing of Benavides's condition, urged him to allow "some officer in rank" to take command of his troops. As a result, his brother Refugio assumed command of the Laredo defenders. Col. Santos Benavides certainly lived up to this appraisal made by Ford: "You have added to the reputation you and your command have already acquired."[24]

During the last week of March, the situation grew worse for the Cavalry of the West. Desertions, supply shortages, and the Federal attack on Laredo compelled Old Rip to hold a council of war with his officers. They decided to continue the march to the Rio Grande. On March 26, they left Camp San Fernando, Ford's men cheering loudly. Four companies under Major Nolan were left near Corpus Christi to protect his left flank and supply lines. Colonel Showalter and four companies of the 4th Arizona Cavalry caught up with the expedition on March 30. On April 15 eighteen hundred men of the Cavalry of the West reached Laredo.[25]

Back on the border at Laredo, Ford grew concerned about keeping the movements of his cavalry a secret. The element of surprise, however, was still on his side. Union intelligence reports stated that he had only 650 men, too small a force to constitute any real threat to the garrison at Brownsville. The Union commander at Fort Brown, Maj. Gen. Francis J. Herron, discredited the news of Ford's movements as mere rumor.[26]

After about a week in Laredo, Ford moved downriver to his next objective, Fort Ringgold, at Rio Grande City. Soldiers from Laredo under Capt. Refugio Benavides joined the campaign. For the next ten days, torrential rains fell in South Texas, greatly relieving this parched region of the state. Around April 22, Ford arrived at Fort Ringgold and discovered that the enemy had evacuated that position. At Rio Grande City, he established his headquarters for the Cavalry of the West. Here he consolidated the different portions of his command, which included more soldiers from Laredo and the 4th Arizona Cavalry. More important, he made final preparations for the assault on Brownsville.[27]

The occupation of Rio Grande City caused grave concern for the Union forces in Brownsville. Because of the Red River campaign in Louisiana, General Herron's troop strength had declined dramatically. One soldier at Fort Brown noted in his diary on April 27 that "There seems to be some uneasiness manifested among our officers regarding a force of rebels which are marching upon some point in this vicinity. Every precaution has been taken against surprise—the first brigade slept on their arms all night. Our generals were out at an early hour this morning and passed around our picket lines. 400 cavalry have been sent out as scouts."[28]

Activities in Louisiana also affected the Rio Grande expedition's march upon Brownsville. Men and supplies destined for the Rio Grande were sent to Louisiana. For six weeks the campaign against Fort Brown stalled at Rio Grande City. Ford's problems included supply procurement, troop transfers, and short-term enlistments. To resolve the supply problem, Ford used the cotton bales his troops had picked up on the march to the Rio Grande. He sold them in Mexico and used the money to purchase supplies for his men. While in Mexico, he established contacts with Matamoros, not only to promote the Confederate cause in that city but also to obtain information about Union forces at Fort Brown. Two of these contacts were Lt. Col. J. J. Fisher and Col. John M. Swisher, both of whom supplied Ford with valuable information and much-needed provisions. Swisher also sent drawings of Fort Brown and estimated the troop strength there at five thousand.[29]

During the six-week stay at Fort Ringgold, everything was placed in a state of readiness for the final advance on Brownsville. Throughout that time, Old Rip suffered from a severe fever. The indisposition required an extraordinary effort on his part to continue making preparations. Despite his illness, the hard work Ford undertook won the hearts of all of the men in his command. A captain serving under him wrote that the troops respected their colonel and would follow him to hell.[30]

June brought news from Ford's spies downriver that the Federals might be planning a general evacuation of Brownsville. One Confederate informant wrote that "about 600 men left Brownsville this morning on the steamer[s] *Mustang* and *Matamoros* for New Orleans on the *Clinton*. I am told three companies of Mexican cavalry—say Vidals, Falcons, and Martines—were the one[s] that left. Four companies of infantry on the boats [left] with them. General Herron is ordered to New Orleans. His successor is Fitz Henry Warren, an old man and no account. Change will be beneficial to us."[31]

The news of a general evacuation of Fort Brown prompted Ford to make an immediate forward movement in the direction of Brownsville. He decided to make a reconnaissance in force to test the validity of the information his spies had provided. While most of the cavalry moved directly overland, Ford and sixty men followed the river and arrived at the ranch of John McAllen, near Edinburg, on June 21. Ford now felt confident that his campaign would be a success. He stated that "now is the first time I can with truth say this country is practicable. The rains have been abundant [and] the grass is becoming plentiful. I can now operate; before it was quite an impossibility."[32]

Ford left the McAllen ranch on June 22. By this time his main force was about 30 miles west of Brownsville. He then brought his men to Las Rucias Ranch, about 24 miles west of Brownsville. The movement of the Confederate cavalry, however, did not go undetected. A Union sympathizer named John Webber sent one of his sons to Fort Brown to warn the Federals of the enemy's advance. The son told Herron that Ford himself had only about 60 men. Webber did not realize that Ford intended to link up with a portion of the 4th Arizona Cavalry under Colonel Showalter at Como Se Llama, where there was a dependable water well, on June 25. Ford's scouting force now numbered about 250 men. In response, General Herron ordered Capt. Phillip E. Temple to take two companies of the 1st Texas Cavalry (U.S.) to Las Rucias Ranch. Presumably, Temple would thus have the element of surprise and deal a mortal blow to the expeditionary forces.[33]

On June 23, Ford met Colonel Showalter and his men at Como Se Llama. The next day they dried beef for emergency rations. At dawn on June 25, the

Confederates advanced toward Las Rucias Ranch. The Union forces at the ranch under Captain Temple consisted of about one hundred soldiers. Temple made a tactical error by failing to station sufficient men along the road leading to Brownsville. He expected the Confederates to attack from the west. Instead, Old Rip arrived from the south and caught the enemy by surprise when the battle began.[34]

The Confederate advance party, led by Capt. James Dunn, came upon the Federals sooner than expected. When fired upon, Dunn charged with his men and was killed. Two officers with him, Capt. Cristobal Benavides and Lt. C. B. Gardiner, had their horses shot out from under them. Two men under Benavides were also killed. On the Union side, Captain Temple was wounded in the bloody first exchange.[35]

As the fighting became more general, Temple and the Union cavalry took refuge in a brick building that served as ranch headquarters. Some of the men took up positions behind a pile of adobe bricks and a large lagoon but were driven from every spot. The brief but fierce battle ended in a complete rout of the Federals. The Union cavalry fought fiercely during the battle, believing that since they were Texas Unionists, the Confederates might execute them as traitors. The Union casualties were 20 killed, 25 wounded, and 36 taken prisoner. The Cavalry of the West suffered 3 killed and 4 wounded. The Confederates also captured two wagons, twenty-eight horses, and a number of saddles, which they desperately needed.[36]

After the Confederate victory at the battle of Las Rucias, the Cavalry of the West anticipated that a larger enemy force would come out to meet them. Ford's men advanced to within five miles of Brownsville, but the Federals did not advance to offer battle. Old Rip's expectation of a Union attack was remote, however. Among the items captured at Las Rucias were official papers indicating that more soldiers were leaving Fort Brown for New Orleans. In addition, General Herron at Fort Brown estimated the enemy's strength at substantially more than a thousand men. He therefore decided to let the rebels attack him.[37]

Although it seemed like an opportune time to attack Brownsville, Ford had no accurate estimate of enemy strength at Fort Brown. As a result, he exercised caution and fell back to Fort Ringgold to regroup. For three weeks, he hesitated to launch an assault for a variety of reasons: the drought, insufficient supplies, and additional desertions. On June 27 four regiments under Gen. J. E. Slaughter arrived from San Antonio, offsetting the desertions. The persistent drought, however, provided little forage for a large cavalry force. Finally, Gov. Juan Cortina of Tamaulipas issued orders preventing the crossing of Mexican goods below Edinburg. Ford would now have to wait longer to receive supplies from Matamoros.[38]

The Confederate victory at Las Rucias put the Federals on alert. Herron wrote that Ford's intentions were "to keep us in as close quarters as possible, which he can do to a certain extent owing to our want of cavalry or horses to mount infantry." The Union soldiers at Fort Brown were placed on high alert, ready to respond to an alarm at a moment's notice. Especially disturbing for the northern soldiers was the rumor that the Confederate flag would be flying over Fort Brown by the Fourth of July.[39]

A military change was indeed about to occur at Fort Brown, but it had nothing to do with the Confederate activity in the region. Maj. Gen. Edward R. S. Canby, commander of the newly formed Military Division of Western Mississippi, ordered the evacuation of Brownsville. The Union troops were commanded to fall back to the island of Brazos Santiago. Confederate spies operating out of Matamoros knew of the evacuation almost as soon as General Herron.[40]

Despite the news, Herron seemed to be in no particular hurry to withdraw from Brownsville. Confederate spies reported that all of the artillery and quartermaster stores were being taken down to the river for shipment to the coast. To hasten the departure of the Federal troops, one spy suggested to Ford that he not "leave without some demonstration against them. If you do, it may injure you—but at the same time be careful. In a stand up fight and open ground, you can do nothing with them—they will move with 3400 infantry, 250 cavalry and two Baltines. Close down on them as soon as you can—don't let them get away without seeing you."[41]

Finally, on July 19, the Cavalry of the West left Fort Ringgold and began the 100-mile march toward Brownsville. After two days, they arrived at Carricitos Ranch, about 22 miles west of Brownsville. Ford outran his supply line and thus had to wait two days at the ranch to be resupplied. By July 25 the Confederates were at the outskirts of Brownsville, where they drove the Union pickets into town. The most advanced Confederate position had the ghoulish name of Dead Man's Hollow, about half a mile above the western edge of town. Wanting to stay out of artillery range, Old Rip advanced no further. A couple of days of outpost firing followed.[42]

As the Confederates closed in on Brownsville, the civilian population of that city expected the worst. Hundreds of Brownsville citizens had taken the oath of loyalty to the Union. They now feared that with the Federal evacuation of the city, the Confederates would look upon them as traitors. Pvt. Benjamin F. McIntyre of the 19th Iowa Infantry Regiment vividly described the panic that gripped the people of Brownsville: "The citizens generally are very much excited. I pity them—all have taken the loyalty oath. We have given them protection and very many aids and secured them every privilege a free people could ask and a bright future seemed dawning upon them. They now feel that their hopes and expectations are blasted—the future to them is dark and dreary with not a ray of light to dawn upon them with a single hope. They cannot remain, for certain death awaits them—if they leave they go as beggars for they must sacrifice every possession of home and the comforts surrounding it."[43]

The Federal officers, aware of the danger many Brownsville citizens faced, offered free passage to New Orleans. Reporting to headquarters on July 23, 1864, Herron reported that 250 refugees, 200 sick, and a number of women had gone or would be going to New Orleans. "Brownsville has been entirely evacuated by the citizens," he wrote, "not one single family remaining." Despite Herron's formal language, the tension in Brownsville increased day by day as many residents fled to Matamoros for safety. Private McIntyre harbored a sense of guilt as he witnessed this mass exodus to Mexico: "The stampede to Matamoros continues—the landings upon both sides of the river is [sic] piled up with household goods of every description. The numbers of people fleeing from those who have compelled them to take the oath who after offering protection and security now leaves them to an uncertain fate. Our forces withdrawing every promise made them—now they are rewarded for their loyalty."[44]

On the afternoon of July 28, thirty to forty Confederates from Matamoros crossed the river to confirm the rumors that the enemy had left Brownsville. They learned that the last troops had left at nine o'clock that morning. Once the Union soldiers were gone, there was almost a repeat of the ransacking and looting that had followed Confederate Gen. Hamilton Bee's evacuation in the fall of the previous year. Fortunately, this small group of Confederate volunteers prevented such activities. One of them, Maj. E. W. Cave, sent out scouts to look for Colonel Ford and the expeditionary forces. Two days later, the advance guard of the Cavalry of the West arrived to take possession of Brownsville. The Confederate forces once again controlled the city.[45]

Ford and the remainder of his cavalry arrived later that day and were met by jubilant citizens. In a letter to his superior, General Slaughter, Ford wrote that "Confidence has been restored, our people are returning to their homes, and commerce is being reestablished, and our relations with Mexican authorities are of the most friendly character."[46]

After capturing Fort Brown, Ford learned that Herron's men were only about eighteen miles below Brownsville. He therefore detached a force under Colonel Showalter to pursue and harass them. When Showalter discovered a body of Federals on August 2, he sent Capt. Refugio Benavides to look them over. However, Benavides exceeded the order and attacked this party of Union soldiers, plunging into the main body before breaking off. Despite this harassment, the Federals made their way safely to Brazos Santiago, where many waited to board ships bound for New Orleans. At Brazos, Herron left behind Col. H. M. Day and fifteen hundred men of the 62nd Colored Infantry Regiment and the 2nd Texas Cavalry to garrison and fortify the island. Although they were not a very reliable force, the island was almost impregnable except with regard to amphibious landings. On the other hand, as long as the Federals stayed where they were, no harm would come to them. Now that Brownsville was again in Confederate hands, the lucrative cotton trade resumed, and that was of course the primary objective of the Confederate Rio Grande expedition.[47]

The Union withdrawal from Brownsville marked the lowest point in its Rio Grande campaign. The Federal soldiers, at one time numbering ten thousand, controlled a large section of the Texas coast for a time. Now they held only Brazos Santiago at the mouth of the Rio Grande. After the failure of the Red River expedition, not to mention the need for troops east of the Mississippi, Halleck directed Banks to break off his Texas operations. Halleck realized that the continued need to impress the French still justified keeping soldiers on the Rio Grande, but he believed this goal could be accomplished "if a single point is held" in Texas.[48]

Despite Ford's successful campaign against Brownsville, a return of the status quo did not automatically ensue. The cotton trade resumed slowly since many Texans were still fearful of the Union troops on Brazos Santiago. The greatest problem, however, concerned Gen. Juan Cortina, the rogue of the Rio Grande. The military situation on the lower Rio Grande allowed him to play a game of cat and mouse with Union, Confederate, and French forces. An international powder keg was about to explode, and Cortina was going to light the fuse.[49]

Six

Troubles South of the Border

"*The* French invasion of Mexico was so closely related to the Rebellion as to be essentially a part of it," commented General in Chief Ulysses S. Grant to Maj. Gen. Phillip H. Sheridan on the relationship between the American and Mexican wars. The Union Rio Grande expedition in November 1863 was designed partly to provide a buffer against the French presence in Mexico and the civil unrest it generated. As the Federal presence in South Texas was reduced to only twelve hundred men on the island of Brazos Santiago by August 1864, incidents at the mouth of the Rio Grande increased. Not only did the river serve as an international boundary, but the mouth of the Rio Grande also became a bustling commercial center for nations supplying these two wars.[1]

Until 1867, the Imperialists and their leader, Emperor Maximilian, had the support of the French under Napoleon III. The Liberals, led by Benito Juarez, established a provisional government in the city that now bears his name. Juarez's agenda included land reform, heavy restrictions on the church, and the suspension of payments to European creditors. Beginning in 1863, the French controlled Mexico City, and the United States, preoccupied with its own war, could do nothing but condemn the French presence in Mexico.[2]

Three important military figures played major roles in the Brownsville-Matamoros region. The first was Col. Henry M. Day, commander of the remaining Union forces on the island of Brazos Santiago. Day, who led the 91st Illinois Infantry Regiment, was one of the original soldiers who occupied Brownsville. His forces on the island included the 91st Illinois, the 34th Indiana, the 1st Texas Cavalry, and the 62nd and 81st Colored troops. Day would later be replaced by Brig. Gen. William A. Pile. Here the Federal forces dug in, determined to hold at least one plot of Texas soil.[3]

The other two figures were Col. John S. Ford and his old adversary, Gen. Juan Cortina, who was also governor of the Mexican state of Tamaulipas. Ford, who served Texas in many capacities, led the Confederate Rio Grande expedition that liberated Brownsville in July 1864. With Brownsville under Confederate control once again, Ford immediately went to work improving Confederate relations in Matamoros. This meant coming to amicable terms with Cortina, whose influence in the region cannot be underestimated. He was born in Camargo, Mexico, on May 16, 1824, and his mother was heiress to a disputed 260,000 acres, which included Brownsville. The grant was involved in controversy, however, because many parties, including the city of Matamoros, made claims to the land. As a result, the true ownership was blurred, which led to legal actions and violent disagreements. It was the land-grant controversy that took Cortina on a path of raiding in the Brownsville-Matamoros region. Because he believed the land had been stolen from his family, he made a career of trying to get it back. Ford, who, as a Texas Ranger, had pursued Cortina in 1859, wrote in 1864 that "Cortina hates Americans; particularly Texans. He has an old and deep seated grudge against Browns-ville." Not surprisingly, Cortina used the volatile environments in both Texas and Mexico to try to reclaim the lost land for his family. As a result, during the years of the Civil War, Cortina sided with any power that might help him achieve his goal.[4]

During the Federal occupation of Brownsville, Cortina sided with the Juarez faction in Mexico. Prior to the Federal invasion of Brownsville in November 1863, the Juarez government had been plagued by the actions of a group of Maximilian adherents in Brownsville. Under the leadership of José M. Cobos, they conspired to capture Matamoros for the Imperialists. Apparently, Juarez sent Cortina to Brownsville to infiltrate this group and kill Cobos. When the Federals moved in to occupy Brownsville, Cortina crossed over into Matamoros with Cobos and helped him capture the city. On November 7, 1863, Cortina had Cobos shot and installed Jesus de la Serna as governor of the Mexican state of Tamaulipas. Eventually, in January 1864, Cortina proclaimed himself both governor and military commandant of Tamaulipas and retained these positions throughout the Union occupation of Brownsville.[5]

Even after the Union retreat from Brownsville, heavy skirmishing continued between Federal and Confederate troops throughout August. This fighting, however, was only a sidelight to the power struggle south of the border between the Mexicans and the French. By late August rumors of a major Imperialist movement against Matamoros were circulating in the border region. These stories became reality when four hundred French legionnaires landed at Bagdad at the mouth of the Rio Grande. Another Imperialist force under Gen. Tomás Mejía was advancing from the interior north to Matamoros. The French troops at Bagdad drove back Cortina's Republican troops toward Matamoros. Ford, realizing that Matamoros would soon be under French control, sent couriers to Bagdad to ascertain the attitude of the French toward the Confederates on both sides of the river. These couriers met with Capt. A. Veron, who commanded the French forces at Bagdad. He assured Ford's representatives that supplies moving through Matamoros would not be hindered in any way. Veron also promised Ford that the Confederate flag and those seeking protection under it would be "the object of his particular care in Matamoros."[6]

Ford's meeting with Veron caused grave concern for Cortina. He feared that Ford was in collusion, if not an actual alliance, with the French. Even Ford believed that French noninterference in the region meant France's recognition of the Confederacy. Cortina's worries were not unfounded. He complained to Ford that whenever the French engaged the Mexicans in battle, the Confederates had fired at the Mexicans. Cortina also suspected that the French at Bagdad supplied the Confederates with weapons and ammunition. Ford of course denied all of Cortina's charges, but there is little doubt that the Confederates occasionally fired on Cortina's men across the river. They saw Cortina and his men as nothing more than bandits, a scourge to both the Confederates and the French.[7]

Cortina's suspicions meant that he and the Federals had a common enemy in the French. This in turn encouraged him to see the American consul in Matamoros, Leonard Pierce. On August 31, 1864, Cortina met with Pierce and informed him that relations with the French and the Confederates were worsening and that he expected open warfare with both groups very shortly. At this meeting Pierce initiated a conspiracy that had as its objective the capture of Brownsville by Cortina. Pierce wrote Colonel Day on September 1 to explain the details of his plan. The day of attack was set for September 6. The strategy was that Cortina would cross some of his men downriver from Brownsville, drawing Ford away from Fort Brown. Before Cortina's crossing, Colonel Day would clear any rebels out of the region to ensure the safety of the crossing. Another body of Cortina's men would cross above Brownsville and then attack Fort Brown once Ford left. As an additional inducement for Cortina to help, Pierce offered him a commission in the U.S. Army as a brigadier general if he captured Brownsville. With the Confederates out of that city, Day would be in a good position to offer hidden support to Cortina to fight the French. Pierce saw Cortina as a tool to maintain the Monroe Doctrine.[8]

A few days after the meeting, on September 3, 1864, Cortina initiated hostilities by closing river traffic to the Confederates. He then wheeled his cannons into place, pointing them directly at Brownsville. The combined U.S.-Mexican operations against Brownsville had begun. Cortina's actions, however, were not entirely unexpected. A man named Combe, an American doctor and Confederate sympathizer in Matamoros, informed Colonel Ford of Cortina's plan to attack Brownsville. Ford realized that, if Cortina attacked from upriver and the Union forces hit from downriver, other Cortina men would swarm across the river from Matamoros. On the appointed day of the crossing, September 6, Colonel Day and nine hundred Federal troops marched west toward Palmito Ranch, fifteen miles from Brazos Santiago. There they engaged a Confederate outpost under the command of Lt. Col. Dan Showalter. Cortina supported Day by firing his cannons at the Confederates from across the river. Showalter, who had been drinking heavily that day, was unnerved by the assault. The Federal commander reported his foe as "flying in confusion." Fortunately, Ford had expected an attack from the coast and sent reinforcements to Palmito. These soldiers, under Capt. G. H. Giddings, relieved Showalter and established a new defensive position that prevented Day's column from advancing any farther west.[9]

On the south bank of the Rio Grande, Cortina ran into difficulties. To prevent interference by France, he attacked the four hundred French at Bagdad. Cortina, with eight hundred men, was defeated by the French and retreated to Burrita Hill, opposite White Ranch on the American side, about ten miles from the mouth of the river. It was here that Cortina and three hundred of his men crossed the river on September 6. Colonel Day offered these men the protection of the U.S. government. Although Cortina's detachment was safely across, Day's attack on Showalter at Palmito Ranch failed to draw Ford away from Fort Brown. This meant that the prospects for a successful attack by Cortina's men from upriver were greatly diminished.[10]

While Confederate soldiers fought east of Brownsville, Ford prepared the city for an attack. Having only three hundred men, Old Rip kept them on the move, which gave the impression that he had more soldiers than he actually commanded. He also kept himself in constant view of the Mexicans across the river, knowing an attack would come if he left the fort. With hostile forces on three sides, the Confederates feared being overrun. As a result, Ford asked for support troops from Gen. John G. Walker, the newly appointed commander of Texas. Instead of reinforcements, Walker sent instructions that, if Cortina were captured, he was to be treated as "a robber and a murderer, and executed immediately." Ford even sought aid from the French, who politely told him, "Our position of perfect neutrality towards the United States as well as towards the Confederacy prevents us from doing the service you request."[11]

The Confederates expected the Mexicans to attack Brownsville at dawn on September 7, but the assault never materialized. One reason was that a heavy rainfall the night before had raised the river to flood stage, preventing the Mexicans from crossing. Another was a near mutiny among Cortina's officer corps. His ranking colonel, Servando Canales, flatly refused to lead his men against Brownsville. In addition, Canales knew Ford before the war and considered him a friend. Three other high-ranking officers also refused to fight with Cortina. To make matters worse, French troops under Gen. Tomás Mejía were fast approaching Matamoros from Monterrey.[12]

As the plans to capture Brownsville rapidly deteriorated for Cortina, a delicate international situation unfolded for Colonel Day near Palmito Ranch. On September 7, Capt. A. Veron, commander of the French units at Bagdad, sent an inquiry to Day concerning the status of the three hundred Mexicans who had crossed the river the day before. Day assured Veron that he would demand the surrender of the arms of these troops and that he desired nothing but harmonious relations with the French.[13]

On September 8, Day addressed a letter to Cortina, demanding the surrender of his arms to U.S. forces, and sent a detachment of the 1st Texas Cavalry under Major E. J. Noyes to meet with Cortina. Day informed Noyes that Cortina must surrender his arms to him. Once this had been accomplished, the Mexicans would be considered refugees under the protection of the U.S. government. Day also told Noyes that, if attacked by the Confederates, the Mexicans were to resume control of their weapons. On September 9, six hundred Confederates attacked the Federals at Palmito Ranch. As a result, the Mexicans were given back their rifles and helped repulse two advances before falling back two miles. On September 11, the Union troops retreated to White Ranch, where Day arrived with two hundred men and some artillery. The Confederates made a third attack at White Ranch, but with the advantage of position and firepower, Day successfully repulsed the assault. The Union soldiers finally returned to Brazos Santiago with their Mexican refugees on September 12. Cpl. James Beverly of the 91st Illinois reported that twenty rebels were killed and that the Union forces suffered only two wounded.[14]

Colonel Day's grant of asylum to Cortina's men was approved by the Department of the Gulf. Day was advised, however, that Cortina's continued presence on American soil would not be tolerated. If Cortina tried to wage war against the French from the American side of the river, Day had orders to attack and, if possible, capture Cortina. Maj. Gen. Edward R. S. Canby, commander of the Military Division of West Mississippi, forwarded reports of Day's activities at Brazos Santiago to Maj. Gen. Henry W. Halleck, chief of staff.[15]

The lack of French intervention during these tension-filled weeks greatly bothered Ford at Brownsville. He reminded the French commander at Bagdad, Captain Veron, that Napoleon III and Maximilian had declared the Juarez government null and void. As a result, Cortina became the responsibility of the French government. He also reminded Veron that when Mexican forces fired on them on September 6, they had violated Confederate neutrality. In addition, Ford warned the French that the Mexicans would cross the river and join the Federals.[16]

By September 11, Colonel Day's troops were back at Brazos Santiago, and Cortina's plan to attack Brownsville no longer seemed feasible. The high water level of the Rio Grande, the defection of his officers, and the convergence of French soldiers on Matamoros forced Cortina to abandon any plan for attacking Brownsville. The next move was up to Cortina. Confederate sources seemed to indicate that he would seek the protection of the Union steamer *Matamoros*, anchored at the mouth of the Rio Grande. Ford warned the French at Bagdad to expect such a move. Cortina, however, returned to Matamoros after the aborted attack on Brownsville. On September 23, Cortina invited Ford to Matamoros to discuss the resumption of commercial and political intercourse between the two governments. Fearing treachery, Ford's men discouraged him from going. Old Rip went to the meeting heavily armed and, for extra protection, placed men with rifles on the roofs of the buildings overlooking the Matamoros ferry, where the meeting was to take place. When the two commanders met, they agreed to resume their former amicable international relationship.[17]

Within a week, however, a new situation emerged across the river that erased the agreement. Cortina, aware of the Confederates' need for artillery, invited Ford to Matamoros on September 29 to discuss the sale of his cannons. Using his artillery as bait, Cortina hoped to snare Ford by having him in Matamoros during its occupation by Imperial troops. Ford's capture would satisfy Cortina's need for revenge on his old adversary. Secretly, Cortina had promised to surrender Matamoros to the Imperialists under certain conditions. One stipulation was that the city be occupied only by Mexican soldiers. In addition, the French forces must leave Bagdad. Cortina then pledged his allegiance to the Imperialists in exchange for a commission in their army. Captain Veron, representing the French, agreed to Cortina's terms. Although it appeared that Cortina had betrayed the Juarez cause, during this time he evidently communicated with Juarez secretly, promising him that he would reassert his control over Matamoros at the first available opportunity. On September 29, Gen. Tomás Mejía occupied Matamoros. Ford, assured by Cortina that the city would not be occupied until September 30, barely escaped capture. With Matamoros occupied, many of the Juaristas fled to Brownsville for protection. That evening, Emperor Maximilian's forces paraded triumphantly through the streets of Matamoros. By the end of September, the Confederate flag flew over Brownsville, the French Imperialist flag over Matamoros and Bagdad, and the U.S. flag over Brazos Santiago.[18]

The Imperialist occupation of Matamoros brought a return of the cotton trade through Brownsville. Mexican refugees told Union commander Day that a Confederate flag flew over Matamoros and that Confederate officers were received with great cordiality by Mejía. Even before the Imperialist occupation, Colonel Ford, who visited Matamoros in late August, reported "millions of dollars of merchandise in the place." Even the American consulate reported that "large quantities of merchandise now cross the river for the interior of Texas." In October and November alone, an estimated six hundred thousand pounds of ordnance were transported from Matamoros to Brownsville. What the Union Rio Grande expedition had hoped to stop a year before was now restored by the Confederate Rio Grande expedition.[19]

The Union army in Texas, at one time nearly 10,000 strong, was now reduced to a 950-man force on Brazos Santiago. Colonel Day made sporadic reports throughout October, describing the still-volatile situation at the mouth of the Rio Grande. On October 14, 1864, Day's men fought a skirmish near Boca Chica, near the mouth of the Rio Grande. The Confederates, 50 in number, were turned away by cannon fire from the Federals. Two weeks later Day reported that Juaristas under General Ortega were advancing on Matamoros. In the last week of October, Juaristas and Imperialists clashed near Matamoros, but the Imperialists still held the city.[20]

In November a change of command occurred on Brazos Santiago. On November 1, Brig. Gen. William A. Pile arrived on the island and relieved Colonel Day. Regiments under Pile's command included the 91st Illinois and the 62nd and 81st U.S. Colored Troops. Pile's first official report described the dilapidated condition of his command. Since the post hospital at the time was constructed of tents, Pile immediately asked for supplies, especially lumber, to build a suitable hospital to protect the wounded against the oncoming winter. If properly supplied, he believed he could render the Brazos garrison efficient in four weeks.[21]

Pile clearly wanted Brazos Santiago to be an effective military post. He continued his negative reports throughout November. In one account, he described how valuable military supplies were damaged because there were only tents in place to store them. He also requested that three companies of heavy artillery plus one battalion of cavalry be sent to Texas. To add insult to injury, he blamed the former commander, Colonel Day, for the sorry condition of the post. Believing that headquarters was ignoring him, Pile eventually asked to be transferred to a more active command.[22]

A change of authority also took place among the Confederates in Texas. Magruder was replaced by Gen. John G. Walker on August 4, 1864. Magruder, who took credit for the success of the Confederate Rio Grande expedition, was appointed to the Arkansas District by Kirby Smith. Smith, who wanted a good combat officer to head the district, was planning a new offensive in Arkansas against the Federals, who controlled the northern half of the state. Magruder, in a farewell address to Texas, exhibited his usual panache: "I found your State in danger, I leave it in security. I found the people in despondency, I leave them in hope. I found traitors exultant; I leave patriots triumphant."[23]

Magruder's transfer stirred mixed emotions in Texas. Some saw him as an administrative tyrant with "an utter disregard for the law." Others thought of him as a dependable warrior who had perhaps done more than anyone to repel the Yankee invaders since the fall of 1863. Would Walker be as effective? Many Texans believed that as long as the enemy maintained a strong garrison on Brazos Santiago, another invasion would surely come. As Confederate defeats mounted in the winter of 1864, invasion jitters developed into statewide paranoia.[24]

In Brownsville, the Confederate command structure was also reorganized. Brig. Gen. James E. Slaughter was assigned to command the Western Subdistrict, replacing Maj. Gen. Hamilton Bee. Slaughter made Fort Brown his headquarters and arrived there around the first of November. Ford resented the appointment of Slaughter, who, in his opinion, had done little for either Texas or the Confederacy. Old Rip's jealousy stemmed from the fact that he himself desired the command of the subdistrict, based upon the success of his Rio Grande expedition. As a result, Slaughter and Ford feuded constantly. They argued over issues such as military strategy, the Mexican policy, and even who should command patrols and where they should operate.

If the Federals had launched an invasion during this period, a Confederate disaster would surely have followed.[25]

It was the Confederates, however, who went on the offensive in the last months of the war. Slaughter and Ford decided to remove the final Union threat to Texas by moving against the Federal garrison stationed at Brazos Santiago. On November 17, around fifteen hundred Confederates gathered at Palmito Ranch, about twelve miles from Brazos. For the next two days, a severe norther hit the lower Rio Grande, hampering operations. The attack called for part of the Confederate force to cross the Boca Chica inlet at night and attack the southern end of the island. Another group would assault the northern part. The harsh weather canceled the offensive from the south, however. As a result, only the attack from the north was carried out. Although no exact date for the battle was recorded, it probably occurred around November 20.[26]

The Federals were ready for a confrontation and fired their artillery at the enemy advancing from the north. General Pile reported two Confederates killed and several wounded. Pile wanted to counterattack, perhaps even make a raid into Brownsville itself, but he hesitated because he was outnumbered and without cavalry. Like other Union commanders, he also wanted to capture Brownsville to stop the extensive cotton trade that was occurring right under his nose. He reported that "large quantities of cotton pass out through Mexico and immense quantities of supplies pass in by the same route." If no effort was to be made to stop this exchange, Pile again requested to be transferred to another command.[27]

General Pile certainly sensed that as the war was drawing to a close, his chances for military glory in Texas were remote. His constant requests for reinforcements led to a sharp rebuke from his superior at New Orleans, Major General Canby, who informed Pile that no support troops would be sent before Christmas. He also reminded the general that it is "the first duty of an officer to do the best he can with the means at his command, and not to ask to be relieved because his superior may find it impracticable or inexpedient to increase his resources."[28]

By the year's end, Union regiments on the Brazos consisted of the 34th Indiana, the 62nd and 81st U.S. Colored Troops, and a detachment of the 1st Texas Cavalry. These soldiers would serve primarily as a watchdog, keeping an eye on the still-turbulent situation in Mexico. The Union high command rejected another invasion of Texas in favor of more tenable objectives in the East. Another reason for the defensive posture was the fact that the Union Rio Grande expedition had failed to stop the cotton trade along the Rio

Grande. As a result, the small Brazos garrison remained inactive for the remainder of the war.[29]

As the year 1864 came to a close, the Confederates in South Texas found their economic situation along the Rio Grande vastly improved. The streets of Brownsville were churned to dust as cotton wagons by the hundreds rolled toward the river. The twin cities of Brownsville and Matamoros once again became a thriving center of commercial activity. An almost feverish traffic in cotton resumed—for two reasons. One was the backlog of business due to the earlier Federal occupation of Brownsville. Second, many feared that the favorable trade situation would not last long. Although their numbers were greatly reduced, the Union troops had withdrawn only to Brazos Santiago. The Mexican side of the river was even more uncertain. Although the Imperialists controlled the cities of Matamoros, Camargo, and Monterrey, bands of Juaristas roamed the countryside undisturbed.[30]

With the return of the status quo in Brownsville, the Cavalry of the West was also reduced in strength. The border was so peaceful that two-thirds of Ford's men were either transferred or furloughed by Ford's superior, General Slaughter. Although friction continued between the two officers, it was Ford who received the admiration and respect of Brownsville's citizens. On November 20, 1864, several Brownsville citizens expressed their gratitude to Ford: "We your undersigned friends and acquaintances take great pleasure in presenting to you the accompanying valise as a small token of our admiration of you as a true patriot and soldier and our high esteem of your important services rendered to the Rio Grande Country, as well as the entire cause. We have the honor to be your friends."[31]

By the start of 1865, the cause of Confederate nationalism seemed to be on a steady decline, and the Confederate armies faced defeat on all fronts. Although the military situation for the Lincoln administration had vastly improved by then, the international situation was still very complicated. In 1864 France had installed Maximilian as Mexico's leader, and rumors circulated that Kirby Smith was negotiating with him. Someone had to be sent to the Trans-Mississippi Department to try to convince the Confederates in those states, but especially Texas, that the Confederate cause was lost and that events in the region could not alter the outcome of the war.[32]

Fortunately, Lincoln did not have to look very far to find the right man for the job. He chose another political general: Maj. Gen. Lew Wallace of Indiana. Suspected of dilatory tactics at Shiloh in 1862, Wallace received an appointment to the Union's Middle Department, headquartered at Baltimore. Ever since the Mexican War, Wallace had maintained a keen interest in the affairs of Mexico. He saw in the war between Juarez and Maximilian, not to

mention the Confederate reoccupation of Brownsville, an opportunity to negotiate a political settlement that would enhance his reputation. If his plan
worked, Wallace hoped to restore Texas to the Union, perhaps the whole
Trans-Mississippi as well, and at the same time provide a joint Union-
Confederate task force to aid Juarez in driving the Imperial troops from
northern Mexico.[33]

General Wallace, therefore, devised a plan to bring about an honorable
peace for the Trans-Mississippi Department. He took inspiration for his
scheme from an old schoolmate, S. S. Brown, a refugee from Texas then living in Monterrey, Mexico. Brown sent Wallace a letter in January 1865, relating to him the importance of Brownsville and Matamoros as a great financial center, "feeding and clothing the rebellion, arming and equipping,
furnishing it materials of war and a specie basis of circulation in Texas that
had almost entirely displaced Confederate money." These twin cities on the
Mexican border, Brown wrote, sustained not only the Trans-Mississippi Department but also the entire Confederacy. In addition, he informed Wallace
that many people in Texas were secretly opposed to the French in Mexico. If
properly approached and offered the right incentives, the Confederates west
of the Mississippi might be persuaded to join the United States in driving
the French out of that country.[34]

On January 14, 1865, Wallace sent a letter to General Grant at City Point,
Virginia, in which he relayed the pertinent information from the Brown letter. Under the guise of making an inspection tour, Wallace proposed going
to Brownsville to observe firsthand whether the economic and international
situation Brown had described was actually true. If the description proved
correct, then Wallace could offer the Confederates at Brownsville an honorable means to reenter the Union. Wallace told Grant that the Confederates
would be informed of a plan to aid Benito Juarez in driving the French out of
northern Mexico. If the Brownsville negotiations were successful, Wallace
could, at the very least, shut down the port of Brownsville with no loss of
life on either side. At the very most, he might procure the surrender of the
whole Trans-Mississippi Department. If the negotiations fell through, however, then Grant could dispatch troops to aid Wallace and shut the port down
by force if necessary. Wallace was so confident of success that he bet Grant
a month's pay he could get the Confederates to support his proposal. Grant
believed Wallace's plan had merit and on January 22 ordered him to the Rio
Grande region of Texas to assess the situation.[35]

Driving the French out of Mexico in defense of the Monroe Doctrine was
not an idea unique to General Wallace. On December 28, 1864, Francis P.
Blair of Maryland had received permission from President Lincoln to visit

Pres. Jefferson Davis at Richmond. Although the mission was classified as unofficial, Lincoln wanted to learn the attitude of the Confederacy toward a proposal of peace. When Blair met with Davis on January 12, 1865, his main proposition was the end of hostilities and the union of military forces for the purpose of maintaining the Monroe Doctrine. Blair pointed out to Davis that Napoleon III intended to conquer the continent of North America. The American Civil War, as long as it continued, would help the French realize that dream. If an armistice were reached, Davis could "transfer such portions of his army as he deemed proper to the banks of the Rio Grande." Here he would join up with the Liberals under Juarez and help drive the French out of Mexico. If necessary, Northern forces would also join in the enterprise. Once the French were repelled, Davis could bring the conquered Mexican states into the Union as new American states. Davis, who realized that an alliance with the French at this stage of the war was hopeless and who was moved also by an old sense of patriotism, seemed sympathetic to Blair's proposals. The Lincoln administration, however, did not support the scheme because, in the words of one historian, "the government councils at Washington were not ruled by the spirit of political adventure."[36]

General Wallace left Washington immediately and went directly to Brownsville. He arrived at Brazos Santiago on March 5, 1865, aboard the steamer *Clifton*. That same day he wrote a letter to his wife describing the immense number of foreign ships he saw at the mouth of the Rio Grande. Wallace also wasted no time in arranging a peace conference with the commander of the Confederate forces at Brownsville, Gen. James E. Slaughter, and his second in command, Colonel Ford. Wallace, through a civilian intermediary, Charles Worthington, arranged to meet with Slaughter and Ford on March 9 at the town of Point Isabel (now Port Isabel). Because a severe storm hit that day, the conference was delayed until March 11.[37]

The Point Isabel conference began on March 11 and lasted until late afternoon of the next day. At the outset, both sides in the negotiations stated that they were not acting in official capacities for their respective governments and that anything that both parties agreed upon would be passed along to higher authorities. Wallace presented ambitious and optimistic proposals to Slaughter and Ford concerning not only Brownsville but also the entire Trans-Mississippi region. First, the Confederates of the Trans-Mississippi would cease all opposition to the United States. If the Confederates took an oath of allegiance to the Union, they would receive amnesty. Second, the Monroe Doctrine would be enforced, and the Federals and former Confederates would join together to aid Juarez in driving the French out of northern

Mexico. Third, ignoring the Emancipation Proclamation, Wallace proposed that the issue of slavery be decided by the United States at a later date. Finally, hostilities in the region would cease, for it was doubtful that the battles in South Texas could alter the outcome of the Civil War.[38]

Wallace emerged from the Point Isabel conference with high expectations. On March 14, 1865, he forwarded a letter to General Grant explaining that both Slaughter and Ford heartily agreed to the Mexican project. Slaughter pointed out that the best way for officers in his situation to get back into the Union honorably was to cross the Rio Grande, wrest two or three Mexican states from the French, and eventually annex them to the United States. Both Confederate officers, however, doubted that such a project would ever be approved by the Confederate government. Privately, Ford told Wallace that he believed Kirby Smith was already negotiating with Maximilian, possibly with a view to the Imperial annexation of Texas. Wallace asked Ford what he would do if such a situation arose. "Old Rip" responded without hesitation: He would lead a counterrevolution against Kirby Smith. Yet despite these rumors, both Slaughter and Ford agreed to forward a copy of the Point Isabel negotiations to General Walker, commander of the Department of Texas, and to Kirby Smith. Before Wallace left Brazos Santiago, all three officers (Wallace, Slaughter, and Ford) agreed to a temporary truce on the lower Rio Grande. They also selected Ford to carry the propositions in person to Kirby Smith.[39]

The Point Isabel meeting concluded one stage of Wallace's mission. The next step was for Wallace to meet Ford in Galveston. Ford was to arrange the landing of Wallace and Brig. Gen. E. J. Davis, commander of the 1st Texas Cavalry. Wallace wanted Davis along because Kirby Smith and Davis were lifelong friends. Davis's presence, Wallace believed, might help persuade Smith to accept Wallace's proposals. An unfortunate turn of events sabotaged this stage of the negotiations, however. Ford could not leave Brownsville because Slaughter, for reasons not officially known, absented himself from the city shortly after Wallace departed. As a result, Ford sent Wallace's proposals "under the seal of secrecy" to Kirby Smith by a courier named Col. Fairfax Gray. Gray was to deliver the sealed letter to Walker, who in turn would deliver it to Smith.[40]

When Gray reached district headquarters in Houston, Walker ignored the seal and made the proposals public. Wallace arrived in Galveston on March 29, 1865, aboard the steamer *Clifton* and informed Walker the following day of his arrival. By this time Walker had already looked over the terms and conditions of the Point Isabel conference. Walker, an officer of the "last ditch school," sent Wallace a firm rebuke regarding his peace mission: "It would be folly of me to pretend that we are not tired of a war that has sown sorrow and desolation over our land; but we will accept no other than an honorable peace. With three hundred thousand men yet in the field, we would be the most abject of mankind if we should now basely yield all that we have been contending for the last four years—namely, nationality and the rights of self-government. With the blessings of God, we will yet achieve these, and extort from your government all that we ask. Whenever you are willing to yield these, and to treat as equal with equal, an officer of your high rank and character, clothed with the proper authority from your government, will not be reduced to the necessity of seeking an obscure corner of the Confederacy to inaugurate negotiations."[41]

Needless to say, Wallace was taken aback by Walker's rather terse letter, especially the implication that he was a sneak. In a sharp rebuttal, Wallace informed Walker that he fully expected the conditions of peace he proposed to be passed along to Kirby Smith. With a hint of sarcasm, Wallace told Walker that it was unfortunate that "all of the sane men of your Confederacy are located in its obscure corners." Wallace also implied that Walker had no right to decide the fate of the Confederates in Texas and prodded him to send the peace conditions on to Smith for final deliberation. Wallace then left for New Orleans, leaving Walker with instructions to forward any response from Kirby Smith to that location.[42]

Dejected and demoralized from his communications with Walker, Wallace left Galveston for New Orleans. He arrived in that city on April 5, 1865, and spoke to Union Gen. A. S. Hurlbut, then commanding the Department of the Gulf. Wallace relayed to Hurlbut the events of the last month and especially the rude reception he had received from Walker in Galveston. Wallace explained to Hurlbut his eventual goal of speaking to Kirby Smith concerning the surrender of the Trans-Mississippi Department. He also told Hurlbut that Walker might still present his peace proposals to Smith. If Smith replied, the response would be forwarded to New Orleans according to the instructions Wallace had given to Walker. Nevertheless, Wallace expected Smith not to take any positive action. He reasoned (correctly, as it later turned out) that the higher up he went in the Confederate chain of command, the greater the defiance. As a result, he left the unfinished project in the hands of General Hurlbut and returned to Washington.[43]

Before Wallace left New Orleans, he sent a letter to Slaughter and Ford at Brownsville, informing them that the peace initiative they had discussed at Point Isabel had stalled. He mentioned Walker's rejection of peace at

Galveston and assured them that, if further bloodshed occurred in Texas, they (Wallace, Slaughter, and Ford) would not be responsible. Wallace then stated that, regardless of the turn of events in Texas, he would always regard Slaughter and Ford as principled men who sought nothing less for Texas than an honorable return to the Union.[44]

As late as April 19, 1865, Wallace remained optimistic concerning the surrender of the Trans-Mississippi Department. On that date, he wrote a letter to General Grant stating that he believed Kirby Smith would surrender "without a shot fired." This optimism was shattered when, on April 21, Smith issued a proclamation to the troops in his department urging them to continue the struggle against the United States. Smith eventually replied to Wallace on May 7. He expressed his desire for an honorable peace but regretted that he had no authority to act on Wallace's peace plan. The letter from Smith to Wallace was very courteous but clearly implied that, as long as Jefferson Davis had not been captured, the combat would continue.[45]

Despite the fact that Wallace failed to procure the surrender of the entire Trans-Mississippi Department, a minor triumph had been achieved by the Point Isabel negotiations. During the conference, it was mutually agreed that further fighting along the lower Rio Grande would not affect the outcome of the war. For two months, then, as Robert E. Lee endured his final agony in Virginia, a gentleman's agreement kept the peace in South Texas.[46]

In war, especially a conflict as bloody as the Civil War, peace often appears as an elusive goal for both combatants. Those who undertake campaigns for peace appear even stranger since glory often goes to the warriors, not to peacemakers. Wallace offered an optimistic solution not only to Texas but to the whole Trans-Mississippi Department as well. Slaughter and Ford knew the situation for the Confederacy was untenable. Stubborn and defiant higher Confederate authorities refused even to consider the olive branch Wallace proffered. In hindsight, even Ford believed that rejection of Wallace's peace overtures had cost the South dearly: "The days of reconstruction as things occurred in the South, were terrible proofs of the evils arising from the contrary course. Better it would have been for the Confederate States to have accepted the terms proposed by General Wallace than to have disbanded its armies, surrendered at discretion, and become the prey of unprincipled men."[47]

Seven

The War Ends in Texas

*D*espite his failed efforts to obtain the surrender of the Trans-Mississippi Department, Maj. Gen. Lew Wallace did procure a two-month truce between Union and Confederate forces on the lower Rio Grande. That cease-fire ended on May 13, 1865, however, when opposing troops clashed at Palmito Hill, about ten miles east of Brownsville. This was the last battle of the Civil War, fought nearly five weeks after Gen. Robert E. Lee surrendered at Appomattox.[1]

Nevertheless, news of Lee's surrender failed to dampen the fighting spirit of the leaders of the Trans-Mississippi Department, whose commander, Lt. Gen. Edmund Kirby Smith, issued a proclamation on April 21, encouraging southerners to fight on despite Lee's admission of defeat. Maj. Gen. John B. Magruder, again in command of the Texas district, issued a stirring appeal to his troops to stand firm and resist the enemy. One of these soldiers, William Heartsill, stationed near Houston, believed the Trans-Mississippi could hold out indefinitely if the people truly united. Political and civilian leaders also worked hard to maintain high morale. Texas governor Pendleton Murrah also called upon the people of Texas to continue the struggle. On April 27 Murrah warned, "Look at the bloody and desolate tracks of the invader through Georgia and South Carolina and see what awaits you. Rally around the battle scarred and well known flag of the Confederacy and uphold your state government in its purity and integrity—There is no other hope of safety for you and yours." E. H. Cushing, editor of the *Houston Daily Telegraph*, encouraged Texans to resort to guerrilla warfare if necessary to defeat the enemy.[2]

Despite the brave front presented by both military and civilian leaders of the Trans-Mississippi, the everyday soldier and civilian knew that the end was near. One Confederate soldier stationed near Shreveport observed the reaction of many soldiers after Kirby Smith's exhortation to continue the fight.

He observed that "the effect of the order upon the troops was marked in the extreme. The men instantly became dejected. Mutiny and wholesale desertion was [sic] talked of. This soon gave way to a general apathy and indifference, but through all could be seen by a close observer that the Army of the Trans-Mississippi was in spirit crushed." A young woman in Tyler, Texas, wrote that "anarchy and confusion reign over all. Jayhawking is the order of the day. The soldiers are disbanding throughout the Department and seizing Government property wherever they can find it. All work is over and all who can are going home."[3]

More bad news continued to reach the Trans-Mississippi. In the second week of May, Texans learned that Gen. Richard Taylor had surrendered his forces to Union Gen. E. R. S. Canby at Citronelle, Alabama, on May 4. This convinced many Texas soldiers that the war was over and that it would be foolish to fight on. More and more soldiers in the Lone Star State began to leave their units and head home. On May 8, Col. John T. Sprague, chief of staff for Union General Pope, who commanded the Federal district of Missouri, was allowed to pass through the Confederate lines to meet with Kirby Smith at Shreveport. Sprague brought a letter from Pope stating that Grant had authorized Pope to offer terms of surrender to Smith similar to the ones offered to Lee at Appomattox. As a result, Smith called together another conference of the governors of his department at Marshall, Texas, to discuss Pope's proposals. The meeting was attended by Governors Thomas C. Reynolds of Missouri, Harris Flanagin of Arkansas, Henry W. Allen of Louisiana, and Col. Guy M. Bryan, representing Texas (Murrah was ill at the time). On May 13 these state executives adopted a series of proposals. They agreed that since resistance was futile, the army would be disbanded without parole, state governments would continue to operate until state conventions established new governments, and the states would keep sufficient troops under arms to maintain order.[4]

Considering the existing military situation, the resolutions adopted by the Trans-Mississippi governors were unrealistic. Colonel Sprague pointed out that neither he nor General Pope could approve anything of a political nature as presented by the governors. As a result, Sprague returned to St. Louis on May 15, having failed in his mission of securing a surrender from Kirby Smith. Before he left, however, Smith advised Sprague that "Many examples of history teach that the more generous the terms proposed by a victorious enemy, the greater is the certainty of a speedy and lasting pacification, and that the imposition of harsh terms leads invariably to subsequent disturbances." When Sprague reported to Pope, he related that the general attitude among civil and military officials was that more lenient terms were merited.[5]

As Kirby Smith delayed the inevitable, the final battle of the Civil War was about to take place near Brownsville. The reasons for this last encounter are not altogether clear but seem strongly related to the personal ambitions of a minor Union officer and the pent-up frustrations of the Confederates following the terrible news from Appomattox. At Brazos Santiago, the Federal garrison was commanded by Col. Theodore H. Barrett of the 62nd Colored Infantry Regiment. Barrett had assumed command in the absence of the post commander, Brig. Gen. E. B. Brown. Other units at Brazos included the 34th Indiana, the Morton Rifles (a New York regiment), several dismounted companies of the 2nd Texas Cavalry, and several artillery companies. Barrett had seen little combat in the Civil War and seemed obsessed with a desire "to establish for himself some notoriety before the war closed." He requested permission from departmental headquarters to make a demonstration against Fort Brown, but headquarters denied his request. Despite the refusal, Barrett resolved to attack the Confederates at Fort Brown anyway. The image of being labeled the "Victor of Brownsville" must have inspired him to do so.[6]

As for the Confederates, it is hard to accept the standard explanation that is generally given concerning the last battle of the Civil War. One of its major figures, Col. John S. Ford, argued that the participants did not know the war was over until they took some prisoners who told them the news. A more plausible explanation would be that, although the Confederates may not have "known" that the war was over, to say that they had not "heard" of Lee's surrender would be untrue. Erroneous reporting of war news from the eastern front was so common that it had conditioned the Texas Confederates to doubt any information from that theater, especially a report as important as that of Lee's surrender. Missionary Melinda Rankin, who arrived in the Mexican town of Bagdad shortly after Lee's capitulation, recorded conversations of Confederate sympathizers who had heard of the laying down of arms at Appomattox Courthouse but doubted the authenticity of the news. One man stated that "It can not be possible that our righteous cause can fail! Justice and right must and will prevail." Another rebel believed that "It is an act of strategy on the part of General Lee. He is feigning to evacuate Richmond, and going to withdraw his army to cut off Sherman and the whole host of Yankees."[7]

This devotion to Lee cannot be underestimated. Since 1862, Lee and the Army of Northern Virginia had come to symbolize the cause of Confederate nationalism. Noted Lee historian Gary Gallagher has pointed out that, in all of the Confederate states, civilians equated Lee's importance in the Civil War to that of George Washington in the American Revolution. Although Pres. Jefferson Davis created a government on paper, it was Lee who instilled a sense of patriotism throughout the Confederacy. A typical statement of Lee's significance came from Virginian Mary Jones in 1862, who said that "the head of our army is a noble son of Virginia, and worthy of the intimate in which he stands connected with our immortal Washington."[8]

News of Lee's admission of defeat reached Brownsville around May 1, 1865. One Confederate officer at Fort Brown mentioned that the *New Orleans Times* ran headlines of Lee's surrender at Appomattox. The officer stated that "The news was soon known to all the troops, and caused them to desert, by the score, and to return home; so that on the morning of May 12, 1865, there was [sic] not more than three hundred men at and below Brownsville." Many of Ford's men also deserted because they had not been paid in more than a year. Both of these factors prompted Ford to believe that his men might ransack Brownsville and seize the cotton that had begun to pile up because of declining international demand. Much of this cotton, though, belonged to the steamboating firm of King, Kenedy, and Stillman of Brownsville, the chief contractors for the government after 1864. Ford, who had friendly relations with this company, especially Richard King, was not going to allow this valuable commodity to fall into the hands of the enemy, much less his own men, should they decide to mutiny. Ford's sense of loyalty to his friends meant that he would fight to protect their property. He also realized that allowing his soldiers to attack the enemy might allow them to release some of the tension and resentment that had built up.[9]

The orders to move on Brownsville were issued by Colonel Barrett on May 11. Two hundred fifty men of the 62nd Colored Infantry Regiment were selected for the operation. These men stood quietly at the Brazos Santiago landing, each loaded down with one hundred rounds of ammunition and rations for five days. The officers leading these troops were Lt. Col. David Branson and acting assistant adjutant general Lt. I. B. Rush. The plan called for moving the regiment by steamboat to Point Isabel on the mainland, then marching overland to Brownsville. As it happened, the steamboat assigned to ferry the men to Point Isabel broke down, and no one knew when it would be operational. As a result, Branson could either cancel the operation, wait, or find another way to get the men to the mainland. Because of technical difficulties, Barrett issued new orders to Branson. He would march his men to the southern end of Brazos Santiago and cross the Boca Chica bridge from that part of the island. Barrett also bulked up the raiding party by adding fifty men of the 2nd Texas Cavalry, unmounted. By 9 : 30 P.M. Branson had crossed all of his men to Boca Chica, despite a blinding rainstorm that suddenly came up.[10]

The Federals' first target was a small Confederate outpost at White's Ranch on the Rio Grande, about six miles inland. Hoping to surprise the rebel position, Branson took what he later described as a "long circuitous" route to this objective. As the troops approached the ranch, Branson divided his column, sending Company F under Capt. Fred Miller about three-quarters of a mile north of the ranch before they doubled back to attack from below. Branson anticipated capturing about sixty Confederates and some much-needed cattle and horses. As Branson and Miller closed in, they discovered no enemy troops and reasoned that they had probably moved upriver to Palmito Ranch, about twelve miles from Brownsville. To preserve some element of surprise, Branson set up camp in a thicket about one mile above White's Ranch in order to conceal his men. Companies H and G under Capt. Harrison Dubois were on sentry duty while the rest of the men slept.[11]

Nevertheless, Branson lost the element of surprise the following morning when he reported that "persons on the Mexican shore seeing us started to give the alarm to the rebels." Around six A.M., the lieutenant colonel continued his march toward Palmito Ranch, deploying Company F as skirmishers. About an hour later, the soldiers reported that they had encountered enemy pickets near Palmito Ranch. These rebels belonged to a Confederate cavalry battalion under Capt. W. N. Robinson. The two sides fought for about an hour before the Confederates retreated through the underbrush, leaving a few horses and some cattle. At noon the rest of the Union soldiers arrived and set fire to the ranch. While Robinson and his men retreated upriver, he sent a dispatch to Fort Brown, informing his superiors that he had engaged the enemy at Palmito Ranch. Colonel Ford told Robinson to hold his position. Robinson then counterattacked around three in the afternoon, forcing the Federals to retreat to White's Ranch. Upon arriving there, Branson requested instructions from Colonel Barrett at Brazos Santiago.[12]

While Branson waited for instructions at White's Ranch, the Confederates at Fort Brown were organizing their forces. When Old Rip received word from Captain Robinson that the enemy was advancing toward Brownsville, he immediately sent out couriers that night to gather all of his cavalry, who were scattered about twenty miles from Brownsville. That same night, Ford ate dinner with his superior, Brig. Gen. James E. Slaughter, to discuss a plan of action. When Ford asked Slaughter what he intended to do, the general replied, "Retreat." Ford replied, "You can retreat and go to hell if you wish. These are my men, and I am going to fight." After Ford composed himself, he said, "I have held this place against heavy odds. If you lose it without a fight the people of the Confederacy will hold you accountable for a base neglect of duty." Slaughter decided to stay and join Ford in this last battle of the war. While Slaughter concentrated the scattered forces at Brownsville, Ford left the fort at 11:00 A.M. on May 13. With him were 250 men and six pieces of artillery. Ford led the Cavalry of the West toward the sound of gunfire in the direction of Palmito Ranch and the last engagement of the Civil War.[13]

That same day, the Union forces under Colonel Barrett arrived at White's Ranch at daybreak to reinforce Colonel Branson. Barrett brought with him two hundred men of the 34th Indiana Volunteer Regiment. Barrett ordered his men forward. As the Union troops approached Palmito Ranch, sharp skirmishing ensued with Confederate pickets, but by noon the ranch was again under Federal control. A halt was made at the ranch to burn enemy supplies that had escaped destruction the day before. While at the ranch, Barrett ordered back to Brazos Santiago a small detail of men, consisting of "all the disabled men, and those not able to make a heavy march, with the wounded men, horses and cattle." He apparently wanted to weed out the slowest-moving elements of his expedition before making an aggressive thrust toward Brownsville. Barrett deployed his men as follows: The 34th Indiana took up a position on the river near Palmito Hill; a company from the 2nd Texas Cavalry held the Union center; and the 62nd Colored Infantry held the Union right. Early that afternoon, as the Union forces advanced westward, they were involved in what Barrett described as a "sharp engagement" about a mile west of Palmito Hill, but suffered only light casualties. Apparently, this engagement indicated to Barrett that the enemy was being reinforced; he thus pulled back his regiments to Palmito Hill to begin a general retreat to Point Isabel.[14]

Around 3 P.M., Confederate reinforcements under Ford arrived to help Captain Robinson, who had taken up a position two miles north of Palmito Hill. Although somewhat nervous about the number of troops opposing him, Ford nonetheless decided to attack. He had at his disposal a force of about 360 men, including six pieces of artillery on loan from the French along with several French cannoneers. (Ford's artillery commander, Captain O. G. Jones, had accepted the offer of an Imperialist artillery company that volunteered its service to the Confederates that day. They played a crucial role in the upcoming battle.) After an hour spent in deploying his men in a line perpendicular to the Rio Grande, the Confederate colonel rode along his main line, encouraging his men before the battle: "Men, we have whipped the enemy in all our previous fights!" he bellowed. "We can do it again." The soldiers responded, shouting "Rip! Rip!" Ford then gave the command: "Charge!" Three hundred horsemen surged forward, shooting everything that moved.[15]

A shell that landed and hit near Barrett's men on Palmito Hill cracked the Federal line. According to one Union officer, this first artillery burst caused "some confusion and disorder" in the ranks of the 34th Indiana. Realizing the rebels had cannon, Barrett stated that "our position became untenable." Turning to the officers around him, Barrett said, "Very well then; we will retreat in good order, and good order let it be. Men, keep your ranks. They can't hurt you; we'll get out of this yet." When Barrett decided to retreat, he ordered the 62nd Colored Infantry to form a skirmish line to cover his men. With shells exploding around them, one officer noted that "the entire regiment moved back with great precision." Trying to pull out in an organized manner, the Federal units became entangled near Palmito Ranch but soon managed to unscramble themselves and give ground with some semblance of order. Three times during the withdrawal, the Union soldiers made temporary stands, but they were dislodged each time by Ford's artillery. Three hours later, Barrett's column reached the safety of Brazos Santiago. Clearly the French artillery played a significant role in forcing the Federals to retreat.[16]

During the confusion of that day's fighting, both armies experienced some embarrassing incidents. On the Confederate side, Colonel Ford, in ordering his artillery into battle formation, did not realize that some of the men were French and could not understand a word of English. When finally informed of their nationality, Ford used his limited French vocabulary and shouted "Allons!" Meanwhile, a steamboat from the firm of M. Kenedy and Company was chugging up the river during the height of the fighting. Fearing that it might be a Yankee gunboat, the gray gunners fired two shells at it but fortunately missed. The vessel was finally able to identify itself as a nonbelligerent before more shells were fired. On the Union side, during its withdrawal to Brazos Santiago, the 34th Indiana Regiment lost both the U.S. flag and the state flag of Indiana, objects of great pride for any regiment. The 34th Indiana had the unfortunate distinction of losing the last regimental battle flag in the Civil War.[17]

Ford's Texans pursued the Federals for seven miles, but, knowing that both men and horses were spent, Ford called off the pursuit and said to his men, "Boys, we have done finely. We will let well enough alone and retire." At this time General Slaughter arrived with a battalion under the command of Capt. W. D. Carrington. Both Ford and Slaughter exchanged heated words over whether to resume the attack. Ford insisted that his men were too tired to continue fighting. He also pointed out that it was almost dark and that the garrison on Brazos Santiago was probably on high alert. Slaughter disagreed and led Carrington's battalion to Boca Chica to continue harassing the Federals as they retreated. By the time Slaughter arrived at Boca Chica, the Union soldiers had already made it safely across the marshy inlet to Brazos Santiago. Out of frustration, the general rode into the bog and emptied his pistol at the retreating enemy, some three hundred yards away. At dusk, as the two exhausted armies faced each other in the marshes off Brazos Santiago, one last artillery shell burst near a young Confederate soldier. Swearing loudly and shaking his fist—which delighted the old veterans—the young rebel fired his rifle at the shadows of Brazos Santiago. It was the last shot of the last battle of the Civil War.[18]

Accounts of the conflict at Palmito Hill have disagreed on the number of casualties for both sides. Ford reported only 5 wounded among the Confederate forces. However, another Confederate officer, Captain Carrington, later stated that the Confederates took time to bury their dead. The Federals suffered 101 captured, 9 wounded, and 2 killed. Although no exact numbers were given for Confederate casualties, their losses approximated those of the Federals. Among the Union soldiers captured, 77 were from the 34th Indiana, 22 from the 2nd Texas Cavalry, and 2 from the 62nd U.S. Colored Troops. Most of these were skirmishers, and when the order to retreat was given, they never received it. Because of the expense of feeding these prisoners, the Confederates paroled them, letting them return to Brazos. The black troops of the 62nd were "agreeably surprised when they were paroled and permitted to depart with the white prisoners." They were astonished because, early in the war, the Confederate government, through various proclamations, had stated that black troops captured in battle faced either reenslavement or possible execution.[19]

The fate of the captured Texans in the Union ranks remains unclear. Twenty years later, with an eye toward posterity, Ford wrote that "Several of them were from Texas. This made no difference in their treatment. Most of these were allowed to escape during the march to Brownsville. The Confederate soldiers were unwilling to see them tried as deserters. There was no disposition to visit upon them a mean spirit of revenge." The paroled Union soldiers told another story, however. When they reached Brazos Santiago on May 17, they reported that "There was a company of Texans [the 2nd Texas] made up mostly of deserters from the rebels. As fast as these were captured they were shot down. Neither would the deserters surrender, for they knew it would be death, and so died fighting."[20]

Both sides displayed a sense of history as the final confrontation of the Civil War ended. Lt. I. B. Foster, who commanded Company I of the 62nd Colored Infantry, claimed the honor of having given the "last command to fire at Confederate troops in this last battle of the war." Lieutenant Colonel Branson, who commanded the 62nd, wrote in 1883 that he had given the final Union command when he ordered his men to cease fire. With a sense of melodramatic finality, Branson allegedly turned to an officer next to him and said, "That winds up the war." Both of these commands were given near dark as the last of the Union soldiers retreated to Brazos Santiago while the 62nd provided cover for them. The last soldier to die in the Civil War was believed to be Pvt. Bill Redman of the 62nd Colored Infantry, who breathed his last breath on June 4, 1865, at the post hospital in Brazos Santiago after being wounded in the battle of Palmito Hill. The victorious Texas Confederates gathered up souvenirs from the Palmito Hill battlefield throughout May 14.[21]

Both combatants also told different stories about what actually brought on the clash at Palmito Hill. In his first official report after the battle, Colonel Barrett, who commanded the Union forces on Brazos, claimed to have sent some of his men to the mainland to procure forage and horses rumored to be in the direction of Brownsville. Many years after the fight, Lieutenant Colonel Branson seemed to confirm Barrett's intentions. Branson commented that Barrett had been motivated by a desire to "stop the clamoring of the troops generally, for fresh beef to eat and lumber to build barracks and for horses to ride while scouting for future supplies." Considering the fact that he had unmounted members of the 2nd Texas Cavalry at Brazos Santiago, Barrett's need for horses seems legitimate. Finally, a Federal soldier captured by the Confederates informed them that Union forces had advanced to Brownsville not to do battle but in expectation of a Confederate capitulation since Lee had surrendered at Appomattox a month before.[22]

The Confederates, Rip Ford specifically, denied that they had ever heard of Lee's surrender and insisted that the Yankees came to Brazos looking for trouble—and certainly found it. Ford also stated that he saw the advance of Union troops on Brownsville as a violation of the truce he had worked out with Maj. Gen. Lew Wallace two months earlier. Ford insisted that he first learned of Lee's surrender from a Union prisoner on the day after the battle of Palmito Hill. The Yankee prisoner also said that they were moving on Brownsville to occupy it, not to engage the Confederates in battle. Ford and his officers denied that version of the story, however. To this day, the motives behind the last battle of the Civil War have never been settled to the satisfaction of both sides. Whatever precipitated it was insignificant as the last chapter of the Civil War came to a close in South Texas. But until Kirby Smith surrendered, the Confederates remained at their posts in and around Brownsville.[23]

If Colonel Barrett undertook the campaign against Brownsville for a last chance at military glory, he was destined to be disappointed: Brownsville was not Richmond, Vicksburg, or Gettysburg. In an effort to deflect responsibility from himself, Barrett brought charges against Lieutenant Colonel Morrison of the 34th Indiana for his alleged poor performance during the battle. Participants in the combat testified later and found Morrison not guilty of wrongdoing. In hindsight, it is hard to absolve Colonel Barrett of his responsibility for the poor results of the Brownsville campaign. When the Federals encountered strong enemy resistance at Palmito Ranch on May 12, Barrett sent the 34th Indiana to reinforce them. When this veteran regiment failed to drive the enemy back to Brownsville, subsequent charges against its commander were not surprising. If Barrett intended only to search for supplies as he indicated in an official report, why send reinforcements? A prudent officer would have pulled his men back to prevent further casualties. Moreover, if the Federals intended only to occupy Brownsville, why not send a courier to Brownsville under a flag of truce to inform the enemy of their peaceful intentions? [24]

A much greater problem presented itself to the Union forces on the Rio Grande than the Confederate victory at Palmito Hill. As the last days of the Civil War were coming to an end, many high-ranking Confederates were making their way to Mexico. The Federal government feared a Confederate resurgence out of Mexico, knowing all too well that the French had been sympathetic to the Southern cause. The Confederate exodus to Mexico therefore had to be stopped. To this end, the Department of the Gulf, under Maj. Gen. Nathaniel P. Banks, put Brig. Gen. Egbert B. Brown in command of the U.S. forces at Brazos Santiago on May 3, 1865. Brown had been wounded twice in fighting at Springfield, Missouri, on January 8, 1863. His later military appointments included commands of military districts in Missouri.[25]

Brown's biggest task concerned the capture of the Confederacy's highest-ranking official, Pres. Jefferson Davis. In a dispatch to Brown, Banks stated that "As a matter of special and important interest your attention is called to the probability of the passage of Jeff Davis, the fugitive President of the Confederacy, across the Mississippi into Texas, with a view to entering Mexico by that route. We have rumors here today that he is at Shreveport. His escape

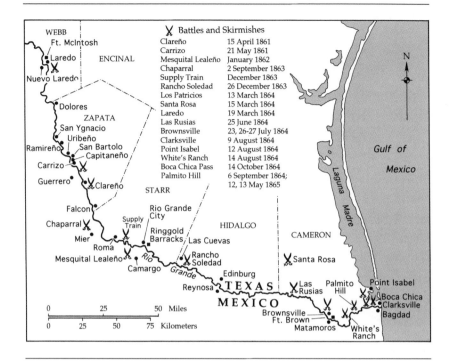

| WEBB | | | | | | | | |

| | X | Battles and Skirmishes | | | | | |

| Ft. McIntosh | Clareño | 15 April 1861 | | | | | |

Clareño   15 April 1861
Carrizo   21 May 1861
Mesquital Lealeño January 1862
Chaparral   2 September 1863
Supply Train   December 1863
Rancho Soledad   26 December 1863
Los Patricios   13 March 1864
Santa Rosa   15 March 1864
Laredo   19 March 1864
Las Rusias   25 June 1864
Brownsville   23, 26-27 July 1864
Clarksville   9 August 1864
Point Isabel   12 August 1864
White's Ranch   14 August 1864
Boca Chica Pass 14 October 1864
Palmito Hill   6 September 1864;
                 12, 13 May 1865

Civil War battles in the Rio Grande Valley. Map by Jerry Thompson.

from Texas into Mexico should be prevented. The Government of the United States has offered a reward of $100,000 dollars for his capture." Banks then went on to point out the possible need of occupying the lower Rio Grande Valley as far as Rio Grande City to prevent the escape of Davis and his associate officers. Liberal forces under Juarez controlled the Rio Grande as far north as Piedras Negras, opposite the town of Eagle Pass. Banks ordered Brown not to start offensive operations against Brownsville, however, unless he could prevent Davis from fleeing. Banks closed his orders to Brown by pointing out that "I have the highest confidence in your faithful discharge of the duties assigned you at that important post, which may become the theater of important events in the progress of the war now near its close." [26]

General in Chief Ulysses S. Grant also grew concerned over the possible continuation of the war west of the Mississippi. As long as Confederate Gen. Kirby Smith had not surrendered, Grant made military preparations to continue the war in the West until those states had formally laid down their arms. Grant also feared that as long as the French were in Mexico, the possibility of collusion between them and the escaped Confederates meant the possible expansion of the war south of the Rio Grande. Grant assigned one of his most trusted generals, Maj. Gen. Philip H. Sheridan, to terminate the hostilities west of the Mississippi as quickly as possible. Grant told Sheridan that "Your duty is to restore Texas, and that part of Louisiana held by the enemy, to the Union in the shortest practicable time, in a way most effectual for securing permanent peace. In case of an active campaign, a hostile one, I think a heavy force should be put on the Rio Grande as a first preliminary. The 25th Corps is now available and to it should be added a force of White troops say those now under Major General Steele." With added emphasis, Grant closed the dispatch by informing Sheridan that "I think the Rio Grande should be strongly held whether the forces in Texas surrender or not and that no time should be lost in getting them there. If war is to be made, they will be in the right place: if Kirby Smith surrenders they will be on the line which is to be strongly garrisoned." Later, in a private conversation with Sheridan, Grant said that he believed that the destruction of secession would never be complete until "the French were compelled to quit the territory of our sister republic" in Mexico. In that regard, Grant urged Sheridan to exercise great caution in the use of troops on the Rio Grande, not wanting to involve the United States in a war with the French.[27]

As Sheridan prepared to move to his new post, the commanding officer at Brazos Santiago, Brigadier General Brown, began making reports to the Department of the Gulf concerning the military and international situation on the lower Rio Grande. On May 23, Brown sent two dispatches to headquarters in New Orleans. The first telegram gave a rather unflattering description of the post at Brazos Santiago. As with previous commanders, what Brown described there was not unusual. He requested rations of beef and other supplies for the troops and then asked for three hundred horses, one battery of artillery, and another regiment of cavalry. The second dispatch gave an evaluation of the military and international situation. Around May 20, Brown sent six officers under a flag of truce to Brownsville to ascertain the enemy's position. They reported the Confederate strength at one thousand, plus six pieces of light artillery. These officers also learned that General Slaughter, the commander of Fort Brown, was pro-French. Colonel Ford, second in command, along with most of the men at Fort Brown, supported the Liberal government of Juarez. In general, the Union officers reported that the majority of men at Fort Brown were eager for peace. Brown's statement also noted that cotton was being moved across the river as quickly as possible to prevent its seizure by the Federals. In closing his dispatch, Brown reported a meeting of archtraitors on May 18 in Austin that Jefferson Davis had supposedly attended.[28]

On a somewhat lighter note, Rip Ford described a cordial gathering with six Union officers. One of them, a major, was invited to Ford's home for a glass of eggnog. As the guest smacked his lips over this welcome beverage, he commented, "If my wife knew that I was at the house of a Confederate colonel, and accepting his friendly hospitality, she would be so mad she would hardly speak to me." To provide his guests further entertainment, Ford took them across the river into Matamoros to observe a review of the Imperial troops under Gen. Tomás Mejía. This mixed group of blue and gray uniforms stationed itself directly across from General Mejía's reviewing stand. Ford recalled with amusement how the Imperial soldiers, when they marched by, could not help staring at these American army officers who were supposedly enemies. Ford continued to arouse suspicion by taking the same officers to breakfast at a restaurant where French officers were known to dine on a regular basis. When Ford's party arrived, many of the French jumped to their feet to engage the American enemies in friendly discourse. When exiting the restaurant, the French besieged Ford, wanting to know the meaning of his visit. Old Rip assured them that nothing north of the Rio Grande had changed. He was only entertaining a few friends. Ford had indeed sprung a diplomatic surprise. As long as the American Civil War continued, the French remained confident of noninvolvement by the United States in Mexico. Ford, resentful of the fact that France had never recognized the Confederacy, wanted to deliver a parting shot at the French before the war officially ended.[29]

The Confederacy breathed its last in Texas. The concluding two weeks of the war were hectic ones for the Trans-Mississippi Department. As mentioned earlier, its commander, Kirby Smith, called a final meeting of the governors of his department. On May 13, as the battle of Palmito Hill was being fought, the governors of the Trans-Mississippi met in Marshall, Texas. Although Smith did not attend the conference, the governors recommended that he consult U.S. authorities "with [a] view to making a complete pacification of the Trans-Mississippi Department." The terms of the surrender, however, had to be ones of honor and not humiliation. On May 15, Smith wrote a letter to Col. John Sprague, a Union officer sent to Shreveport from New Orleans to feel Smith out for his surrender. In the letter Smith charged that the Federal authorities at New Orleans sought to humiliate, not conciliate, the Confederates west of the Mississippi. He told Sprague that the United States must offer more generous conditions if they expected the surrender of the Trans-Mississippi Department.[30]

On May 16 Smith received a frantic telegram from General Magruder, commander of the Department of Texas. Magruder stated, "For God's sake *act* or let me *act!* I have excited myself more than I ever did to instill a spirit of resistance into the men, but in vain. I but make myself antagonistic to the army and an object of their displeasure." He also mentioned that on the night of May 14, four hundred soldiers had left the garrison at Galveston en masse. Upon hearing this distressing news from Texas, Smith announced that, on May 18, he was moving his headquarters from Shreveport to Houston. Before leaving Shreveport, he appointed Generals Simon Buckner, Sterling Price, and J. L. Brent to meet with Maj. Gen. E. R. S. Canby, the Union commander of the Military Division of West Mississippi in New Orleans, to negotiate more favorable terms of surrender.[31]

Smith left Shreveport on May 20. As he made his way to Texas, Magruder continued to send him gloomy reports of the worsening military situation there. Rioting occurred in Galveston and Houston as soldiers, whose pay had been in arrears for more than a year, looted government buildings. The lawlessness spread to other cities such as Austin, San Antonio, La Grange, Gonzalez, and Henderson. General Slaughter, commanding the Western Subdistrict at Brownsville, sent word to Houston that his men were leaving in droves. Slaughter went on to comment, "They say we are whipped. It is useless for the Trans-Mississippi Department to accomplish what the Cis-Mississippi has failed to do." Despite the deteriorating situation in Texas, Smith ordered Magruder to abandon Galveston but to concentrate as many soldiers as possible near Houston, his new headquarters. When Smith reached Houston on May 27, he found he had no army to command. Little did he realize that, at the St. Charles Hotel in New Orleans on May 26, the Trans-Mississippi Department had ceased to exist.[32]

Smith's despondency over the end of the war is reflected in the dispatches he continued to send at the end of May. On May 30 he wired Gov. Pendleton Murrah of Texas: "I found on my arrival here that the Troops of this District had disbanded and were making their way home. That they had possessed themselves of the public property; that much of this had been scattered here, and there over the State; and that some of it in the shape of ordnance stores, artillery, etc., remains unmolested." Smith urged Murrah to use state troops to protect what Confederate property he could. Smith then sent a message to Gen. John Sprague, who commanded the Federal forces along the Red River in North Texas. Two weeks earlier, Sprague had approached Smith concerning the surrender of the Trans-Mississippi Department. With no department left, Smith stated, "When I gave you, at Shreveport, a memorandum which I hoped might be the basis of negotiations with the United States Government, I commanded an army of over 50,000 and a department rich in resources. I am now without either." With nothing to command, Smith concluded, "The department is now open to occupation by your Government. I plan to go abroad until future policy of the United States Government is announced." This last statement clearly suggested that Smith and the other officers that served with him in the department intended to join Maximilian south of the Rio Grande in Mexico.[33]

On June 2, 1865, Smith, accompanied by Magruder, went aboard the Union steamer *Fort Jackson* off Galveston harbor and signed the articles of surrender. In doing so, he understood that "officers observing their parole are permitted to make their homes either in or out of the United States." Smith then ordered Magruder to appoint commissioners for various districts within the Department of Texas to carry out the parole of those troops that had remained to surrender. For the Western Subdistrict, which encompassed the region from San Antonio to the lower Rio Grande, Magruder appointed Colonel Ford as commissioner. Ford received the appointment because the former commander of the subdistrict, General Slaughter, had transferred command of the area to Ford on May 26.[34]

After the surrender, both Smith and Magruder headed for San Antonio with plans to cross over into Mexico. When they arrived at the Menger Hotel, Smith checked in under the name William Thompson. By mid-June the Menger Hotel had become the meeting place for other Confederates, civilian and military, bound for Mexico. The civilian arrivals included three governors: Henry W. Allen, the last Confederate governor of Louisiana; Thomas Reynolds of Missouri; and Texas governor Pendleton Murrah. Besides Smith and Magruder, the Confederate generals at San Antonio included Brig. Gen. Joseph Shelby, who commanded the "Iron Brigade" of the Missouri Cavalry. Others were Maj. Gen. Sterling Price and Maj. Gen. Cadmus M. Wilcox, one of Lee's lieutenants. On June 26, Shelby's Brigade, Governors Reynolds and Allen, and Generals Smith and Magruder arrived at Eagle Pass. Before entering Mexico, five colonels of Shelby's Brigade took out their last battle flag, attached weights to it, and lowered it into the muddy water of the Rio Grande. With tears in their eyes, this last organized force of the Confederacy crossed the river, closing the final chapter of the Civil War. They now marched straight into the middle of someone else's fight.[35]

In the last days of Confederate authority in Brownsville, the rebel commander, General Slaughter, made plans to join the Imperialists in Mexico. Needing personal funds, Slaughter sold the artillery he had at Fort Brown to the Imperialist general in Matamoros, Tomás Mejía. Before Slaughter completed the transaction, his second in command, Colonel Ford, intervened on May 25. The soldiers at Brownsville had not been paid for well more than a year, so Ford used these troops to confine Slaughter to his tent until he paid them twenty thousand dollars in silver. Once this was done, Slaughter was allowed to leave and cross into Mexico, transferring the Brownsville command to Ford. On the following day, May 26, Ford moved his family to Matamoros. Ford and Mejía had been on cordial terms during the war, and, as a result, Mejía allowed Ford's family to take up residence in Matamoros. Before leaving, Ford left a home guard in Brownsville to prevent looting and rioting. Although a few disturbances occurred, there was not the mass hysteria that had gripped Brownsville's citizens before Gen. Hamilton Bee's evacuation in November 1863. On May 29, 1865, eighteen hundred Union troops under Brigadier General Brown occupied Brownsville.[36]

That same day, Philip H. Sheridan assumed command of the newly created Military Division of the Southwest, which was headquartered in New Orleans. Sheridan was amassing a large Federal force in Texas for the primary purpose of policing the still-volatile situation along the Rio Grande. With the exodus of so many prominent Confederates into Mexico, not to mention the menacing presence of Imperial forces in northern Mexico, the United States was taking no chances of a possible Confederate resurgence from that country. An estimated 50,000 soldiers were under Sheridan's command, 30,000 of whom were to be stationed in Texas. Most of the 30,000 were elements of the IV and XXV Army Corps. The IV Corps was stationed at San Antonio, while the XXV Corps, composed of black troops, occupied a line from Indianola to Brazos Santiago. Sheridan believed it was absolutely necessary to assemble a large body of soldiers in Texas to have "an army strong enough to move against the invaders of Mexico if occasion demanded."[37]

Perhaps the greatest proponent of assertive action against the French in Mexico was General Grant. In a letter to Pres. Andrew Johnson, he wrote that a truly permanent peace for the United States would not be a reality until the French were driven from Mexico. This peace must be secured while "we still have in service a force sufficient to insure it." As a result, Grant urged that Union armies not be mustered out until the French danger in Mexico had subsided. He also pointed out to Johnson that, ever since the establishment of the Maximilian empire in Mexico, the Rio Grande region had been pro-Confederate. In this letter to Johnson, Grant specifically mentioned the lower Rio Grande Valley: "Matamoros and the whole Rio Grande has been an open port to those in rebellion against this government. It is notorious that every article held by the rebels for export was permitted to cross the Rio Grande and from there go[es] unmolested to all parts of the world and they in turn to receive in pay all articles, and arms, munitions of war."[38]

Sheridan also supported taking stronger action against the Imperialists in Mexico. He arrived at Brazos Santiago on June 26 to investigate the international situation firsthand. There he observed that Matamoros supplied the Imperialists with numerous supplies. Consequently, Sheridan ordered Maj. Gen. Frederick Steele, the Union commander at Brownsville, to "make demonstrations along the lower Rio Grande," believing that "a formidable show of force . . . [would create] much agitation and demoralization among the Imperial troops." Sheridan thought that his presence on the border plus the increasing number of troops in Texas would cause the Imperialists to pull back from the Rio Grande into the interior of Mexico.[39]

With no significant Imperial movement away from the Rio Grande, however, Sheridan staged a second demonstration along the border. Wanting to give the impression that these soldiers were preparing for an invasion of northern Mexico, in late September he made a very public inspection of the IV Corps stationed at San Antonio. Sheridan then moved southward toward Fort Duncan near Eagle Pass to open negotiations with Juarez. Upon arriving at Fort Duncan, he sent a staff officer across the river to Piedras Negras to begin the communications, "taking care not to do this in the dark." Sheridan's posturing in Texas had the desired impact on the Imperialists in northern Mexico. He later commented that his actions in Texas were "spreading like wildfire, the greatest significance was ascribed to my action, it being reported most positively and with many specific details that I was only awaiting the arrival of troops, then under marching orders at San Antonio, to cross the Rio Grande in behalf of the Liberal cause." His actions caused the Imperialists to pull their forces back as far as Monterrey, with the exception of a stubborn force at Matamoros under General Mejía.[40]

Sheridan also spoke of how the Liberal forces in northern Mexico received material aid from the U.S. forces on the lower Rio Grande. It became common practice to leave guns and ammunition at selected points along the north bank of the Rio Grande, knowing that the Juaristas would come along to claim these precious supplies. Liberal troops under Gen. Mariano Escobedo received an estimated thirty thousand rifles from an arsenal in Baton Rouge. When news of Sheridan's active sympathy reached Washington, the French minister protested vigorously to Secretary of State William Seward. The French minister pointed out that Sheridan's truculence at

Brownsville and other points along the Rio Grande violated the strict neutrality Washington had agreed to observe concerning the affairs in Mexico. As a result of the minister's protest, Seward directed Sheridan to observe a strict neutrality along the Rio Grande.[41]

Although Sheridan felt handcuffed by the State Department's policy, he proved himself to be quite a shrewd politician. He believed that the immense show of force on the north bank of the Rio Grande gave Juarez and the Liberals renewed confidence in their war against the French. All of northern Mexico supported Juarez, and the last Imperialist stronghold, Matamoros, was about to fall. In late September 1865 Sheridan wrote two letters to Grant expressing his concern over the possible recognition of Maximilian by the United States. One letter stated that "I consider the Liberal cause as in better condition than at any other period since the advent of Maximilian. I further say that nearly the whole of Mexico is against Maximilian in feeling and that . . . the government recognizes the power of Louis Napoleon and not the will of the Mexican people." In another letter he noted the impact of the U.S. Army on the events in northern Mexico: "The liberals are anxious that the United States Government refuse to recognize the Empire; they are now beginning to realize that they can accomplish the work themselves. The appearance of our large force in Texas has dispelled their despondency, now they know we are strong and think our people sympathize with them."[42]

The Liberal forces indeed increased their activity against Matamoros shortly after the Federal occupation of Brownsville in May 1865. From May through November 1865, the Juaristas made three separate attacks on Matamoros in an attempt to dislodge the Imperialist general Mejía. These assaults continued to weaken the Imperialists' hold on Matamoros. In one dispatch to General Grant, Sheridan pointed out the importance of Matamoros. On October 25 he told Grant that "Should the liberals get Matamoros, northern and eastern Mexico will pass into the hands of the Liberals."[43]

One incident that confirmed the decline of the Imperialists' power near Matamoros involved American troops. On January 5, 1866, soldiers of the 108th U.S. Colored Infantry stationed at Clarksville, near the mouth of the Rio Grande, crossed the river and entered the town of Bagdad. A small group of adventurers claiming to be anti-Imperialists had seized control of the community. For about five days they had looted and terrorized Bagdad, causing the death of twenty people. Order was restored on January 10, when additional American troops, under orders, entered the village and restored peace until proper Mexican authority could be established. Evidence given at a later court of inquiry suggested that some of the soldiers joined these adventurers because they were attracted by the prospect of booty. Although the Imperialists demanded reparations, the U.S. military claimed that these men were no longer soldiers since they had been mustered out of service. As a result, no damages were paid. Regardless of the causes of the Bagdad raid, the Liberal forces saw the event as a sign that Imperial power in the region had definitely waned.[44]

What plagued the Liberal forces in the spring of 1866 was the lack of a leader who could unite their various factions. When Sheridan telegraphed Grant about this problem, Grant suggested Gen. José M. Carvajal, the exiled governor of the Mexican state of Tamaulipas. Since April 1865 Carvajal had been in Washington seeking financial and military support for the Liberal cause. He had been assisted in this matter by Maj. Gen. Lew Wallace of Indiana, who was keenly interested in the republican cause in Mexico. Sheridan spent much of the spring at Fort Brown, convincing the Liberal generals Juan Cortina and Servando Canales to accept Carvajal's leadership in the spirit of Juarista unity. In mid-June 1866 a Liberal offensive was launched against Matamoros. On June 23, Imperialist forces under General Mejía surrendered Matamoros to General Carvajal. The Liberals under Juarez now firmly controlled northern Mexico.[45]

In November 1866 Napoleon III announced that French soldiers were to be withdrawn from Mexico at six-month intervals. Several months later, on June 19, 1867, Maximilian was executed by his enemies in the city of Queretaro. Sheridan always believed that the presence of a large American army on the Rio Grande delivered a death blow to the Mexican Imperialists. He stated, "I doubt very much whether such results could have been achieved without the presence of an American army on the Rio Grande, which, be it remembered, was sent there because, in General Grant's words, the French invasion of Mexico was so closely related to the rebellion as to be essentially a part of it."[46]

Thus, from 1861 to 1867, two sister republics fought their own bloody civil wars, one to preserve republican principles and the other to throw off the yoke of monarchy. In the end, the sustained occupation of Texas soil, begun by the Union Rio Grande expedition in November 1863, helped Juarez to achieve victory over the French.

Eight

War and the Lower Rio Grande Valley

$\mathcal{T}$exas, especially the lower Rio Grande Valley, has a distinctive place in American history. The first battle of the Mexican War was fought there, and the last engagement of the Civil War took place in the same region. In the Mexican War, the Rio Grande served as a disputed boundary between the United States and Mexico. In the Civil War, the Rio Grande divided not just two nations but also two nations that were engulfed in civil wars. Texas was the only rebelling Confederate state that bordered a foreign country. Mexico, with the French occupation, presented a complicated international and military problem for the United States. In Pres. Abraham Lincoln's strategy, the Confederacy was not to be recognized or sustained by a foreign power. The French presence in Mexico thus represented a threat.

During the Civil War, President Lincoln concerned himself with anything that might allow the Confederacy to sustain its war effort. Texas presented two problems to the federal government: a potential French alliance and the Confederate cotton trade in the Brownsville-Matamoros area. The Lincoln administration sought to neutralize both dangers by occupying the Lone Star State. This task was left up to Gen. Nathaniel P. Banks, commander of the Department of the Gulf. Banks eventually launched four expeditions toward Texas, all four of which aimed to establish a sizable Union force there, partly to intimidate the French in Mexico. The third, the Rio Grande expedition, also had the formidable assignment of blocking the lucrative Confederate cotton trade.[1]

The campaign began with an unopposed landing at the mouth of the Rio Grande on November 2, 1863. By the end of December, the Federals controlled the Texas coastline from Brownsville to the Matagorda Peninsula. Before moving up the coast, Banks contemplated linking up with Brig. Gen. James H. Carleton, commander of the Union forces in New Mexico.

This move would have given the Federals control of the Rio Grande from Brownsville to El Paso. Distance, however, made such a project impracticable. Guarding 804 miles from Brownsville to El Paso would have required many more regiments than the Union could spare. Even a daring commander would hesitate to launch such an operation in the drought-stricken region along the Rio Grande. Banks opted for coastal operations because he knew the Texas shoreline was more vulnerable than the Rio Grande border. He expected to then penetrate the Texas interior, capturing cities such as Houston, San Antonio, Austin, and Galveston, thus crushing the civilian and military resistance. This would have accomplished the diplomatic and economic goals of the Rio Grande expedition. Unfortunately for Banks, his vision of conquering Texas from the coast was not shared by his superior, General in Chief Henry W. Halleck. Halleck, who opposed the Rio Grande campaign, pressured Banks in January 1864 to switch to the Red River route into Texas.[2]

Despite Halleck's reluctance to push deeper into Texas from the coast, the Rio Grande expedition had already achieved some of its objectives. Diplomatically, Banks established a significant Union presence in Texas for the French to consider. Second, the export of Confederate cotton, though not severely crippled, was slowed. The Confederates were forced to divert the cotton to the upriver ports of Laredo and Eagle Pass, where the traffic continued to be quite heavy, but the increased distance over which the trade items had to travel added greatly to their cost. This caused considerable distress for the Confederate commanders who were waiting to receive valuable supplies. Politically, the expedition placed into power A. J. Hamilton, whom Lincoln had appointed as the military governor of Texas in November of 1862. Perhaps the strongest civilian advocate of a Union occupation of the Lone Star State, Hamilton arrived in Brownsville in December of 1863 to begin his duties. With Federal forces occupying only the Texas coastline, however, his political power did not extend to the state's major population centers.[3]

The presence of Federal troops on the Texas coast had a sobering impact on Texas' civilian and military population. Texans believed that the heavy hand of war they had read about in other theaters had finally come to their state. Texas newspapers, especially the *Houston Tri-Weekly Telegraph*, wrote about the great fear and anxiety the invasion generated. One account described the situation on the middle Texas coast this way: "We and the entire country [are] in great excitement. The majority of planters have removed their negroes towards the interior, and many families have left them all behind, in fleeing from the perils of invasion. We see families flying in every direction from the coast. The people feel they have nothing to hope for [and pray] that the scenes of outrage perpetrated in Louisiana will not be re-enacted in Texas." Apprehension also developed as far inland as Austin, where a newspaper reported that "Their purpose is evidently to overrun Texas, and the occupation of the capital will be their first object."[4]

Confederate soldiers too were discouraged during this operation. Nothing illustrates this better than their letters. One trooper stationed near Houston in the spring of 1864 wrote the following report: "Cannonading heavy off the coast. Boom upon boom shakes the solid ground. Have to fight soon I suppose. I have a hell of a headache tonight. This day has been cloudy and cold winds. I spread my blankets and fall recumbent on my hard pallet. My poor and pensive soul is weighed down at seeing our nation in tears and trouble."[5]

Morale, with a few exceptions, was never a serious problem among the Federal soldiers in Texas. Since the summer of 1863, the Union armies had achieved great victories, and this instilled a sense of pride in the Federal units. A good example of this appeared in a newspaper published by soldiers at Brownsville, the *Loyal National Union Journal.* The paper regularly reported the sense of dignity the men maintained, despite the fact that they were the Union's most distant and isolated fighting force. The paper pointed out that the men in the Union armies were the very foundation of the war effort. Their work, even though by the spring of 1864 it was primarily occupation duty, was still a major contribution to the eventual defeat of the Confederacy. In their own eyes, they were a distinct breed of men who deserved the respect and admiration of a grateful nation.[6]

Although the soldiers in the Union ranks maintained relatively high morale, some of the generals associated with the expedition became decidedly uneasy by the spring of 1864. Many of them believed all of Texas might fall that year. Maj. Gen. Napoleon J. T. Dana, who briefly commanded the XIII Army Corps, supported more aggressive military action in Texas. He maintained that the inactive status of the Union troops on the Texas coast caused these veteran soldiers to lose their fighting edge. Another prominent officer associated with the expedition, Maj. Gen. C. C. Washburn, also wanted to continue the successful march up the Texas coast and requested additional troops and supplies. Unfortunately for the Union, by the end of December 1863, the Rio Grande campaign had ground to a halt. Federal operations on the Texas coast would not be expanded.[7]

Standing in the way was General Halleck's insistence that the Red River was the best route for an expedition into Texas. The death blow to the Rio Grande campaign came in March 1864, when the new general in chief of all U.S. armies, Ulysses S. Grant, ordered the abandonment of the entire Texas shoreline except for the Brownsville area. As long as the French were in Mexico, Lincoln wanted a Union force kept in the Lone Star State, even a small one. Banks, not wanting to tip his hand to the enemy, actually kept Federal soldiers on the Texas coast until June, thus preventing an immediate transfer of some of the Confederate troops from Texas to Louisiana. This move, he hoped, would increase the chances of military success in Louisiana.[8]

Unfortunately for the Union, the Red River campaign failed, and Banks, as the commander of the Department of the Gulf, had another defeat marked against him. After his important victory at Port Hudson, nothing went right for Banks. The strike at Sabine Pass and the Texas Overland expedition had both failed in their attempts to penetrate Texas in 1863. When Banks successfully occupied the lower Texas coast in the fall of that year, his immediate superior, General Halleck, refused to provide logistical support for continued operations. Halleck's obsession with the Red River route into Texas undermined the possible success of the Rio Grande expedition. A common criticism leveled against many Union generals during the Civil War was their failure to follow up their victories by relentlessly pursuing the enemy army until it was completely destroyed. When Banks attempted to extend his success in Texas, Halleck refused any further support for the Rio Grande operation. Banks had generals under him who not only had good combat records but also were confident of victory in the Lone Star State. General Dana, in particular, knew South Texas fairly well, having been stationed near Corpus Christi during the Mexican War.[9]

Another reason for the failure of the Rio Grande expedition was Halleck's low opinion of political generals. Halleck told General Sherman that "Banks's operations in the West are about what should have been expected from a general so utterly destitute of military education and military capacity. It seems but little better than murder to give important commands to such men as Banks, Butler, McClernand, Sigel, and Lew Wallace, and yet it seems impossible to prevent it." In May 1864, Halleck also suggested that Grant petition Lincoln to replace Banks as a military necessity. Halleck knew that Banks was a political asset to Lincoln but realized that a request from Grant for a reorganization of the Union command west of the Mississippi would carry more weight. Even before Grant received Halleck's letter, he had suggested to Halleck (on April 25) that Banks be replaced by Maj. Gen. Joseph Reynolds, then commander of the New Orleans defenses. The petitions for Banks's removal by Grant and Halleck forced Lincoln to make a politically difficult decision. On May 8, 1864, he appointed Maj. Gen. Edward R. S. Canby to command the newly created Division of West Mississippi, which encompassed the Department of the Gulf and the Department of Arkansas.[10]

The failed Red River campaign finished Banks's military career. His removal became official when General Canby took command on May 19, 1864. Banks was then little more than a head clerk under Canby. His duties dealt primarily with the political sphere, but even in that arena Canby did not hesitate to overrule him. In the fall of 1864, Banks traveled to Washington to visit with Lincoln in a desperate attempt to have his authority restored. Lincoln, recently elected to a second term, refused to give Banks his old command. With the crucial presidential election behind him, Lincoln could afford to be firm.[11]

Banks's adversary on the Rio Grande, Hamilton P. Bee, also suffered as a result of the Red River campaign. At Monett's Ferry, Louisiana, on April 22, 1864, he angered his superiors by retreating at a critical moment. A similar situation had occurred at Brownsville, Texas, in November 1863, when Bee had retreated from a numerically superior force. In both instances he was censured but later exonerated for his actions. Bee could do little to redeem his name after Monett's Ferry since operations against Texas ceased after the Red River campaign. After the war ended, however, the spirit of the Lost Cause embraced all of its defenders as gallant and courageous heroes.[12]

After the war, nearly thirty thousand Federal soldiers were sent to Texas, in part to monitor the ever-turbulent situation in Mexico. They were there to uphold the Monroe Doctrine, and many of them were stationed in South Texas. Some of these men had been part of the Rio Grande operation. Without official permission, they provided war materiel to the Juaristas in northern Mexico. The United States never officially intervened in Mexico, but the strong presence of Federal soldiers in Texas clearly indicated to the French that the United States could still mobilize a large army and move into Mexico if necessary. It also encouraged the forces under Juarez to continue their struggle against the French. In the end, the occupation of Texas, achieved first by the Union Rio Grande expedition, affected events not only in Texas but in Mexico as well.[13]

Shortly after the war ended, the extensive cotton trade across the Rio Grande, the primary cause of the military activity in Texas, collapsed. As in Western boomtowns, when the source of the residents' livelihood disappeared (for example, when a vein of gold ran out), the towns collapsed as well. Thus thousands who had swarmed to the lower Rio Grande Valley to take advantage of the wartime cotton boom now quickly departed. All that remained was the vague memory of a period of abounding financial opportunity that the Mexicans called "los algodones," the time of the cotton.[14]

The cotton trade in the lower Rio Grande Valley helped some Texans thrive financially after the Civil War. Richard King, Miflin Kenedy, and

Charles Stillman had operated a steamboat company on the lower Rio Grande since 1850, and their business venture made an enormous profit during the Civil War years, much of it in gold. After the war, both King and Kenedy went on to invest their profits in cattle and other enterprises and became rich and powerful in South Texas.[15]

The Union Rio Grande campaign, an often-overlooked chapter of the Civil War, led to the only sustained occupation of any part of Texas. The Federal army disrupted the cotton trade, discouraged French meddling in the war north of the Rio Grande, and installed a military governor, Andrew J. Hamilton. In the postwar period, many of these Federals served with the occupation forces along the Rio Grande. The expedition also created a fear among soldiers and civilians that the ravages of war had now descended upon the Lone Star State. Civilians along the Gulf coast and up the Rio Grande Valley knew all too well that the Civil War had arrived.

Of Banks's four campaigns against Texas, only the Rio Grande expedition led to any significant Federal presence on Texas soil for an extended period of time. Although most of Texas remained unconquered during the Civil War, the blame should not fall on the soldiers of the Department of the Gulf, most of whom were seasoned veterans. The men associated with the Rio Grande operation did their duty well despite the fact that they were not led by a successful general or involved in a famous battle. Dispute over strategy between Banks and Halleck doomed the Rio Grande campaign. And even though General Grant ordered the abandonment of the Texas operations in the spring of 1864, he maintained a thousand-man force at Brazos Santiago until the end of the war. When the war in the East ended, Grant's only major concern west of the Mississippi was the presence of the French in Mexico. He feared a continuation of the war south of the Rio Grande since so many Confederates had fled to Mexico. As a result, the garrison at Brazos Santiago provided a valuable service to Grant at this time. The troops there monitored the international border and reported any suspicious activity to the Union high command.

In the final analysis, the sustained occupation of Texas, achieved only by the Rio Grande expedition, warned against French flirtations with the Confederacy out of Mexico. By planting the American flag in Texas and keeping it there until the end of the war, the Lincoln administration was able to concentrate on defeating the Confederate forces east of the Mississippi.

NOTES

CHAPTER 1

1. William Watson, *Adventures of a Blockade Runner*, 20–21; James Daddysman, *Matamoros Trade*, 18–20; Bill Winsor, *Texas in the Confederacy*, 82.

2. Bern Anderson, *By Sea and by River*, 228–29.

3. Pat Kelley, *River of Lost Dreams*, 45.

4. Tom Lea, *King Ranch*, vol. 1, 183–86; John Salmon Ford, *Rip Ford's Texas*, 463–65; Chauncey D. Stillman, *Charles Stillman, 1810–1875*, 27; Kelley, *River of Lost Dreams*, 45.

5. Watson, *Adventures of a Blockade Runner*, 19–23.

6. Robert L. Kerby, *Kirby Smith's Confederacy*, 181; Watson, *Adventures of a Blockade Runner*, 19.

7. Daddysman, *Matamoros Trade*, 24–25, 107; Watson, *Adventures of a Blockade Runner*, 25.

8. Daddysman, *Matamoros Trade*, 107–109.

9. Ibid.

10. Ibid., 107–108; Harry S. Drago, *Steamboaters*, 110.

11. Watson, *Adventures of a Blockade Runner*, 16; Sir Arthur James Lyon Fremantle, *Fremantle Diary*, 6.

12. Kerby, *Kirby Smith's Confederacy*, 178–79, 182; U.S. War Department, *War of the Rebellion*, series 1, vol. 9, 674 (hereafter cited as *ORA*).

13. Lew Wallace, *Lew Wallace*, 820–21.

14. James A. Irby, "Line of the Rio Grande," 5; Paul Horgan, *Great River*, 837; *New Orleans Daily True Delta*, Mar. 5, 1863, Dec. 16, 1864; *New York Herald*, Jan. 9, 1865; Daddysman, *Matamoros Trade*, 20–21.

15. *New York Tribune*, Feb. 7, 1863.

16. Andrew Jackson Hamilton was born in Alabama in 1815. He had lived in Texas since 1846, holding various political offices. Suspected by some fellow Texans of plotting to overthrow the Confederate state government in Austin, Hamilton fled to Mexico in the summer of 1862. During the Civil War he would be one of the strongest civilian promoters of a Union invasion of Texas (William C. Harris, *With Charity for All*, 87; Richard Lowe, *Texas Overland Expedition of 1863*, 16).

17. *Washington National Intelligencer*, Oct. 18, 1862; *New York Tribune*, Feb. 7, 1863; Harris, *With Charity for All*, 90; John L. Waller, *Colossal Hamilton of Texas*, 36–38, 42–46.

18. Robert W. Delaney, "Matamoros, Port for Texas during the Civil War," 470, 480.

19. Roy P. Basler, ed., *Collected Works of Abraham Lincoln*, vol. 8, 164 (hereafter cited as *CWAL*).

20. Ford, *Rip Ford's Texas*, 359; Horgan, *Great River*, 837; Kevin R. Young, *To the Tyrants Never Yield*, 150.

21. *ORA*, series 1, vol. 9, 648; U.S. Navy Department, *Official Records of the Union and Confederate Navies in the War of the Rebellion*, series 1, vol. 20, 201 (hereafter cited as *ORN*); Ludwell H. Johnson, *Red River Campaign*, 34.

22. Basler, *CWAL*, vol. 6, 354–55.

23. Nathaniel Banks was one of the most active of the higher-ranking political generals. Born in Massachusetts in 1816, Banks was elected to various state offices, including governor. At the outbreak of the Civil War, Lincoln appointed him major general of volunteers. Serving at various posts in the Virginia theater, he saw some combat against Gen. Thomas J. ("Stonewall") Jackson. In November 1862 Banks was appointed to head the Department of the Gulf. In July 1863 he captured Port Hudson after the fall of Vicksburg. From September 1863 to April 1864, Banks launched four unsuccessful campaigns in an effort to capture Texas (Ezra J. Warner, *Generals in Blue*, 17–18).

24. Basler, *CWAL*, vol. 6, 364, 374.

25. Lowe, *Overland Expedition*, 16; Frank H. Smyrl, "Texans in the Union Army, 1861–1865," 240.

26. Kerby, *Kirby Smith's Confederacy*, 186; Basler, *CWAL*, vol. 5, 357; Harris, *With Charity for All*, 88–89; Smyrl, "Texans in the Union Army," 240–41.

27. *ORA*, series 1, vol. 15, 152; Lowe, *Overland Expedition*, 19; Smyrl, "Texans in the Union Army," 236–37.

28. Basler, *CWAL*, vol. 6, 354–55; Harris, *With Charity for All*, 92–93.

29. *ORA*, series 1, vol. 15, pt. 2, 590; Kurt Hackemer, "Strategic Dilemma," 193–94.

30. Kerby, *Kirby Smith's Confederacy*, 187; James M. McPherson, *Battle Cry of Freedom*, 683; Basler, *CWAL*, vol. 6, 364.

31. *ORA*, series 1, vol. 26, pt. 1, 672–73.

32. Hackemer, "Strategic Dilemma," 196; Rowena Reed, *Combined Operations in the Civil War*, 323.

33. Johnson, *Red River Campaign*, 41; Kerby, *Kirby Smith's Confederacy*, 187–88; *ORA*, series 1, vol. 26, pt. 1, 673.

34. *ORA*, series 1, vol. 26, pt. 1, 673, 682–83, 697.

35. Ibid., 287–90, 311–12; T. R. Fehrenbach, *Lone Star*, 370; Andrew F. Muir, "Dick Dowling and the Battle of Sabine Pass," 193–94.

36. *ORA*, series 1, vol. 26, pt. 1, 768; Johnson, *Red River Campaign*, 39; Lowe, *Overland Expedition*, 47.

37. Lowe, *Overland Expedition*, 47–48; Johnson, *Red River Campaign*, 39; *ORA*, series 1, vol. 26, pt. 1, 292; James G. Hollandsworth Jr., *Pretense of Glory*, 141; *New Orleans Times*, Dec. 31, 1863.

38. James G. Hollandsworth Jr., *Pretense of Glory*, 141.

39. Lowe, *Overland Expedition*, 61–62; Hackemer, "Strategic Dilemma," 204; *ORN*, vol. 20, 632; *ORA*, series 1, vol. 26, pt. 1, 871.

40. Hamilton Prioleau Bee was born in Charleston, South Carolina, on July 22, 1822. His brother, Gen. Bernard E. Bee, was killed at the First Battle of Bull Run, or First Manassas. Hamilton Bee came to Texas in 1837. After fighting in the Mexican War, he served in the Texas legislature from 1849 to 1859. At the outbreak of the Civil War in 1861, Bee was appointed brigadier general of state troops. In March 1862 he was commissioned a brigadier general in the Confederate army and placed in command at Brownsville. He later saw action in the Red River campaign, fighting at the battles of Mansfield and Pleasant Hill. By war's end, Bee was paroled as a major general, although no record of this appointment has been found (Harold B. Simpson, ed., and Marcus J. Wright, comp., *Texas in the Civil War, 1861–1865*, 75–76; Hollandsworth, *Pretense of Glory*, 141).

41. John B. Magruder was born in Virginia in 1811. A West Pointer, he fought in Mexico, receiving two brevets. At the outbreak of the Civil War, he was made a colonel in the Confederate army. Serving in the Virginia theater, he rose to major general on Oct. 7, 1861. Magruder was later criticized for his actions during the Seven Days' Battle. He was then appointed to command the District of Texas, New Mexico, and Arizona on Oct. 10, 1862. He was kept busy in this theater of operations by the numerous Union invasions launched by Gen. Nathaniel Banks. When the war ended, Magruder refused a parole and went on to serve as a major general under Maximilian in Mexico. He died in 1871 (Ezra J. Warner, *Generals in Gray*, 207–208).

42. *ORA*, series 1, vol. 26, pt. 1, 395, 439, 565; Daddysman, *Matamoros Trade*, 90–91; Fred H. Harrington, *Fighting Politician*, 131.

43. *ORA*, series 1, vol. 26, pt. 1, 398; Mark M. Boatner, *Civil War Dictionary*, 221; Hollandsworth, *Pretense of Glory*, 141.

44. *ORN*, series 1, vol. 20, 643–47; Charles Dana Gibson and E. Kay Gibson, *Assault and Logistics*, vol. 2, 336.

45. *ORA*, series 1, vol. 26, pt. 1, 20, 397–98, 425; *ORN*, series 1, vol. 20, 643–47; Edward Gee Miller, *Captain Edward Gee Miller of the 20th Wisconsin*, 19–20; Michael A. Mullins, *Fremont Rifles*, 236; Henry A. Shorey, *Story of the Maine Fifteenth*, 55.

46. *Chicago Evening Journal*, Nov. 17 and 19, 1863; *Houston Telegraph*, Nov. 1, 1863.

47. James S. Clark, *Life in the Middle West*, 103–104.

48. Ibid.

49. *ORA*, series 1, vol. 26, pt. 1, 20, 397–98, 425; Tilley, *Federals on the Frontier*, 248–50; William J. Hughes, *Rebellious Ranger*, 211; John W. Hunter, "Fall of Brownsville on the Rio Grande, November, 1863," 17; James M. Beverly, *History of the Ninety-first Regiment Illinois Volunteer Infantry, 1862–1865*, 11.

50. *ORA*, series 1, vol. 26, pt. 1, 20, 399, 425; Tilley, *Federals on the Frontier*, 253–55; Boatner, *Civil War Dictionary*, 833; Daddysman, *Matamoros Trade*, 91; Brian Robertson, *Wild Horse Desert*, 116; Mullins, *Fremont Rifles*, 238, 240; muster roll and regimental papers of the 94th Illinois Volunteer Infantry Regiment, dated Nov.–Dec. 1863, stationed at Brownsville, Texas (M594, roll #28).

51. *ORA*, series 1, vol. 4, and vol. 15, 966; Daddysman, *Matamoros Trade*, 22–24; Stambaugh and Stambaugh, *Lower Rio Grande Valley of Texas*, 117; Simpson and Wright, *Texas in the Civil War*, 141.

52. *ORA*, series 1, vol. 26, pt. 1, 433.

53. Ibid., 432–35, 439–45; Robertson, *Wild Horse Desert*, 116; Stambaugh and Stambaugh, *Lower Rio Grande Valley*, 117.

54. Stambaugh and Stambaugh, *Lower Rio Grande Valley*, 117; Robertson, *Wild Horse Desert*, 116; *ORA*, series 1, vol. 26, pt. 1, 432–35, 439–45.

55. Hunter, "Fall of Brownsville," 22.

56. Ibid., 9–10.

57. Ibid., 10–12.

58. Ibid., 13–15; Robertson, *Wild Horse Desert*, 116; Stambaugh and Stambaugh, *Lower Rio Grande Valley*, 117.

59. Hunter, "Fall of Brownsville," 15–17; *ORA*, series 1, vol. 26, pt. 1, 399–401, 405.

60. *ORA*, series 1, vol. 26, pt. 1, 399–401, 405; Lea, *King Ranch*, 207–10; Stambaugh and Stambaugh, *Lower Rio Grande Valley*, 117; Kerby, *Kirby Smith's Confederacy*, 192; Robertson, *Wild Horse Desert*, 116; Our Special Correspondent, "The Rio Grande Expedition," *New York Herald*, Nov. 23, 1863.

61. *ORA*, series 1, vol. 26, pt. 1, 448–49; Fehrenbach, *Lone Star*, 377; Kerby, *Kirby Smith's Confederacy*, 191; Hunter, "Fall of Brownsville," 23; Jerry Don Thompson, *Wild and Vivid Land*, 110.

CHAPTER 2

1. Fred H. Harrington, *Fighting Politician*, 133; James G. Hollandsworth Jr., *Pretense of Glory*, 143.

2. Harrington, *Fighting Politician*, 131–32; Rowena Reed, *Combined Operations in the Civil War*, 323; U.S. War Department, *War of the Rebellion* (hereafter cited as *ORA*; unless otherwise indicated, all future *ORA* references in this chapter come from series 1, vol. 26, pt. 1); Hollandsworth, *Pretense of Glory*, 143.

3. Gilbert D. Kingsbury to his sister Mariah, Nov. 10, 1863.

4. James Daddysman, *Matamoros Trade*, 93; *ORA*, 410–11; Ezra Warner, *Generals in Blue*, 390; Hobart Huson, *Refugio*, 37; James S. Clark, *Life in the Middle West*, 105; J. D. Barnes, *What I Saw You Do*, 32; Chester Barney, *Recollections of Field Service with the 20th Iowa Infantry Volunteers*, 247–48.

5. *ORA*, 409; U.S. Navy Department, *Official Records of the Union and Confederate Navies in the War of the Rebellion* (hereafter cited as *ORN*); Nueces County Historical Society, *History of Nueces County*, 37; Henry A. Shorey, *Story of the Maine Fifteenth*, 59; muster rolls for the 13th and 15th Maine Volunteer Infantry Regiments stationed at Matagorda Island, dated Dec. 1863 (M594, roll #70).

6. *ORN*, series 1, vol. 20, 681; *ORA*, 409–10; Alwyn Barr, "Texas Coastal Defense, 1861–1865," 28; *Houston Tri-Weekly Telegraph*, Dec. 15, 1863; Alfred T. Mahan, *Gulf and Inland Waters*, 188; regimental returns of the 8th Texas Infantry, dated Jan. 10 and 19, 1864, stationed at Galveston Island (M861, roll #60); Barnes, *What I Saw You Do*, 33; Edwin B. Lufkin, *History of the Thirteenth*

Maine, 58; Shorey, *Maine Fifteenth*, 59; Barney, *Twentieth Iowa*, 247–48; *Corpus Christi Caller Times*, May 28, 1961.

7. *ORN*, series 1, vol. 20, 681–82; Kurt Hackemer, "Strategic Dilemma," 207. Fred H. Harrington, in his biography of Banks, states that Banks failed to arrange effective cooperation with his navy escort on the Rio Grande expedition (*Fighting Politician*, 131).

8. John Salmon Ford, *Rip Ford's Texas*, 352; *ORA*, series 1, vol. 26, pt. 2, 850–51; Eugenia R. Briscoe, "Narrative History of Corpus Christi, Texas, 1519–1875," 430.

9. Bill Winsor, *Texas in the Confederacy*, 40–41; Hackemer, "Strategic Dilemma," 208; Lester N. Fitzhugh, "Saluria, Fort Esperanza, and Military Operations on the Texas Coast," 96–97; Harold B. Simpson, ed., and Marcus J. Wright, comp., *Texas in the Civil War, 1861–1865*, 143; Walter Prescott Webb, ed., *Handbook of Texas*, vol. 2, 158. For more information on Civil War artillery, consult James C. Hazlett, Edwin Olmstead, and M. Hume Parks, *Field Artillery Weapons of the Civil War*.

10. Warner, *Generals in Blue*, 542–43; Mark M. Boatner, *Civil War Dictionary*, 892; Richard Lowe, *Texas Overland Expedition of 1863*, 30; *ORA*, 896.

11. Hackemer, "Strategic Dilemma," 208; *ORA*, 418–19, 427; Barr, "Texas Coastal Defense," 28; Clark, *Life in the Middle West*, 106; Lufkin, *Thirteenth Maine*, 59; Shorey, *Maine Fifteenth*, 61–62.

12. *ORA*, 419; Albert O. Marshall, *Army Life*, 309–37; *Houston Tri-Weekly Telegraph*, Dec. 5, 1863; Lufkin, *Thirteenth Maine*, 60; Clark, *Life in the Middle West*, 106; Shorey, *Maine Fifteenth*, 62–63.

13. Barr, "Texas Coastal Defense," 28; *ORA*, 427–28; *Houston Tri-Weekly Telegraph*, Dec. 5, 1863; *Galveston Weekly News*, Dec. 9 and 14, 1863; Lufkin, *Thirteenth Maine*, 61; Marshall, *Army Life*, 318–30, Clark, *Life in the Middle West*, 106; Shorey, *Maine Fifteenth*, 65; Silas I. Shearer, *Dear Companion*, 63.

14. *ORA*, 418, 420–23; Clark, *Life in the Middle West*, 106–107; Lufkin, *Thirteenth Maine*, 60.

15. Daddysman, *Matamoros Trade*, 24; Lillian Stambaugh and J. Lee Stambaugh, *Lower Rio Grande Valley of Texas*, 88–90; Brian Robertson, *Wild Horse Desert*, 86–87; Simpson and Wright, *Texas in the Civil War*, 146.

16. Col. J. C. Black to his mother and sister, Nov. 21 and 28, 1863, J. C. Black correspondence; Tom Lea, *King Ranch*, vol. 1, 213–14; Frank H. Smyrl, "Texans in the Union Army, 1861–1865," 235–43; Michael A. Mullins, *Fremont Rifles*, 244; Ronald N. Gray, "Edmund J. Davis," 53.

17. Mullins, *Fremont Rifles*, 245.

18. Ibid., 246.

19. Daddysman, *Matamoros Trade*, 93; Mullins, *Fremont Rifles*, 246; muster rolls of the 37th Illinois Volunteer Infantry Regiment stationed at Brownsville, Texas, dated Dec. 1863 (M594, roll #19).

20. Mullins, *Fremont Rifles*, 246.

21. Col. J. C. Black to his sister, Nov. 29, 1863, J. C. Black correspondence.

22. Andrew L. Swap, *A. L. Swap in the Civil War*, 21; petition of Ramijo Garza to the Commissioner of Claims, Apr. 11, 1872 (microfiche M1407, fiche #4451).

23. *ORA*, 423–24, 430; Lea, *King Ranch*, 213–14; Smyrl, "Texans in the Union Army," 235–43; Boatner, *Civil War Dictionary*, 224; Warner, *Generals in Blue*, 115; Mullins, *Fremont Rifles*, 247.

24. *ORA*, 830, 843, 865.

25. Ella Lonn, *Salt as a Factor in the Confederacy*, 31, 109; Stambaugh and Stambaugh, *Lower Rio Grande Valley*, 134; Wallace Hawkins, *El Sal del Rey*, 45.

26. James A. Irby, "Line of the Rio Grande," 72; Robertson, *Wild Horse Desert*, 118–19; Lonn, *Salt as a Factor*, 109. For some unknown reason, a second raid was ordered against El Sal del Rey in late December 1863. The attack was led by Col. Henry M. Day of the 91st Illinois Volunteer Infantry Regiment. Although finding no equipment to destroy, one soldier commented that "About seventy serviceable horses and mules were seized and driven in for the use of the Government in accordance with orders" (muster roll from the 91st Illinois Volunteer Infantry Regiment, dated Jan.–Feb. 1864, Brownsville, Texas, National Archives (M594, roll #28).

27. *Houston Tri-Weekly Telegraph*, Feb. 1, 1864; Jerry Don Thompson, *Mexican-Texans in the Union Army*, 10–23; Bruce S. Cheeseman, "'Let us have 500 good determined Texans,'" 91. The Military Board of Texas designated King Ranch as an official receiving, storage, and shipping depot for Confederate cotton. Thousands of bales, both government and private, passed through the ranch on their way to the Rio Grande. They came from East Texas, Arkansas, and Louisiana and as far away as Missouri (Lea, *King Ranch*, vol. 1, 182–92).

28. Cheeseman, "'Let us have 500 good determined Texans,'" 78–79; *Houston Tri-Weekly Telegraph*, Feb. 1, 1864; Lea, *King Ranch*, vol. 1, 218.

29. Lea, *King Ranch*, vol. 1, 217–18; Robertson, *Wild Horse Desert*, 117; *ORA*, 856; Cheeseman, "'Let us have 500 good determined Texans,'" 91; *Houston Tri-Weekly Telegraph*, Feb. 1, 1864.

30. A. E. Sweet and J. A. Knox, *On a Mexican Mustang through Texas from the Gulf of Mexico to the Rio Grande*, 477–83; Winsor, *Texas in the Confederacy*, 133; *ORA*, 853.

31. Winsor, *Texas in the Confederacy*, 133; Sweet and Knox, *On a Mexican Mustang*, 498–99.

32. Robert Marmion, *Texas Soldier and Marine during the Civil War, 1861–1865*, 16; *ORA*, 482; Lufkin, *Thirteenth Maine*, 64–65.

33. *ORA*, 482–85; Stanley S. McGowen, "Augustus Buchel," 9; Lufkin, *Thirteenth Maine*, 63.

34. *ORA*, 485; Marmion, *Texas Soldier and Marine*, 17–19; Stanley S. McGowen, "Horsesweat and Powdersmoke," 197–201; Lufkin, *Thirteenth Maine*, 65–66.

35. *ORA*, 485; Marmion, *Texas Soldier and Marine*, 17–19; McGowen, "Horsesweat and Powdersmoke," 197–201; Lufkin, *Thirteenth Maine*, 64–65.

36. Marmion, *Texas Soldier and Marine*, 19; *ORA*, 482–84; Lufkin, *Thirteenth Maine*, 65–66; muster rolls of the 13th Maine Volunteer Infantry Regiment stationed at Matagorda Island, dated Jan. 1864 (M594, roll #70).

37. *ORA*, 480–81; Winsor, *Texas in the Confederacy*, 108, 114; Shorey, *Maine Fifteenth*, 67.

38. *ORA,* 849–60, 416–17; Hackemer, "Strategic Dilemma," 208; Col. Oran M. Roberts, *Confederate Military History,* 120; Shearer, *Letters of Silas I. Shearer,* 64.

39. Hackemer, "Strategic Dilemma," 209–10; *ORA,* 834–35; General Halleck to General Banks, Sept. 30, 1863, Nathaniel P. Banks Papers.

40. Joseph T. Woods, *Services of the 96th Ohio Volunteers,* 50; Sweet and Knox, *On a Mexican Mustang,* 479–81; McGowen, "Horsesweat and Powder-smoke," 197; *ORA,* 418–20; Clark, *Life in the Middle West,* 107.

41. Fitzhugh, "Operations on the Texas Coast," 98–99; *ORA,* 418–20, 876–77; Winsor, *Texas in the Confederacy,* 60; Reuben A. Scott, *History of the 67th Regiment, Indiana Infantry Volunteers,* 67.

42. Winsor, *Texas in the Confederacy,* 40; Daddysman, *Matamoros Trade,* 98; Robert L. Kerby, *Kirby Smith's Confederacy,* 367–68.

43. Winsor, *Texas in the Confederacy,* 40; *ORA,* 898.

44. Winsor, *Texas in the Confederacy,* 40–41; Marmion, *Texas Soldier and Marine,* 15; *ORA,* 431, 897; Clark, *Life in the Middle West,* 107–108.

45. Kerby, *Kirby Smith's Confederacy,* 193; *ORA,* 879; Charles D. Gibson and E. Kay Gibson, *Assault and Logistics,* vol. 2, 340; Tilley, *Federals on the Frontier,* 34; Jerry Don Thompson, *Vaqueros in Blue and Gray,* 84–93.

46. Sherrill L. Dickeson, "Texas Cotton Trade during the Civil War," 24–25; Lea, *King Ranch,* 214; Hackemer, "Strategic Dilemma," 207–208; *ORA,* 414–15, 830; Gilbert D. Kingsbury to the editor of the *New York Herald,* Mar. 1, 1864, Gilbert D. Kingsbury Papers.

47. Smyrl, "Texans in the Union Army," 242; Simpson and Wright, *Texas in the Civil War,* 140; *ORA,* 865.

48. *ORA,* 865–66.

49. Ibid., 859.

50. William C. Harris, *With Charity for All,* 95; *ORA,* 846.

51. Harris, *With Charity for All,* 95; Smyrl, "Texans in the Union Army," 243; Frank C. Pierce, *Brief History of the Lower Rio Grande Valley,* 47; Andrew Jackson Hamilton, "Address of A. J. Hamilton, Military Governor, to the People of Texas."

52. *Texas State Gazette,* Mar. 23 and Apr. 6, 1864.

53. Harris, *With Charity for All,* 95; Hackemer, "Strategic Dilemma," 211–13; Ludwell H. Johnson, *Red River Campaign,* 45.

54. Chester Barney, *Recollections of Field Service with the 20th Iowa Infantry Volunteers,* 258; Marshall, *Army Life,* 340; George Crooke, *Twenty-first Regiment of Iowa Volunteers,* 125; J. Irvine Dungan, *History of the 19th Regiment Iowa Volunteer Infantry,* 118; J. D. Barnes, *What I Saw You Do,* 33.

55. Winsor, *Texas in the Confederacy,* 7.

CHAPTER 3

1. Ezra J. Warner, *Generals in Gray,* 279–80; Joseph H. Parks, *General Edmund Kirby Smith,* 311.

2. Robert L. Kerby, *Kirby Smith's Confederacy,* 137; Parks, *Kirby Smith,* 311; Francis R. Lubbock, *Six Decades in Texas,* 493–501; Ralph A. Wooster, *Texas and Texans in the Civil War,* 101.

3. Sherrill L. Dickeson, "Texas Cotton Trade during the Civil War," 48–49; Williamson S. Oldham, "Memoirs," 369–70.

4. Kerby, *Kirby Smith's Confederacy*, 142–43; newspaper clipping, "To the People of Louisiana, Texas, Arkansas, Missouri, and the Allied Indian Nations," dated Aug. 16, 1863, Edmund K. Smith Papers (M786.209, roll 209 A); Florence E. Holladay, "Powers of the Commander of the Confederate Trans-Mississippi Department, 1863–1865," 279–98.

5. Dickeson, "Texas Cotton Trade," 49–52; U.S. War Department, *War of the Rebellion*, series 1, vol. 26, pt. 2, 136, 437–38 (hereafter cited as *ORA*); Charles W. Ramsdell, "Texas State Military Board, 1862–1865," 270; Gen. Edmund K. Smith to Guy M. Bryan, Nov. 1, 1863, Guy M. Bryan Papers.

6. Bill Winsor, *Texas in the Confederacy*, 59.

7. *ORA*, series 1, vol. 26, pt. 1, 432–33; James W. Daddysman, *Matamoros Trade*, 91–92.

8. John Warren Hunter, "Fall of Brownsville on the Rio Grande, November 1863," 19–21.

9. *ORA*, series 1, vol. 26, pt. 2, 384–86. (All further references to *ORA* in this chapter are to series 1, vol. 26, pt. 2, unless otherwise indicated.)

10. *ORA*, 412; Kerby, *Kirby Smith's Confederacy*, 192–93; *Houston Tri-Weekly Telegraph*, Jan. 20, 1864.

11. *ORA*, 411.

12. Kerby, *Kirby Smith's Confederacy*, 193.

13. Ibid., 193–94; William C. Nunn, ed., *Ten Texans in Gray*, 129; H. P. N. Gammel, comp., *Laws of Texas, 1822–1897*, vol. 5, 829–30; Maj. W. Hyllested, "To the Citizens of Houston," *Houston Tri-Weekly Telegraph*, Dec. 9, 1863; Jan. 11 and 13; Feb. 29, 1864; Frank L. Owsley, *State Rights in the Confederacy*, 61.

14. *ORA*, 396.

15. Ibid., 399–400; Jerry Don Thompson, *Vaqueros in Blue and Gray*, 12; Harold B. Simpson, ed., and Marcus J. Wright, comp., *Texas in the Civil War, 1861–1865*, 121; Gilberto M. Hinojosa, *Borderlands Town in Transition*, 85; Jerry Don Thompson, *Sabers on the Rio Grande*, 197.

16. *ORA*, 400; J. Fred Rippy, "Mexican Projects of the Confederates," 298–99.

17. *ORA*, 404.

18. Ibid., 406–407; Milo Kearney and Anthony Knopp, *Boom and Bust*, 126–27.

19. *ORA*, 409; Joseph B. Wilkinson, *Laredo and the Rio Grande Frontier*, 283; *ORA*, series 1, vol. 26, pt. 1, 423–24, 430; *Corpus Christi Ranchero*, Jan. 21, 1864; Hinojosa, *Borderlands Town*, 85.

20. Bruce S. Cheeseman, "'Let us have 500 good determined Texans,'" 81–83.

21. *ORA*, 413; Winsor, *Texas in the Confederacy*, 7.

22. *ORA*, 414, 420.

23. Ibid., 421.

24. Mary Maverick to her son, Capt. Lewis Maverick, Nov. 16 and Dec. 1, 1863, Maverick Family Papers.

25. *Austin State Gazette*, Nov. 16, 20, and 25; Dec. 2, 1863; Frank Brown, "Annals of Travis County and of the City of Austin," vol. 23, 40–41.

26. Getulius Kellersberger, *Memoirs of an Engineer in the Confederate Army in Texas*, 32; Brown, "Annals of Travis County," vol. 23, 21; *Austin State Gazette*, Dec. 14, 18, 21, and 23, 1863; James A. Marten, *Texas Divided*, 47.

27. Laura P. DuVal to Thomas H. DuVal, Jan. 31, 1864, Diaries of Thomas H. Duval. At the time of Mrs. DuVal's letter, Thomas DuVal was in Brownsville, having just returned from a trip to Washington, D.C., where, in a meeting with President Lincoln, he continued to urge aggressive military action Texas.

28. Ibid.

29. "To the People of Arkansas, Louisiana, and Texas," *Austin State Gazette*, Nov. 20, 1863.

30. "Fall of Aransas Pass," *Houston Tri-Weekly Telegraph*, Nov. 23, 1863.

31. "Fall of Fort Esperanza," *Houston Tri-Weekly Telegraph*, Dec. 4, 1863. In its attempt to paint a stoic picture of the fall of Fort Esperanza, the *Tri-Weekly Telegraph* failed to see a glaring contradiction in the article. If a determined spirit of resistance prevailed everywhere as it claimed, why were people fleeing to the interior?

32. *Houston Tri-Weekly Telegraph*, Dec. 7, 1863.

33. Sioux, "From the West," *Houston Tri-Weekly Telegraph*, Dec. 9, 1863.

34. Sioux, "From the Front," *Houston Tri-Weekly Telegraph*, Dec. 11, 1863.

35. Ibid.

36. Maj. W. Hyllested, "To the Citizens of Houston," *Houston Tri-Weekly Telegraph*, Dec. 9, 1863.

37. Entry of Jan. 23, 1864, Diaries of Thomas H. DuVal.

38. Patsy M. Spaw, *Texas Senate*, vol. 2, 39.

39. Ibid., 42–49.

40. *ORA*, 422–25; Paul Horgan, *Great River*, 838.

41. *ORA*, 437; diary of Thomas J. Noakes (Confederate rancher who lived near Corpus Christi), 17 Nov. 1863 (hereafter cited as Noakes Diary); *Corpus Christi Ranchero*, Dec. 17, 1863.

42. Col. A. T. Rainey to Capt. E. P. Turner, Nov. 28, 1863, correspondence and circulars, 1863–1865, Ashbel Smith Papers; Ralph A. Wooster, *Lone Star Regiments in Gray*, 324.

43. Minetta A. Goyne, *Lone Star and Double Eagle*, 110–12; *ORA*, 443–46; Carl L. Duaine, *Dead Men Wore Boots*, 46–47.

44. Brian Robertson, *Wild Horse Desert*, 116–17; John S. Ford, *Rip Ford's Texas*, 342–43; Alvin M. Josephy, *Civil War in the American West*, 187; Kerby, *Kirby Smith's Confederacy*, 195; *ORA*, 446–50.

45. Horgan, *Great River*, 838; Daddysman, *Matamoros Trade*, 93–94.

46. Col. P. C. Woods to his wife, Georgia, Nov. 26, 1863, unpublished letters of Col. P. C. Woods and his wife, Georgia Woods; Kerby, *Kirby Smith's Confederacy*, 195. The 32nd Texas Cavalry was actually the 36th Texas cavalry, although it was often referred to as the 32nd at this time in the war.

47. Stanley S. McGowen, "Horsesweat and Powdersmoke," 196, 198; Wooster, *Texas and Texans in the Civil War*, 134; Elizabeth Silverthorne, *Ashbel Smith of Texas*, 161.

48. Lubbock, *Six Decades in Texas,* 528–33; Paul D. Casdorph, *Prince John Magruder,* 262; *ORA,* 491–93; *Houston Tri-Weekly Telegraph,* Dec. 2, 4, 9, and 11, 1863.

49. Troops of the 96th Ohio serving on Matagorda Peninsula indicated that a Colonel Decrow, who owned most of the peninsula, lived at its south end. This is where DeCrow's Point gets its name. Joseph T. Woods, *Services of the 96th Ohio Volunteers,* 50; Casdorph, *Prince John Magruder,* 262; *ORA,* 487, 515.

50. Casdorph, *Prince John Magruder,* 262.

51. Winsor, *Texas in the Confederacy,* 63–64; Robert Marmion, *Texas Soldier and Marine during the Civil War, 1861–1865,* 12; U.S. Navy Department, *Official Records of the Union and Confederate Navies in the War of the Rebellion,* series 1, vol. 20, 847 (hereafter cited as *ORN*).

52. Marmion, *Texas Soldier and Marine,* 15; Winsor, *Texas in the Confederacy,* 65. Matagorda Bay extends approximately forty miles southwest to northeast, roughly parallel to the Texas mainland. It is shielded from the Gulf of Mexico by the Matagorda Peninsula (Frank H. Gille, ed., *Encyclopedia of Texas,* 367–68); James M. Day, "Leon Smith."

53. *ORN,* series 1, vol. 20, 853–54; Winsor, *Texas in the Confederacy,* 64; Marmion, *Texas Soldier and Marine,* 15.

54. Lubbock, *Six Decades in Texas,* 172; McGowen, *Horsesweat and Powdersmoke,* 202; *ORA,* series 1, vol. 26, pt. 1, 482–85; Marmion, *Texas Soldier and Marine,* 17–18.

55. Jeff Morgan to his wife, Dec. 7, 1863, unpublished letters of Jeff Morgan.

56. Goyne, *Lone Star and Double Eagle,* 115; Col. P. C. Woods to his wife, Georgia, Nov. 26, 1863, unpublished letters of Col. P. C. Woods and his wife, Georgia Woods.

57. *ORA,* series 1, vol. 26, pt. 1, 878; Maj. William G. Thompson to his wife, Dec. 3, 1863, unpublished letters of Maj. William G. Thompson to his wife concerning his tour of duty on Mustang Island; J. D. Barnes, *What I Saw You Do,* 33.

58. Briscoe, "Narrative of Corpus Christi," 432–33.

59. Maj. William G. Thompson to his wife, Dec. 25, 1863, unpublished letters of Maj. William G. Thompson.

60. Noakes Diary, Dec. 21, 1863; Briscoe, "Narrative of Corpus Christi," 433–34.

61. Maj. William G. Thompson to his wife, Mar. 3, 1864, unpublished letters of Maj. William G. Thompson.

62. Eli Merriman, "Memoirs."

63. Noakes Diary, Dec. 27, 1863; Maj. William G. Thompson to his wife, Feb. 21, 1864, unpublished letters of Maj. William G. Thompson.

64. Gary B. Mills, *Southern Loyalists in the Civil War,* ix–x.

65. Petitions to the Southern Claims Commission by Francisco Solis, Nicholas Champion, and Pauline Victoria Butler, Sept. 27, 1871 (Solis), Oct. 7, 1871 (Champion), Oct. 16, 1871 (Butler) (M1407, fiche #4737, #4365, #4379 respectively).

66. Petition to the Southern Claims Commission by Alvin C. Priest, Sept. 28, 1876 (M1407, fiche #4677).

67. U.S. Treasury Department, petition of Louisa Steinberg to the Commissioner of Claims, July 7, 1871.

CHAPTER 4

1. William S. McFeeley, *Grant*, 157; James M. McPherson, *Battle Cry of Freedom*, 683; Fred H. Harrington, *Fighting Politician*, 133; U.S. War Department, *War of the Rebellion*, series 1, vol. 34, pt. 1, 190 (hereafter cited as *ORA*).

2. Harrington, *Fighting Politician*, 151; Henry A. Shorey, *Story of the Maine Fifteenth*, 70–71; Ludwell H. Johnson, *Red River Campaign*, 45; *ORA*, series 1, vol. 34, pt. 2, 133; Paul Casdorph, *Prince John Magruder*, 269; Joseph H. Parks, *General Edmund Kirby Smith*, 37.

3. Roy P. Basler, ed., *Collected Works of Abraham Lincoln*, vol. 8, 89–90 (hereafter cited as *CWAL*); Johnson, *Red River Campaign*, 47.

4. Norman D. Brown, ed., *Journey to Pleasant Hill*, 171; T. Michael Parrish, *Richard Taylor*, 320–24; Casdorph, *Prince John Magruder*, 270; Harrington, *Fighting Politician*, 152–53; Johnson, *Red River Campaign*, 47.

5. Ralph J. Smith, *Reminiscences of the Civil War and Other Sketches*, 31–37; Elizabeth Silverthorne, *Ashbel Smith of Texas*, 162; U.S. Navy Department, *Official Records of the Union and Confederate Navies in the War of the Rebellion*, series 1, vol. 21, 23–24 (hereafter cited as *ORN*).

6. *ORA*, series 1, vol. 24, pt. 2, 899, 913–16, 932; Stanley S. McGowen, *Horsesweat and Powdersmoke*, 115–19.

7. *ORN*, series 1, vol. 21, 23–24.

8. Smith, *Reminiscences of the Civil War*, 34–37; *ORN*, series 1, vol. 21, 24, 859, 864; *ORA*, series 1, vol. 26, pt. 1, 80–81; morning reports, Jan. 1–15, 1864, 1st Texas Cavalry Regiment, unit reports, National Archives, Microfilm M861, Box 488, (hereafter cited as unit reports, 1st Texas Cavalry).

9. William Kuykendall, Civil War diary, Kuykendall Family Papers, 1822–1891 (hereafter cited as Kuykendall Diary), 17; unit reports, 1st Texas Cavalry; *ORA*, series 1, vol. 26, pt. 2, 564.

10. Frank E. Vandiver, ed., "Letters from the Confederate Medical Service, 1863–1865," 381–82.

11. Ibid., 384.

12. Joseph E. Chance, *From Shiloh to Vicksburg*, 141.

13. *ORN*, series 1, vol. 21, 24, 48–51; Edwin B. Lufkin, *History of the Thirteenth Maine Regiment*, 68–69.

14. Lufkin, *History of the Thirteenth Maine Regiment*, 69.

15. Shorey, *Maine Fifteenth*, 68.

16. Diary entry of Thomas J. Noakes, Dec. 29, 1863 (hereafter cited as Noakes Diary); John S. Ford, *Rip Ford's Texas*, 346–50.

17. Maj. William R. Thompson to his wife, Jan. 11 and 25, 1864, unpublished letters of Maj. William R. Thompson (hereafter cited as Thompson Letters); *Corpus Christi Caller Times*, July 16, 1961.

18. Minetta Goyne, *Lone Star and Double Eagle*, 119; Bill Winsor, *Texas in the Confederacy*, 136; *ORN*, series 1, vol. 21, 74–76; muster rolls of the 2nd Texas

Infantry stationed at Camp Sidney Johnston, Jan. and Feb. 1864, National Archives (M861, roll #59).

19. Capt. E. P. Turner to Gen. Hamilton Bee, Feb. 17, 1864, military order book, Ashbel Smith Papers; Gen. Hamilton Bee to Col. Ashbel Smith, Feb. 18 and 20, 1864, Hamilton Bee Papers.

20. *ORA*, series 1, vol. 34, pt. 1, 135–36; Winsor, *Texas in the Confederacy*, 134.

21. Bruce S. Cheeseman, "'Let us have 500 good determined Texans,'" 81–83.

22. Jacob C. Switzer, "Reminiscences of Jacob Switzer of the 22nd Iowa," 44–45; Brownson Malsch, *Indianola*, 176–77; *ORA*, series 1, vol. 34, pt. 1, 150–51; George Crooke, *Twenty-first Regiment of Iowa Volunteer Infantry*, 125.

23. Switzer, "Reminiscences," 45.

24. Joseph T. Woods, *Services of the 96th Ohio Volunteers*, 50–51; Malsch, *Indianola*, 178–80; Johnson, *Red River Campaign*, 89–95.

25. Switzer, "Reminiscences," 45–46; Malsch, *Indianola*, 180; *ORA*, series 1, vol. 34, pt. 2, 1058, 1097; Ralph A. Wooster, *Texas and Texans in the Civil War*, 135.

26. John Salmon Ford, *Memoirs and Reminiscences of Texas History from 1836–1888*, vol. 5, 1027; *San Antonio Weekly Herald*, Mar. 19, 1864; *ORA*, series 1, vol. 34, pt. 1, 638–39, 653.

27. *ORA*, series 1, vol. 34, pt. 1, 543–44.

28. Maj. William R. Thompson to his wife, Mar. 22, 1864, Thompson Letters; *ORA*, series 1, vol. 34, pt. 1, 543–44, 653.

29. *Texas State Gazette*, Mar. 23 and Apr. 6, 1864; *ORA*, series 1, vol. 34, pt. 1, 543–45.

30. Maj. William R. Thompson to his wife, May 7, 1864, Thompson Letters.

31. Rebecca W. Smith and Marion Mullins, eds., "Diary of H. C. Medford, Confederate Soldier, 1864," 121–23; Alwyn Barr, "'Queen City of the Gulf' Held Hostage," 124–25.

32. Casdorph, *Prince John Magruder*, 279; *ORA*, series 1, vol. 34, pt. 1, 652–53.

33. S. C. Jones, *Reminiscences of the Twenty-second Iowa Volunteer Infantry*, 64; Switzer, "Reminiscences," 46; *ORA*, series 1, vol. 34, pt. 1, 885–86.

34. Alwyn Barr, "Texas Coastal Defense, 1861–1865," 29; Casdorph, *Prince John Magruder*, 279; *ORA*, series 1, vol. 34, pt. 3, 779, 833–34.

35. Marmion, *Texas Soldier and Marine*, 25; *ORA*, series 1, vol. 34, pt. 1, 189, 1011; *ORA*, series 1, vol. 34, pt. 4, 686.

36. *ORA*, series 1, vol. 34, pt. 2, 278–80.

37. Gilbert D. Kingsbury to the editor of the *New York Herald*, Mar. 1, 1864, Gilbert D. Kingsbury Papers, 1855–1874.

38. Diary entries of Thomas H. DuVal, Feb. 23 and 29, 1864, Diaries of Thomas H. DuVal, 1857–1879.

39. *ORA*, series 1, vol. 34, pt. 2, 278–80; Malsch, *Indianola*, 287.

40. Jones, *Reminiscences of the Twenty-second Iowa*, 62; Winsor, *Texas in the Confederacy*, 135; *ORA*, series 1, vol. 34, pt. 3, 804.

41. Edward Gee Miller, *Captain Edward Gee Miller of the 20th Wisconsin*, 22; Tilley, *Federals on the Frontier*, 355–60; Jerry Don Thompson, *Vaqueros in Blue and Gray*, 81–89.

42. Thompson, *Vaqueros in Blue and Gray*, 91–92.

43. Miller, *Captain Edward Gee Miller of the 20th Wisconsin*, 22; Tilley, *Federals on the Frontier*, 355–56; Thompson, *Vaqueros in Blue and Gray*, 90–91; Robert I. Alotta, *Civil War Justice*, 115, 205; list of soldiers executed by U.S. military authorities during the late war, 8–9, National Archives (M1523, roll #1); muster roll, Company E, 1st Texas Cavalry, compiled service records of volunteer Union soldiers who served in organizations from the state of Texas, National Archives (M402, roll #3, frame 889).

44. Tilley, *Federals on the Frontier*; Miller, *Captain Edward Gee Miller of the 20th Wisconsin*, 22; Allan C. Ashcraft, "Union Occupation of the Lower Rio Grande Valley during the Civil War," 18–19.

45. Harold B. Simpson, ed., and Marcus J. Wright, comp., *Texas in the Civil War, 1861–1865*, 163; Robert Hoekstra, "Historical Study of the Texas Ports during the Civil War," 90; Milo Kearney and Anthony Knopp, *Boom and Bust*, 126; *ORA*, series 1, vol. 36, pt. 1, 447–49.

46. *ORA*, series 1, vol. 36, pt. 1, 449; Thompson, *Vaqueros in Blue and Gray*, 75; Jerry Don Thompson, "Mutiny and Desertion on the Rio Grande, 160–67.

47. Wright, *Texas in the War*, 163; *ORA*, series 1, vol. 36, pt. 1, 449; Thompson, *Vaqueros in Blue and Gray*, 72–75; Kearney and Knopp, *Boom and Bust*, 126.

48. *ORA*, series 1, vol. 34, pt. 4, 685; Thompson, *Vaqueros in Blue and Gray*, 77–78.

49. Frank H. Smyrl, "Texans in the Union Army, 1861–1865," 240; Thompson, *Vaqueros in Blue and Gray*, 78–79.

50. Silas I. Shearer, *Dear Companion*, 65–66.

51. Ashcraft, "Union Occupation of the Lower Rio Grande Valley," 17; Miller, *Captain Edward Gee Miller of the 20th Wisconsin*, 22; Tilley, *Federals on the Frontier*, 357.

52. Basler, *CWAL*, vol. 7, 192–93; Tilley, *Federals on the Frontier*, 320–25; General Banks to General Halleck, Mar. 6, 1864, Nathaniel P. Banks Papers (M786.26, roll #26A).

53. Leonard Pierce to William Seward, Jan. 16, 1864, U.S. State Department, consular dispatches, Matamoros, vol. 7, consular correspondence, 150–51; Simeon Barnett, *History of the Twenty-second Regiment Iowa Volunteer Infantry*, 14; Chester Barney, *Recollections of Field Service with the Twentieth Iowa Infantry Volunteers*, 266–73; James M. Beverly, *History of the Ninety-first Regiment Illinois Infantry, 1862–1865*, 27; John A. Bering, *Forty-eighth Ohio Veteran Volunteer Infantry*, 116; Miller, *Captain Edward Gee Miller of the 20th Wisconsin*, 21.

54. *Loyal National Union Journal*, Mar. 12 and May 21, 1864 (hereafter cited as *Union Journal*), Thompson, *Vaqueros in Blue and Gray*, 84–93; *New Orleans True Delta*, Feb. 17, 1864; *Houston Tri-Weekly Telegraph*, Mar. 4, 1864.

55. James S. Clark, *Life in the Middle West*, 107–108; J. T. Woods, *Services of the 96th Ohio Volunteers*, 50–51; Bering, *Forty-eighth Ohio*, 116.

56. W. H. Bentley, *History of the 77th Illinois Volunteer Infantry*, 240–41.

57. Barney, *Recollections of Field Service*, 282; Bering, *Forty-eighth Ohio*, 116.

58. Albert O. Marshall, *Army Life*, 349–51; Bell I. Wiley, *Life of Billy Yank*, 179–83; James Marten, "For the Army, the People, and Abraham Lincoln," 131.

59. *Union Journal*, Mar. 5, 1864; Marten, "For the Army," 132. The *New Orleans Times*, which copied some of the articles from the *Union Journal*, commented on the newspaper's long name but also pointed out that the *Indianola Horn* would contest its claim to being the first loyal paper in Texas. See also Jacob D. Brewster to Louisa Brewster, Dec. 31, 1863, Brewster Papers.

60. *Union Journal*, Mar. 5, 1864.

61. Ibid., Mar. 5, 12, 19; Apr. 26, and May 2, 9, and 21, 1864; Marten, "For the Army," 133.

62. *Union Journal*, Mar. 5 and 12, May 21, 1864.

63. Ibid., Mar. 5, 1864.

64. Ibid., Mar. 19, 1864.

65. Ibid.; muster rolls of the 94th Illinois Volunteer Infantry Regiment stationed at Brownsville, Texas, dated April 1864, National Archives (M594, roll #28).

66. Attached to the Rio Grande expedition were the 1st Engineers and 16th Infantry of the Corps d'Afrique. A private in the 37th Illinois, describing the November landing of his regiment on Brazos Santiago, commented on the actions of black troops during the process. The private observed them and commented that the men were "waist, and often neck deep" as they struggled to carry equipment and supplies through the rough surf. The private noted that "the scales dropped from the eyes of some of the most rabid nigger-haters, and they had to acknowledge that a negro was just as good for soldiering" (Michael A. Mullins, *Fremont Rifles*, 239–40).

67. *Union Journal*, Mar. 12 and 26, 1864; Marten, "For the Army," 135.

68. *Union Journal*, Mar. 12 and 19, Apr. 9, and May 21, 1864.

69. *Union Journal*, Mar. 12 and 19, Apr. 9, and May 7, 1864; Frank H. Smyrl, "Texans in the Union Army, 1861–1865," 234–50.

70. *Union Journal*, Mar. 19, 1864.

71. Diary entry of Thomas H. DuVal, Mar. 5, 1864, Diaries of Thomas H. DuVal. By March 1864 DuVal had become exasperated at the lack of offensive action in Texas by Federal forces. This diary passage clearly shows that continuing frustration.

72. Harrington, *Fighting Politician*, 159–60; *ORA*, series 1, vol. 34, pt. 4, 610; Max L. Heyman Jr., *Prudent Soldier*, 206; *New Orleans Times*, May 18, 1864.

73. Thomas H. DuVal to James Guthrie, May 30, 1864, Diaries of Thomas H. DuVal.

CHAPTER 5

1. John Salmon Ford, *Memoirs and Reminiscences of Texas History from 1836 to 1888*, vol. 5, 1007–1008 (hereafter cited as *Memoirs*); Bruce S. Cheeseman, "'Let us have 500 good determined Texans,'" 86; James Irby, *Backdoor at Bagdad*, 30; U.S. War Department, *War of the Rebellion*, series 1, vol. 36, pt. 2, 525–35 (hereafter cited as *ORA*).

2. William John Hughes, *Rebellious Ranger*, 243–45; Stephen B. Oates, "John S. 'Rip' Ford," 290–91.

3. *Austin State Gazette,* Dec. 23, 1863. The man the article referred to was probably Henry Clay Davis, founder of Rio Grande City and a resident of Roma. San Antonio resident Mary Maverick wrote a letter to her son Lewis in which she stated that "H. Clay Davis an old friend of ours and resident at Roma passed thro [sic] here to Austin to get Ford to go down and join Benavides on the Rio Grande." Mary Maverick to Lewis Maverick, Dec. 13, 1863, Maverick Family Papers, Center for American History (hereafter cited as Maverick Family Papers).

4. Ford, *Memoirs,* vol. 5, 1010, 1035; Oates, "John S. Ford," 299; *ORA,* series 1, vol. 26, pt. 2, 525-26.

5. Ford, *Memoirs,* vol. 6, 11; John Salmon Ford, *Rip Ford's Texas,* 344. The "mongrel force of abolitionists, negroes, plundering Mexicans, and perfidious renegades" Ford referred to was the column that invaded Brownsville, which included two black regiments and the 1st Texas Cavalry, led by Edmund J. Davis. This regiment contained Mexicans and Texas Unionists, including Davis (T. R. Fehrenbach, *Lone Star,* 378).

6. Ford, *Memoirs,* vol. 6, 11; Ford, *Rip Ford's Texas,* 344; *ORA,* series 1, vol. 36, pt. 2, 540-41; Jerry Don Thompson, *Vaqueros in Blue and Gray,* 102; *Austin State Gazette,* Dec. 23, 1863.

7. Ford, *Rip Ford's Texas,* 346; Hughes, *Rebellious Ranger,* 213; *ORA,* series 1, vol. 26, pt. 1, 529-31; Ralph A. Wooster, *Lone Star Regiments in Gray,* 210-11.

8. Oates, "John S. Ford," 299; Fehrenbach, *Lone Star,* 378; Hughes, *Rebellious Ranger,* 213; *ORA,* series 1, vol. 26, pt. 1, 525-26.

9. Orders from Col. John S. Ford to Col. Santos Benavides, San Antonio, Dec. 28, 1863, Military Correspondence Collection (hereafter cited as Military Correspondence); Ford, *Memoirs,* vol. 6, 1039-42; *ORA,* series 1, vol. 53, pt. 1, 922.

10. Richard King to Col. John S. Ford, San Patricio, Texas, Jan. 30, 1864, Military Correspondence; Irby, *Backdoor at Bagdad,* 31; Hughes, *Rebellious Ranger,* 215.

11. *San Antonio Weekly Herald,* Mar. 19, 1864; Ford, *Memoirs,* vol. 6, 11-12; *ORA,* series 1, vol. 34, pt. 2, 946-47, 1074-75.

12. Ford, *Memoirs,* vol. 6, 1036; Fehrenbach, *Lone Star,* 378-79; Hughes, *Rebellious Ranger,* 215; *ORA,* series 1, vol. 34, pt. 2, 961-62. Although Ford was always addressed as "Colonel," he was never commissioned by the Confederate War Department with that rank. For some reason, he twice refused to hold regimental elections that would have made him a colonel. Nevertheless, he claimed the rank of colonel of cavalry, C.S.A., throughout the war, and his superiors recognized him as such (Ford, *Rip Ford's Texas,* 346).

13. *Houston Daily Telegraph,* Feb. 13, 1864; Ford, *Rip Ford's Texas,* 352; Fehrenbach, *Lone Star,* 379; Hughes, *Rebellious Ranger,* 216; Ralph A. Wooster, *Texas and Texans in the Civil War,* 136.

14. Mary Maverick to Lewis Maverick, Jan. 15 and Feb. 2, 1864, Maverick Family Papers.

15. Ibid., Feb. 7, 1864.

16. B. F. Dye to Lewis Maverick, Mar. 4, 1864; Mary Maverick to Lewis Maverick, Mar. 6 and 13, 1864, both in Maverick Family Papers.

17. Ford, *Rip Ford's Texas*, 350; Irby, *Backdoor at Bagdad*, 32; Fehrenbach, *Lone Star*, 379.

18. Oates, "John S. Ford," 300; Fehrenbach, *Lone Star*, 378; Ford, *Rip Ford's Texas*, 349; Wooster, *Texas and Texans*, 136.

19. Jerry Don Thompson, "Santos Benavides and the Battle for Laredo"; Wooster, *Texas and Texans*, 136; Joseph B. Wilkinson, *Laredo and the Rio Grande Frontier*, 295–96; *ORA*, series 1, vol. 34, pt. 1, 647–49.

20. Wilkinson, *Laredo and the Rio Grande Frontier*, 295–96; Thompson, "Battle for Laredo," 30; Wooster, *Texas and Texans*, 136; Ford, *Rip Ford's Texas*, 355–56.

21. Gilberto M. Hinojosa, *Borderlands Town in Transition, Laredo, 1755–1870*, 85–86; *ORA*, series 1, vol. 34, pt. 1, 649.

22. Oates, "John S. Ford," 300; Wilkinson, *Laredo and the Rio Grande Frontier*, 296; Hinojosa, *Borderlands Town*, 86; *ORA*, series 1, vol. 34, pt. 1, 649.

23. Ford, *Memoirs*, vol. 6, 13–14; Wooster, *Texas and Texans*, 136; Wilkinson, *Laredo and the Rio Grande Frontier*, 296; Wooster, *Regiments in Gray*, 222–23.

24. Ford, *Rip Ford's Texas*, 357; Thompson, "Battle for Laredo," 33.

25. James A. Irby, "Line of the Rio Grande," 152; Ford, *Memoirs*, vol. 6, 1036–40; Brian Robertson, *Wild Horse Desert*, 119; Fehrenbach, *Lone Star*, 379–80; Ford, *Rip Ford's Texas*, 358.

26. Wooster, *Texas and Texans*, 136; Hughes, *Rebellious Ranger*, 220–21; Ford, *Rip Ford's Texas*, 362–63; *ORA*, series 1, vol. 34, pt. 3, 176.

27. Tilley, *Federals on the Frontier*, 329; Ford, *Rip Ford's Texas*, 360; Robertson, *Wild Hose Desert*, 119; Irby, *Backdoor at Bagdad*, 33; Fehrenbach, *Lone Star*, 383.

28. Tilley, *Federals on the Frontier*, 332.

29. Col. J. M. Swisher to Col. John S. Ford, Matamoros, Mexico, May 25 and June 10, 1864, Military Correspondence; Fehrenbach, *Lone Star*, 383–84; Ford, *Rip Ford's Texas*, 361; Hughes, *Rebellious Ranger*, 218–19.

30. Ford, *Rip Ford's Texas*, 361–62; Fehrenbach, *Lone Star*, 384.

31. Agent #2 to Col. John S. Ford, Matamoros, Mexico, June 21, 1864, Military Correspondence.

32. Ford, *Rip Ford's Texas*, 362; *ORA*, series 1, vol. 53, pt. 1, 1001.

33. Ford, *Memoirs*, vol. 5, 1013; Tom Lea, *King Ranch*, vol. 1, 225; Irby, *Backdoor at Bagdad*, 30; *ORA*, series 1, vol. 34, pt. 1, 1053.

34. Frank C. Pierce, *Brief History of the Lower Rio Grande Valley*, 48–49; Ford, *Memoirs*, vol. 5, 1014; Robertson, *Wild Horse Desert*, 120.

35. *ORA*, series 1, vol. 34, pt. 1, 1053–56; Thompson, *Vaqueros in Blue and Gray*, 114–15; Ford, *Rip Ford's Texas*, 362–63; Hughes, *Rebellious Ranger*, 220; Tilley, *Federals on the Frontier*, 358.

36. Robert Hoekstra, "Historical Study of the Texas Ports in the Civil War," 96; Irby, "Line of the Rio Grande," 160–61; Pierce, *Brief History*, 49; Tilley, *Federals on the Frontier*, 358; Ford, *Rip Ford's Texas*, 362–63; Milo Kearney and Anthony Knopp, *Boom and Bust*, 133.

37. Kearney and Knopp, *Boom and Bust*, 133; Ford, *Memoirs*, vol. 6, 1080–85; Wooster, *Texas and Texans*, 136; *Austin Weekly State Gazette*, June 29, 1864; *ORA*, series 1, vol. 34, pt. 1, 1054–56.

38. Ford, *Memoirs*, vol. 6, 1009, 1102; *ORA*, series 1, vol. 41, pt. 2, 1001; Robertson, *Wild Horse Desert*, 120–21.

39. Allen C. Ashcraft, "Union Occupation of the Lower Rio Grande Valley in the Civil War," 18–19; Tilley, *Federals on the Frontier*, 360–61; Daddysman, *Matamoros Trade*, 98–99.

40. Agent #2 to Col. John S. Ford, July 5, 1864, Matamoros, Mexico, Military Correspondence; *ORA*, series 1, vol. 41, pt. 2, 46.

41. Agent #2 to Col. John S. Ford, July 15, 1864, Matamoros, Mexico; Military Correspondence; Irby, *Backdoor at Bagdad*, 36.

42. Edward Gee Miller, *Captain Edward Gee Miller of the 20th Wisconsin*, 23; Ford, *Memoirs*, vol. 6, 1009, 1102; *ORA*, series 1, vol. 41, pt. 2, 1001; Keith Guthrie, *Texas' Forgotten Ports*, vol. 2, 240; Hughes, *Rebellious Ranger*, 221–22; Kearney and Knopp, *Boom and Bust*, 136.

43. Quoted in Tilley, *Federals on the Frontier*, 371–72.

44. *ORA*, series 1, vol. 41, pt. 2, 352–53; Tilley, *Federals on the Frontier*, 372.

45. Report by Maj. E. W. Cave to Col. John S. Ford, Brownsville, Texas, July 31, 1864, Military Correspondence; Guthrie, *Texas' Forgotten Ports*, 240; Walter W. Hildebrand, "History of Cameron County, Texas," 49; Margaret Petrovich, "Civil War Career of Colonel John Salmon 'RIP' Ford," 90; muster rolls of the 91st and 94th Illinois Volunteer Infantry Regiments stationed at Boca Chica, Texas, and Mobile Point, Alabama, respectively; both rolls dated July–Aug. 1864 (M594, roll #28).

46. *ORA*, series 1, vol. 41, pt. 2, 989; Petrovich, "Civil War Career, Ford," 91; Kearney and Knopp, *Boom and Bust*, 134; LeRoy P. Graf, "Economic History of the Lower Rio Grande Valley, 1820–1875," 593.

47. Ford, *Rip Ford's Texas*, 365–68; Graf, "Economic History," 593–94; Lillian Stambaugh and J. Lee Stambaugh, *Lower Rio Grande Valley of Texas*, 119–20; Wilkinson, *Laredo and the Rio Grande Frontier*, 298; Thompson, *Vaqueros in Blue and Gray*, 118; Tilley, *Federals on the Frontier*, 371.

48. *ORA*, series 1, vol. 41, pt. 2, 46; Kerby, *Kirby Smith's Confederacy*, 194–95.

49. Kearney and Knopp, *Boom and Bust*, 134–35.

CHAPTER 6

1. Phillip Sheridan, *Personal Memoirs of P. H. Sheridan*, vol. 2, 210.

2. Kevin R. Young, *To the Tyrants Never Yield*, 150; Gabriel Saldivar, *Historia compendiada de Tamaulipas*, 314–15. For more information on the French occupation, see Alfred J. Hanna and Kathryn T. Hanna, *Napoleon and Mexico*.

3. U.S. War Department, *War of the Rebellion*, series 1, vol. 41, pt. 4, 366, 449, 978 (hereafter cited as *ORA*); James M. Beverly, *History of the Ninety-first Regiment Illinois Volunteer Infantry, 1862–1865*, 12.

4. Col. John S. Ford to Capt. J. E. Dwyer, acting adjutant general, Brownsville, Texas, Sept. 3, 1864, John S. Ford, Military Correspondence Collection (hereafter cited as Military Correspondence); Brian Robertson, *Wild Horse Desert*, 98–106; Jerry Don Thompson, *Juan Cortina and the Texas-Mexico Frontier, 1859–1877*, 49.

5. *ORA*, series 1, vol. 26, pt. 1, 882–85; Frank C. Pierce, *Brief History of the Lower Rio Grande Valley*, 44–45.

6. Capt. A. Veron, Corps expeditionnaire de la marine français a Bagdad, Aug. 25, 1864, John S. Ford, Military Correspondence; *Austin State Gazette*, Sept. 7, 1864; Leonard Pierce to William Seward, Sept. 1, 1864, U.S. State Department, consular dispatches, Matamoros, vol. 7; Hubert H. Bancroft, *History of the North Mexican States and Texas*, vol. 2, 468; *ORA*, series 1, vol. 41, pt. 2, 1088-89.

7. Gen. Juan N. Cortina to Col. John S. Ford, Matamoros, Mexico, Sept. 8, 1864, and Col. John S. Ford to Gen. J. N. Cortina, Brownsville, Texas, Sept. 8, 1864, Military Correspondence; William J. Hughes, *Rebellious Ranger*, 225-26; Richard T. Marcum, "Fort Brown, Texas," 171; *Austin State Gazette*, Sept. 28, 1864.

8. Leonard Pierce to William Seward, Sept. 1, 1864, U.S. State Department, consular dispatches, Matamoros, vol. 7; Milo Kearney and Alfred Knopp, *Boom and Bust*, 135-36; U.S. Navy Department, *Official Records of the Union and Confederate Navies in the War of the Rebellion*, series 1, vol. 21, 652-53; James A. Irby, "Line of the Rio Grande," 177-78; *ORA*, series 1, vol. 41, pt. 3, 102; Margaret W. Petrovich, "Civil War Career of Col. John Salmon 'RIP' Ford," 123-26.

9. John Salmon Ford, *Memoirs and Reminiscences of Texas from 1836-1888*, vol. 5, 1023 (hereafter cited as *Memoirs*); Kearney and Knopp, *Boom and Bust*, 136; *ORA*, series 1, vol. 41, pt. 1, 742; Stephen B. Oates, "John S. 'Rip' Ford, Prudent Cavalryman, C.S.A," 306; Hughes, *Rebellious Ranger*, 227; Petrovich, "Civil War Career, Ford," 123-26, 129. Although the ranch's name was often spelled "Palmetto" in many official battle reports, local usage favored the spelling "Palmito." The Texas Historical Commission also used that spelling in its historical marker near Brownsville.

10. Lillian J. Stambaugh and J. Lee Stambaugh, *Lower Rio Grande Valley of Texas*, 120; Robertson, *Wild Horse Desert*, 122; Kearney and Knopp, *Boom and Bust*, 136.

11. *San Antonio News*, Sept. 3, 1864; Ford, *Memoirs*, vol. 5, 1026; Col. John S. Ford to Capt. A. Veron, Brownsville, Texas, Sept. 6, 1864, Military Correspondence; Oates, "John S. Ford," 307; *ORA*, series 1, vol. 41, pt. 2, 972.

12. Official statement of the officers who defied General Cortina to Col. John S. Ford, Brownsville, Texas, Oct. 4, 1864, Military Correspondence; Kearney and Knopp, *Boom and Bust*, 136; Marcum, "Fort Brown, Texas," 171-73; John S. Ford, *Rip Ford's Texas*, 371; Joseph B. Wilkinson, *Laredo and the Rio Grande Frontier*, 298-99.

13. *ORA*, series 1, vol. 41, pt. 3, 100-101.

14. Robert Hoekstra, "Historical Study of the Texas Ports during the Civil War," 97-98; Ford, *Memoirs*, vol. 6, 1137; Young, *To the Tyrants Never Yield*, 158; *ORA*, series 1, vol. 41, pt. 3, 184-85; Beverly, *History of the Ninety-first Illinois*, 12.

15. *ORA*, series 1, vol. 41, pt. 3, 184-85, 198.

16. Col. John S. Ford to Capt. A. Veron, Brownsville, Texas, Sept. 8, 1864, Military Correspondence; Ford, *Rip Ford's Texas*, 373.

17. Col. John S. Ford to Capt. A. Veron, Brownsville, Texas, Sept. 13, 1864, Military Correspondence; Ford, *Memoirs*, vol. 5, 1028-29; Petrovich, "Civil War Career, Ford," 124-29; Fehrenbach, *Lone Star*, 386-87.

18. *Austin State Gazette*, Oct. 12, 1864; Young, *To the Tyrants Never Yield*, 158; Oates, "John S. Ford," 309; Ford, *Memoirs*, vol. 6, 1143-44; Kearney and

Knopp, *Boom and Bust*, 136–37; *ORA*, series 1, vol. 41, pt. 3, 722; Marcum, "Fort Brown, Texas," 171–73.

19. *ORN*, series 1, vol. 21, 652–53; *Dallas Times Herald*, Oct. 15, 1864; *ORA*, series 1, vol. 41, pt. 3, 722; Ford, *Rip Ford's Texas*, 403, Fehrenbach, *Lone Star*, 388; Daddysman, *Matamoros Trade*, 182; Kearney and Knopp, *Boom and Bust*, 136–37.

20. *ORA*, series 1, vol. 41, pt. 1, 888; Kearney and Knopp, *Boom and Bust*, 137; Daddysman, *Matamoros Trade*, 182.

21. *ORA*, series 1, vol. 41, pt. 4, 366, 449.

22. Ibid., 555, 675, 746.

23. Stephen B. Oates, *Visions of Glory*, 134–35; Paul D. Casdorph, *Prince John Magruder*, 282–83; *ORA*, series 1, vol. 34, pt. 2, 868–70; Robert L. Kerby, *Kirby Smith's Confederacy*, 334.

24. Joseph Blessington, *Campaigns of Walker's Texas Division*, 73–74; Oates, *Visions of Glory*, 135; Casdorph, *Prince John Magruder*, 282.

25. John P. Felgar, "Texas in the War for Southern Independence," 198; Ford, *Rip Ford's Texas*, 386; Hughes, *Rebellious Ranger*, 231–32; Wilkinson, *Rio Grande Frontier*, 300.

26. Ford, *Rip Ford's Texas*, 386–87; Wilkinson, *Rio Grande Frontier*, 300.

27. *ORA*, series 1, vol. 41, pt. 4, 768; Ford, *Rip Ford's Texas*, 386–87.

28. *ORA*, series 1, vol. 41, pt. 4, 768.

29. James A. Irby, "Line of the Rio Grande," 189; Young, *To the Tyrants Never Yield*, 158; *ORA*, series 1, vol. 41, pt. 4, 978.

30. *Houston Tri-Weekly Telegraph*, Dec. 9, 12, and 16, 1864; Charles D. Dillman, "Functions of Brownsville, Texas, and Matamoros, Tamaulipas," 66; LeRoy P. Graf, "Economic History of the Lower Rio Grande Valley, 1820–1875," 594–95.

31. Ford, *Rip Ford's Texas*, 387; *Austin State Gazette*, Sept. 28, 1864; Kerby, *Kirby Smith's Confederacy*, 371; Kearney and Knopp, *Boom and Bust*, 138; Petrovich, "Civil War Career, Ford," 135.

32. J. Fred Rippy, "Mexican Projects of the Confederates," 308–309; Alfred J. Hanna and Kathryn T. Hanna, *Napoleon III and Mexico*, 164; Lew Wallace, *Lew Wallace*, 812.

33. Irving McKee, *Ben-Hur Wallace*, 90; Wallace, *Autobiography*, 812–13; Ezra Warner, *Generals in Blue*, 535–36.

34. Wallace, *Autobiography*, 812–13; McKee, *Ben-Hur Wallace*, 91.

35. Rippy, "Mexican Projects," 296–97; Irby, "Line of the Rio Grande," 198; Wallace, *Autobiography*, 813–14; *ORA*, series 1, vol. 46, pt. 2, 201; McKee, *Ben-Hur Wallace*, 91.

36. Rippy, "Mexican Projects," 295–96; Jefferson Davis, *Rise and Fall of the Confederate Government*, 614–17.

37. Wallace, *Autobiography*, 820–21, 828; Ford, *Rip Ford's Texas*, 388; McKee, *Ben-Hur Wallace*, 93; Rippy, "Mexican Projects," 297; Petrovich, "Civil War Career, Ford," 144; Ford, *Memoirs*, vol. 6, 1030–31; *ORA*, series 1, vol. 48, pt. 1, 1276–79; Hughes, *Rebellious Ranger*, 233.

38. Wallace, *Autobiography*, 828–30; Ford, *Rip Ford's Texas*, 388; Irby, "Line of the Rio Grande," 198–99, Kearney and Knopp, *Boom and Bust*, 138; Hughes, *Rebellious Ranger*, 234.

39. Wallace, *Autobiography*, 821–22; Ford, *Rip Ford's Texas*, 389; Hughes, *Rebellious Ranger*, 235; *Houston Post*, June 25, 1922; *ORA*, series 1, vol. 48, pt. 1, 1167, 1277–79; Oates, "John S. Ford," 310.

40. McKee, *Ben-Hur Wallace*, 94; Irby, "Line of the Rio Grande," 199–200; Hughes, *Rebellious Ranger*, 236; Wallace, *Autobiography*, 831–32; Rippy, "Mexican Projects," 297.

41. Wallace, *Autobiography*, 832–37; Ford, *Memoirs*, vol. 7, 1181; T. R. Fehrenbach, *Lone Star*, 388; Irby, "Line of the Rio Grande," 200; Ralph A. Wooster, *Texas and Texans in the Civil War*, 172.

42. Ford, *Memoirs*, vol. 7, 1181; *ORA*, series 1, vol. 48, pt. 2, 457–58; Hughes, *Rebellious Ranger*, 236; Wallace, *Autobiography*, 834–35.

43. Rippy, "Mexican Projects," 297; Wallace, *Autobiography*, 835–36; *ORA*, series 1, vol. 48, pt. 2, 120–22.

44. *ORA*, series 1, vol. 48, pt. 2, 463; Wallace, *Autobiography*, 834.

45. *Shreveport Semi-Weekly News*, Apr. 22, 1865; Wallace, *Autobiography*, 840–41; *ORA*, series 1, vol. 48, pt. 2, 122, 1283; Joseph H. Parks, *General Edmund Kirby Smith, C.S.A.*, 456.

46. Ford, *Memoirs*, vol. 7, 1174–81, 1185–86, 1189.

47. Ibid.

CHAPTER 7

1. John S. Ford, *Memoirs and Reminiscences of Texas History from 1836–1888*, vol. 7, 1178–89 (hereafter cited as *Memoirs*); T. R. Fehrenbach, *Lone Star*, 388–89; Ralph A. Wooster, *Texas and Texans in the Civil War*, 172; James A. Irby, "Line of the Rio Grande," 201.

2. W. Buck Yearns, ed., *Confederate Governors*, 214; *Shreveport Semi-Weekly News*, Apr. 22, 1865; Joseph H. Parks, *General Edmund Kirby Smith, C.S.A.*, 456–59; Wooster, *Texas and Texans*, 179; Emory Thomas, "Rebel Nationalism," 349; W. W. Heartsill, *Fourteen Hundred and 91 Days in the Confederate Army*, 239.

3. Parks, *Kirby Smith*, 457; John Q. Anderson, ed., *Brokenburn*, 347–48; William T. Windham, "Problem of Supply in the Trans-Mississippi Confederacy," 160–68.

4. Yearns, *Confederate Governors*, 106, 205; Wooster, *Texas and Texans*, 180; Parks, *Kirby Smith*, 468–69; Kevin R. Young, *To the Tyrants Never Yield*, 186; U.S. War Department, *War of the Rebellion*, series 1, vol. 48, pt. 1, 189 (hereafter cited as *ORA*).

5. Robert L. Kerby, *Kirby Smith's Confederacy*, 418–19; Parks, *Kirby Smith*, 468–70; *ORA*, series 1, vol. 48, pt. 1, 188–93; Paul D. Casdorph, *Prince John Magruder*, 294–95; Wooster, *Texas and Texans*, 180.

6. *New York Times*, June 18, 1865; Noah A. Trudeau, *Out of the Storm*, 298–310; William J. Hughes, *Rebellious Ranger*, 237; Wooster, *Texas and Texans*, 180; Young, *To the Tyrants Never Yield*, 190; Fehrenbach, *Lone Star*, 389; Jeffrey W. Hunt, *Last Battle of the Civil War*, 53–55.

7. *San Antonio Express*, Oct. 10, 1890; Melinda Rankin, *Twenty Years among the Mexicans*, 116–18; Irby, "Line of the Rio Grande," 194, 202.

8. Gary W. Gallagher, *Confederate War*, 85–89, 146–47.

9. Ford, *Memoirs*, vol. 5, 1031–33; *Houston Tri-Weekly Telegraph*, June 16, 1865; Leroy P. Graf, "Economic History of the Lower Rio Grande Valley," 600; Irby, "Line of the Rio Grande," 203–205.

10. Annual Circular of the 62nd Regiment, U.S. Colored Infantry, no. 6 (hereafter cited as Annual Circular no. 6); *ORA*, series 1, vol. 48, pt. 1, 267–68; Irby, "Line of the Rio Grande," 205; Wooster, *Texas and Texans*, 180; reports of Lt. Col. David Branson and Col. Theodore H. Barrett, 62nd U.S. Colored Troops (USCT), expedition from Brazos Santiago, Texas, May 18, 1865, Aug. 10, 1865, Regimental Books and Papers USCT, 62nd USCT Papers, Records of the Adjutant General's Office, 1780s–1917, National Archives (hereafter cited as 62nd USCT Papers).

11. Annual Circular no. 6; *ORA*, series 1, vol. 48, pt. 1, 267–68; Young, *To the Tyrants Never Yield*, 190; Stephen B. Oates, "John S. 'Rip' Ford, Prudent Cavalryman, C.S.A.," 310; 62nd USCT Papers.

12. John S. Ford, *Rip Ford's Texas*, 389; Annual Circular no. 6; *ORA*, series 1, vol. 48, pt. 1. 267–68; Margaret W. Petrovich, "Civil War Career of John Salmon 'RIP' Ford," 146–54; Walter W. Hildebrand, "History of Cameron County, Texas," 49; 62nd USCT Papers.

13. Ford, *Rip Ford's Texas*, 389–90; Oates, "John S. Ford," 311; Fehrenbach, *Lone Star*, 389; Milo Kearney and Anthony Knopp, *Boom and Bust*, 140; James H. Thompson, "Nineteenth-century History of Cameron County, Texas," 99.

14. Sixty-second USCT Papers; Ford, *Memoirs*, vol. 5, 1031–33; John H. Brown, *History of Texas from 1685 to 1892*, vol. 2, 436; *ORA*, series 1, vol. 48, pt. 1, 265–69; *New York Herald*, May 29, 1865; Frank C. Pierce, *Brief History of the Lower Rio Grande Valley*, 54.

15. *New York Times*, June 18, 1865; Col. Oran M. Roberts, *Confederate Military History*, 126–27; Brown, *History of Texas*, 432, 436; Ford, *Rip Ford's Texas*, 390; Young, *To the Tyrants Never Yield*, 194.

16. Sixty-second USCT Papers; Hondon B. Hargrove, *Black Union Soldiers in the Civil War*, 202; Irby, "Line of the Rio Grande," 207; *ORA*, series 1, vol. 48, pt. 1, 266–69; Roberts, *Confederate Military History*, 127; Ford, *Memoirs*, vol. 5, 1031–33; Oates, "John S. Ford," 312; Trudeau, *Like Men of War*, 447–50; Hughes, *Rebellious Ranger*, 239.

17. Roberts, *Confederate Military History*, 128; Ford, *Rip Ford's Texas*, 390–91; *New York Times*, June 18, 1865; Young, *To the Tyrants Never Yield*, 195; *San Antonio Express*, Oct. 10, 1890; *ORA*, series 1, vol. 48, pt. 1, 269; Trudeau, *Like Men of War*, 448–50; Irby, "Line of the Rio Grande," 208.

18. Ford, *Memoirs*, vol. 5, 1032–33; Brown, *History of Texas*, 431–36; *New York Times*, June 18, 1865; Roberts, *Confederate Military History*, 128–29; *San Antonio Express*, Oct. 10, 1890; Oates, "John S. Ford," 312–13; *ORA*, series 1, vol. 48, pt. 1, 267.

19. *New York Times*, June 18, 1865; Joseph T. Glatthaar, *Forged in Battle*, 202; Trudeau, *Like Men of War*, 451–52; Ford, *Memoirs*, vol. 7, 1197; Brown, *History of Texas*, 433–35; Hughes, *Rebellious Ranger*, 240.

20. Ford, *Memoirs*, vol. 7, 1197; *New York Times*, June 18, 1865; Irby, "Line of the Rio Grande," 210.

21. *National Tribune*, May 10, 1883; *ORA*, series 1, vol. 48, pt. 1, 267–69; Hargrove, *Black Union Soldiers*, 202; Trudeau, *Like Men of War*, 450–52.

22. *New York Times*, June 18, 1865; *San Antonio Express*, Oct. 10, 1890; Annual Circular no. 6; Ford, *Rip Ford's Texas*, 396.

23. Ford, *Rip Ford's Texas*, 396; *San Antonio Express*, Oct. 10, 1890; Hughes, *Rebellious Ranger*, 241; Roberts, *Confederate Military History*, 129; Wooster, *Texas and Texans*, 181.

24. *Supplement to the Official Records of the Union and Confederate Armies*, vol. 10, 131; Trudeau, *Like Men of War*, 451.

25. Mark M. Boatner, *Civil War Dictionary*, 90; Wooster, *Texas and Texans*, 181–83; *ORA*, series 1, vol. 48, pt. 2, 300; Young, *To the Tyrants Never Yield*, 195–97.

26. *ORA*, series 1, vol. 48, pt. 2, 381–83.

27. Ulysses S. Grant, *Papers of Ulysses S. Grant*, vol. 15, 43–45 (hereafter cited as *Papers of USG*); Philip H. Sheridan, *Personal Memoirs of P. H. Sheridan*, vol. 2, 210.

28. *ORA*, series 1, vol. 48, pt. 2, 564–65.

29. Ford, *Memoirs*, vol. 7, 1197–99.

30. B. P. Gallaway, ed., *Texas*, 255; Casdorph, *Prince John Magruder*, 295; Parks, *Kirby Smith*, 470; *ORA*, series 1, vol. 48, pt. 1, 189; *ORA*, series 1, vol. 48, pt. 2, 1293.

31. Casdorph, *Prince John Magruder*, 295–96; Parks, *Kirby Smith*, 472; Wooster, *Texas and Texans*, 182; Boatner, *Civil War Dictionary*, 118.

32. Parks, *Kirby Smith*, 472–73; *ORA*, series 1, vol. 48, pt. 2, 1038, 1313–14; Casdorph, *Prince John Magruder*, 296–97; Max L. Heyman, *Prudent Soldier*, 235; Charles W. Ramsdell, "Texas from the Fall of the Confederacy to the Beginning of Reconstruction," 205–207; Wooster, *Texas and Texans*, 182; John S. Bowman, ed., *Civil War Almanac*, 268–69.

33. *ORA*, series 1, vol. 48, pt. 1, 193–94; Parks, *Kirby Smith*, 474–76; *Galveston Tri-Weekly News*, June 5, 1865; Casdorph, *Prince John Magruder*, 297–98; Kerby, *Kirby Smith's Confederacy*, 425–26; *Papers of USG*, vol. 15, 60, 96–97; *Ten Texans in Gray*, 133.

34. Ford, *Memoirs*, vol. 7, 1212; *Houston Tri-Weekly Telegraph*, June 20, 1865; *Papers of USG*, vol. 15, 349; Sheridan, *Memoirs*, vol. 2, 211; *ORA*, series 1, vol. 48, pt. 2, 727–28.

35. John N. Edwards, *Shelby's Expedition to Mexico*, 17–18; Alexander W. Terrell, *From Texas to Mexico and the Court of Maximilian*, 3–10; Parks, *Kirby Smith*, 481–82; Daniel O. Flaherty, *General Jo Shelby*, 243–45; Boatner, *Civil War Dictionary*, 668, 918; W. C. Nunn, *Escape from Reconstruction*, 31–32.

36. *Papers of USG*, vol. 15, 147; Ford, *Memoirs*, vol. 7, 1211; *New York Times*, June 18, 1865; *Houston Tri-Weekly Telegraph*, June 16, 1865; James R. Crews, "Reconstruction in Brownsville," 61–64; Ford, *Rip Ford's Texas*, 401.

37. Sheridan, *Memoirs*, vol. 2, 213; Gallaway, *Dark Corner of the Confederacy*, 255; Alfred J. Hanna and Kathryn T. Hanna, *Napoleon III and Mexico*, 238; Trudeau, *Like Men of War*, 458; *Papers of USG*, vol. 15, 148.

38. *Papers of USG*, vol. 15, 156–57.

39. Sheridan, *Memoirs*, vol. 2, 214–15.

40. Ibid.; Carl C. Rister, *Border Command*, 18–19.

41. Hanna and Hanna, *Napoleon III and Mexico*, 238–39; Sheridan, *Memoirs*, vol. 2, 216–18, 223–26; Rister, *Border Command*, 19.

42. *Papers of USG*, vol. 15, 367.

43. Ibid., 367–68.

44. Ibid.; John C. Rayburn and Virginia K. Rayburn, *Century of Conflict, 1821–1913*, 93–98.

45. Sheridan, *Memoirs*, vol. 2, 219–21; Robert E. Morsberger and Katherine Morsberger, *Lew Wallace*, 195–98; Richard T. Marcum, "Fort Brown, Texas," 186; *Papers of USG*, vol. 15, 154.

46. Hanna and Hanna, *Napoleon III and Mexico*, 272, 300; Sheridan, *Memoirs*, vol. 2, 227–28.

CHAPTER 8

1. Kevin R. Young, *To the Tyrants Never Yield*, 150; Ronnie C. Tyler, "Cotton on the Border, 1861–1865," 477; Ludwell H. Johnson, *Red River Campaign*, 34; Ezra J. Warner, *Generals in Blue*, 17–18.

2. Fred H. Harrington, *Fighting Politician*, 133; General Halleck to General Banks, Sept. 30, 1863, Nathaniel P. Banks Papers; Kurt Hackemer, "Strategic Dilemma," 209–13; *ORA*, series 1, vol. 26, pt. 1, 834–35; William C. Harris, *With Charity for All*, 95; Johnson, *Red River Campaign*, 45.

3. Robert L. Kerby, *Kirby Smith's Confederacy*, 195; Basler, *CWAL*, vol. 5, 357; Harris, *With Charity for All*, 87–89; Frank H. Smyrl, "Texans in the Union Army, 1861–1865," 240; Sherrill L. Dickeson, "Texas Cotton Trade during the Civil War," 48–59.

4. Sioux, "From the Front," *Houston Tri-Weekly Telegraph*, Dec. 11, 1863; *Austin State Gazette*, Nov. 16, 20, and 25, and Dec. 2, 1863.

5. Rebecca W. Smith and Marion Mullins, eds., "The Diary of H. C. Medford, Confederate Soldier, 1864," *Southwestern Historical Quarterly* 34 (Oct. 1930): 117.

6. *Loyal National Union Journal*, Mar. 5 and 19, 1864.

7. *ORA*, series 1, vol. 34, pt. 2, 278–80; *ORA*, series 1, vol. 26, pt. 1, 849–60, 416–17; Col. Oran M. Roberts, *Confederate Military History*, 120; Hackemer, "Strategic Dilemma," 208.

8. William S. McFeeley, *Grant*, 157; James M. McPherson, *Battle Cry of Freedom*, 683; Harrington, *Fighting Politician*, 133, 152–53; *ORA*, series 1, vol. 34, pt. 1, 190; Johnson, *Red River Campaign*, 47; *ORA*, series 1, vol. 34, pt. 4, 686.

9. James G. Hollandsworth Jr., *Pretense of Glory*, 257; Hackemer, "Strategic Dilemma," 208–13; *ORA*, vol. 26, pt. 1, 14, 47, 416–17, 526–27, 546–49, 554–55, 849–60; *ORA*, vol. 34, pt. 2, 278–80; Harris, *With Charity for All*, 95; Johnson, *Red River Campaign*, 45; *U.S.-Mexican War* (Alexandria, Va.: PBS documentary, 1998–1999. 4 videocassettes).

10. Halleck, quoted in Hollandsworth, *Pretense of Glory*, 205–206, 257; Philip Sheridan, *Personal Memoirs of P. H. Sheridan*, vol. 2, 208; Gideon Welles,

Diary, vol. 2, 26; *ORA*, series 1, vol. 34, pt. 3, 244–46, 331–33, 408–409, 490–92; Ulysses S. Grant, *Papers of Ulysses S. Grant*, vol. 15, 43–45 (hereafter cited as *Papers of USG*); Brooks D. Simpson, *Ulysses S. Grant*, 314.

11. Basler, vol. 8, 121; Welles, *Diary*, vol. 2, 26; Johnson, *Red River Campaign*, 283–84.

12. *ORA*, series 1, vol. 34, pt. 1, 610–12; Johnson, *Red River Campaign*, 221–29; *Houston Tri-Weekly Telegraph*, May 2, 1864; Fredericka Meiners, "Hamilton Bee in the Red River Campaign," 23–38, 44; Kerby, *Kirby Smith's Confederacy*, 192; *ORA*, series 1, vol. 26, pt. 1, 399–401, 405.

13. Sheridan, *Memoirs*, vol. 2, 213–15, 223–26; *Papers of USG*, vol. 15, 148, 156–57.

14. Daddysman, *Matamoros Trade*, 187–89; Irby, *Backdoor at Bagdad*, 52; Windham, "Problem of Supply," 167.

15. Stephen A. Townsend, "Steamboating on the Lower Rio Grande River," 54–59.

BIBLIOGRAPHY

DOCUMENTS AND ARCHIVAL COLLECTIONS

Banks, Nathaniel P. Papers. Center for American History, University of Texas, Austin. Microfilm #786.26, roll 26A.

Bee, Hamilton P. Papers. Center for American History, University of Texas, Austin.

Black, Col. J. C. Correspondence. U.S. Military Institute, Carlisle, Pennsylvania.

Brewster, Jacob D. Papers. Center for American History, University of Texas, Austin.

Brown, Frank. "Annals of Travis County and of the City of Austin (from the Earliest Times to the Close of 1875)." 24 vols. Austin History Center, Austin Public Library, Austin, Texas.

Bryan, Guy M. Center for American History, University of Texas, Austin.

Duval, Thomas H. Diaries, 1857–1879. Center for American History, University of Texas, Austin.

Ford, John Salmon. *Memoirs and Reminiscences of Texas History from 1836 to 1888.* 8 vols. Center for American History, University of Texas, Austin.

———. Military Correspondence Collection. Daughters of the Confederacy Museum, Austin, Texas.

Hamilton, Andrew Jackson. Governor's Papers and Records. Record group 301. Texas State Archives, Austin, Texas.

Hunter, John W. "The Fall of Brownsville on the Rio Grande, November, 1863." Arnulfo L. Oliveira Memorial Library, University of Texas at Brownsville, Brownsville, Texas. [Typescript]. ·

Kingsbury, Gilbert D. Papers, 1855–1874. Center for American History, University of Texas, Austin.

Kuykendall, William. Kuykendall Family Papers, 1822–1891. Center for American History, University of Texas, Austin.

Maverick, Mary. Maverick Family Papers. Center for American History, University of Texas, Austin.

Merriman, Eli. Memoirs. Local History Room, La Retama Library, Corpus Christi, Texas. [Typescript].

Morgan, Jeff. Unpublished letters of Jeff Morgan, 35th Texas Cavalry Regiment. Confederate Research Center, Hillsboro, Texas.

National Archives. Compiled service records of volunteer Union soldiers who served in organizations from Texas (1st Cavalry Regiment, Companies E–G). Record group 94. Microfilm 402.

———. List of soldiers executed by U.S. military authorities during the late war. Proceedings of U.S. Army Courts Martial and Military Commissions of Union Soldiers Executed by Military Authorities, 1861–1866. Record group 94. Microfilm M1523. Washington, D.C.

———. Muster rolls and regimental papers (94th Illinois, 37th Illinois, 91st Illinois, 15th Maine, 13th Maine, 62nd USCT). Compiled records showing service of military units in volunteer Union organizations. Record group 94. Microfilm M594.

———. Muster rolls, morning reports, and regimental returns (2nd and 8th Texas Infantry, 1st Texas Cavalry). Compiled records showing service of military units in Confederate organizations. Record group 109. Microfilm M861, Box 488. Washington, D.C.

———. Petitions to the Southern Claims Commission (Francisco Solis, Nicholas Champion, Pauline Butler, Alvin Priest, Ramijo Garza). Cases filed for barred and disallowed claims, Records of the U.S. House. Record group 233. Microfiche M1407.

Noakes, Thomas J. Diary. Original copy. Local History Room, La Retama Library, Corpus Christi, Texas.

Oldham, Williamson S. Memoirs. Center for American History, University of Texas, Austin.

Smith, Ashbel. Papers. Correspondence and circulars, 1863–1865. Center for American History, University of Texas, Austin.

———. Military order book. Papers. Center for American History, University of Texas, Austin.

Smith, Edmund Kirby. Papers. Ramsdell Collection. Center for American History, University of Texas, Austin.

Thompson, Maj. William G. Unpublished letters to his wife concerning his tour of duty on Mustang Island, 20th Iowa Regiment. Local History Room, La Retama Library, Corpus Christi, Texas.

U.S. Navy Department. *Official Records of the Union and Confederate Navies in the War of the Rebellion.* 30 vols. Washington, D.C.: Government Printing Office, 1894–1922.

U.S. State Department. Consular dispatches and correspondence, 1864–1865. Record group 59. National Archives, Washington, D.C. Microfilm roll #4.

U.S. Treasury Department. Records of settled case files for claims approved by the Southern Claims Commission, 1871–1880 (Petition of Louisa Steinberg). Records of the accounting officers of the Department of the Treasury. Record group 217. National Archives, College Park, Md.

U.S. War Department. *War of the Rebellion: A Compilation of the Official Records of the Union and Confederate Armies,* 128 vols. (Washington: Government Printing Office, 1880–1901), series 1, vol. 9, p. 674 (hereafter cited as *ORA*).

Woods, Col. P. C., and Georgia Woods. Unpublished letters of Col. P. C. Woods and his wife, Georgia Woods, 32nd Texas Cavalry Regiment. Confederate Research Center, Hillsboro, Tex.

BOOKS, ARTICLES, AND PAMPHLETS

Alotta, Robert I. *Civil War Justice: Union Army Executions under Lincoln.* Shippensburg, Penn.: Beidel Printing House, 1989.

Anderson, Bern. *By Sea and by River: The Naval History of the Civil War.* Westport, Conn.: Greenwood Press, 1977.

Anderson, John Q., ed. *Brokenburn: The Journal of Kate Stone, 1861–1868.* Baton Rouge: Louisiana State University Press, 1955.

Annual Circular of the 62nd Regiment, U.S. Colored Infantry, no. 6. Minerva, Ohio: Weaver Brothers Steam Printing Works, 1872.

Ashcraft, Allan C. "The Union Occupation of the Lower Rio Grande Valley during the Civil War." *Texas Military History* 8(1) (1970): 18–19.

Bancroft, Hubert H. *History of the North American States and Texas.* 2 vols. San Francisco: History Company, 1890.

Barnes, J. D. *What I Saw You Do: A Brief History of the Battles, Marches, and Sieges of the Twentieth Iowa Volunteer Infantry, during Their Three Years of Active Service in the War of the Rebellion.* Port Byron, Ill.: Owen and Hall, 1896.

Barnett, Simeon. *A History of the Twenty-second Regiment, Iowa Volunteer Infantry.* Iowa City, Iowa: N. H. Brainerd, 1865.

Barney, Chester. *Recollections of Field Service with the Twentieth Iowa Infantry Volunteers: or, What I Saw in the Army.* Davenport, Iowa: Gazette Job Rooms, 1865.

Barr, Alwyn. "The 'Queen City of the Gulf' Held Hostage: The Impact of the War on Confederate Galveston." *Military History of the West* 27 (Fall 1997): 124–25.

———. "Texas Coastal Defense, 1861–1865." *Southwestern Historical Quarterly* 65 (July 1961): 28.

Basler, Roy P., ed. *The Collected Works of Abraham Lincoln.* 9 vols. New Brunswick, N.J.: Rutgers University Press, 1953.

Bentley, W. H. *History of the 77th Illinois Volunteer Infantry.* Peoria, Ill.: Edward Hine, 1883.

Bering, John A. *Forty-eighth Ohio Veteran Volunteer Infantry.* Hillsboro, Ohio: *Highland News* Office, 1880.

Beverly, James M. *A History of the Ninety-first Regiment, Illinois Volunteer Infantry, 1862–1865.* White Hall, Ill.: Pearce Printing, 1913.

Blessington, Joseph. *The Campaigns of Walker's Texas Division.* New York: Lang, Little, 1875.

Boatner, Mark M. *The Civil War Dictionary.* New York: David McKay, 1959.

Bowman, John S., ed. *The Civil War Almanac.* New York: Gallery Books, 1983.

Brown, John H. *History of Texas from 1685 to 1892.* 2 vols. St. Louis: Becktold, 1893.

Brown, Norman D., ed. *Journey to Pleasant Hill: The Civil War Letters of Captain Elijah P. Petty, Walker's Texas Division, CSA.* San Antonio: Institute of Texan Cultures, 1982.

Casdorph, Paul D. *Prince John Magruder: His Life and Campaigns.* New York: John Wiley and Sons, 1996.

Chance, Joseph E. *From Shiloh to Vicksburg: The Second Texas Infantry.* Austin: Eakin Press, 1984.

Cheeseman, Bruce S. "'Let us have 500 good determined Texans': Richard King's Account of the Union Invasion of South Texas, November 12, 1863, to January 20, 1864." *Southwestern Historical Quarterly* 101 (July 1997): 91.

Clark, James S. *Life in the Middle West: Reminiscences of J. S. Clark.* Chicago: Advance, 1916.

Crooke, George. *The Twenty-first Regiment of Iowa Volunteer Infantry.* Milwaukee: King, Fowle, 1891.

Daddysman, James. *The Matamoros Trade: Confederate Commerce, Diplomacy, and Intrigue.* Newark: University of Delaware Press, 1984.

Davis, Jefferson. *The Rise and Fall of the Confederate Government.* New York: D. Appleton, 1881.

Day, James M. "Leon Smith: Confederate Mariner." *East Texas Historical Journal* 3 (March 1965): 41–43.

Delaney, Robert W. "Matamoros, Port for Texas during the Civil War." *Southwestern Historical Quarterly* 58 (April 1955): 470, 480.

Drago, Harry S. *The Steamboaters.* New York: Dodd, Mead, 1967.

Duaine, Carl L. *The Dead Men Wore Boots: An Account of the 32nd Texas Volunteer Cavalry, C.S.A., 1862–1865.* Austin: San Felipe Press, 1966.

Dungan, Irvine. *History of the 19th Regiment Iowa Volunteer Infantry.* Davenport, Iowa: Luse and Griggs, 1865.

Edwards, John N. *Shelby's Expedition to Mexico.* Austin: Steck, 1964.

Fehrenbach, T. R. *Lone Star: A History of Texas and Texans.* New York: American Legacy Press, 1983.

Fitzhugh, Lester N. "Saluria, Fort Esperanza, and Military Operations on the Texas Coast." *Southwestern Historical Quarterly* 61 (July 1957): 96–99.

Flaherty, Daniel O. *General Jo Shelby: Undefeated Rebel.* Chapel Hill: University of North Carolina Press, 1954.

Ford, John Salmon. *Rip Ford's Texas,* ed. Stephen B. Oates. Austin: University of Texas Press, 1963.

Fremantle, Sir Arthur James Lyon. *The Fremantle Diary,* ed. Walter Lord. 1864. Reprint, Boston: Little, Brown, 1954.

Gallagher, Gary W. *The Confederate War.* Cambridge: Harvard University Press, 1997.

Gallaway, B. P., ed. *Texas, The Dark Corner of the Confederacy: Contemporary Accounts of the Lone Star State in the Civil War.* Lincoln: University of Nebraska Press, 1994.

Gammel, H. P. N. *Laws of Texas, 1822–1897.* 31 vols. Austin: Gammel Book, 1898.

Gibson, Charles D., and E. Kay Gibson. *Assault and Logistics: Union Army Coastal and River Operation, 1861–1865.* 2 vols. Camden, Maine: Ensign Press, 1995.

Gille, Frank G., ed. *Encyclopedia of Texas.* St. Claire Shores, Mich.: Somerset, 1982.

Glatthaar, Joseph T. *Forged in Battle: The Civil War Alliance of Black Soldiers and White Officers.* New York: Free Press, 1990.

Goyne, Minetta A. *Lone Star and Double Eagle: Civil War Letters of a German-Texas Family.* Fort Worth: Texas Christian University Press, 1982.

Grant, Ulysses S. *The Papers of Ulysses S. Grant,* ed. John Y. Simon. 18 vols. to date. Carbondale, Ill.: Southern Illinois University Press, 1988.

Guthrie, Keith. *Texas' Forgotten Ports.* 3 vols. Austin: Eakin Press, 1993.

Hackemer, Kurt. "Strategic Dilemma: Civil-Military Friction and the Texas Coastal Campaign of 1863." *Military History of the West* 26 (Fall 1996): 193–94.

Hanna, Alfred J., and Kathryn T. Abbey Hanna. *Napoleon III and Mexico: American Triumph over Monarchy.* Chapel Hill: University of North Carolina Press, 1971.

Hargrove, Hondon B. *Black Union Soldiers in the Civil War.* Jefferson, N.C.: McFarland, 1988.

Harrington, Fred H. *Fighting Politician: Major General Nathaniel P. Banks.* Philadelphia: University of Pennsylvania Press, 1948.

Harris, William C. *With Charity for All: Lincoln and the Restoration of the Union.* Lexington: University Press of Kentucky, 1997.

Hawkins, Wallace. *El Sal Del Rey.* Austin: State Historical Association, 1947.

Hazlett, James C., Edwin Olmstead, and M. Hume Parks. *Field Artillery Weapons of the Civil War.* Newark: University of Delaware Press, 1988.

Heartsill, W. W. *Fourteen Hundred and 91 Days in the Confederate Army; or Camp Life, Day by Day, of the W. P. Lane Rangers from April 19, 1861, to May 20, 1865,* ed. Bell I. Wiley. 1876. Reprint, Jackson, Tenn.: McCowat-Mercer Press, 1954.

Heyman, Max L., Jr. *Prudent Soldier: A Biography of Major General E. R. S. Canby, 1817–1873.* Glendale, Calif.: Arthur H. Clark, 1959.

Hinojosa, Gilberto M. *A Borderlands Town in Transition: Laredo, 1755–1870.* College Station: Texas A&M University Press, 1983.

Holladay, Florence E. "The Powers of the Commander of the Confederate Trans-Mississippi Department, 1863–1865." *Southwestern Historical Quarterly* 21 (October 1918): 279–98.

Hollandsworth, James G., Jr. *Pretense of Glory: The Life of General Nathaniel P. Banks.* Baton Rouge: Louisiana State University Press, 1998.

Horgan, Paul. *Great River: The Rio Grande in North American History.* New York: Rinehart, 1954.

Hughes, William J. *Rebellious Ranger: Rip Ford and the Old Southwest.* Norman: University of Oklahoma Press, 1964.

Hunt, Jeffrey W. *The Last Battle of the Civil War: Palmetto Ranch.* Austin: University of Texas Press, 2002.

Huson, Hobart. *Refugio: A Comprehensive History of Refugio County from Ab-original Times to 1953.* Houston: Guardsman, 1953.

Irby, James A. *Backdoor at Bagdad: The Civil War on the Rio Grande.* El Paso: Texas Western Press, 1977.

Johnson, Ludwell H. *Red River Campaign: Politics and Cotton in the Civil War.* Baltimore: Johns Hopkins Press, 1958.

Jones, S. C. *Reminiscences of the Twenty-second Iowa Volunteer Infantry, Giv-ing Its Organization, Marches, Skirmishes, Battles, and Sieges, as Taken from the Diary of Lieutenant S. C. Jones of Company A.* Iowa City, Iowa, 1907.

Josephy, Alvin M. *The Civil War in the Southwest.* New York: Knopf, 1992.

Kearney, Milo, and Anthony Knopp. *Boom and Bust: The Historical Cycles of Matamoros and Brownsville.* Austin: Eakin Press, 1991.

Kellersberger, Getulius. *Memoirs of an Engineer in the Confederate Army in Texas,* trans. Helen S. Sundstrom. Austin: privately printed, 1957.

Kelley, Pat. *River of Lost Dreams.* Lincoln: University of Nebraska Press, 1986.

Kerby, Robert L. *Kirby Smith's Confederacy: The Trans-Mississippi South, 1863–1865.* New York: Columbia University Press, 1972.

Lea, Tom. *The King Ranch.* 2 vols. Boston: Little, Brown, 1957.

Lonn, Ella. *Salt as a Factor in the Confederacy.* New York: Walter Neal, 1933.

Lowe, Richard. *The Texas Overland Expedition of 1863.* Fort Worth: Ryan Place, 1996.

Lubbock, Francis R. *Six Decades in Texas: Memoirs of Francis R. Lubbock.* Austin: Ben C. Jones, 1900.

Lufkin, Edwin B. *History of the Thirteenth Maine.* Bridgton, Maine: H. A. Shorey and Son, 1898.

Mahan, Alfred T. *The Gulf and Inland Waters.* New York: Charles Scribner's Sons, 1883.

Malsch, Brownson. *Indianola: The Mother of Western Texas.* Austin: State House Press, 1988.

Marmion, Robert. *A Texas Soldier and Marine during the Civil War, 1861–1865.* Melbourne, Australia, 1985.

Marshall, Albert O. *Army Life; From a Soldier's Journal.* Joliet: Chicago Legal News, 1884.

Marten, James A. "For the Army, the People, and Abraham Lincoln: A Yankee Newspaper in Occupied Texas." *Civil War History* 39 (June 1993): 131.

———. *Texas Divided: Loyalty and Dissent in the Lone Star State, 1856–1874.* Lexington: University Press of Kentucky, 1990.

McFeeley, William S. *Grant: A Biography.* Norwalk, Conn.: Easton Press, 1981.

McGowen, Stanley S. "Augustus Buchel: A Forgotten Texas Patriot." *Military History of the West* 25 (Spring 1995): 9.

———. *Horsesweat and Powdersmoke: The First Texas Cavalry in the Civil War.* College Station: Texas A&M University Press, 1999.

McKee, Irving. *Ben-Hur Wallace: The Life of General Lew Wallace.* Berkeley: University of California Press, 1947.

McPherson, James M. *Battle Cry of Freedom: The Civil War Era.* New York: Oxford University Press, 1988.

Meiners, Fredericka. "Hamilton Bee in the Red River Campaign." *Southwestern Historical Quarterly* 78 (July 1974): 23–38, 44.

Miller, Edward Gee. *Captain Edward Gee Miller of the 20th Wisconsin: His War, 1862–1865,* ed. W. J. Lemke. Fayetteville, Ark.: Washington County Historical Society, 1960.

Mills, Gary B. *Southern Loyalists in the Civil War: The Southern Claims Commission.* Baltimore: Genealogical Publishing, 1994.

Morsberger, Robert E., and Katherine Morsberger. *Lew Wallace: Militant Romantic.* New York: McGraw-Hill, 1980.

Muir, Andrew F. "Dick Dowling and the Battle of Sabine Pass." *Civil War History* 4 (December 1958): 193–94.

Mullins, Michael A. *The Fremont Rifles: A History of the 37th Illinois Veteran Volunteer Infantry.* Wilmington, N.C.: Broadfoot, 1990.

Nueces County Historical Association. *The History of Nueces County.* Austin: Jenkins, 1975.

Nunn, W. C. *Escape from Reconstruction.* Fort Worth: Leo Potishman, 1956.

———, ed. *Ten Texans in Gray.* Hillsboro, Tex.: Hill Junior College Press, 1968.

Oates, Stephen B. "John S. 'Rip' Ford, Prudent Cavalryman, C.S.A." *Southwestern Historical Quarterly* 64 (January 1961): 290–91.

———. *Visions of Glory: Texans on the Southwestern Frontier.* Norman: University of Oklahoma Press, 1970.

Owsley, Frank L. *State Rights in the Confederacy.* 1925. Reprint, Gloucester, Mass.: Peter Smith, 1961.

Parks, Joseph H. *General Edmund Kirby Smith.* Baton Rouge: Louisiana State University Press, 1954.

Parrish, T. Michael. *Richard Taylor: Soldier Prince of Dixie.* Chapel Hill: University of North Carolina Press, 1992.

Pierce, Frank C. *A Brief History of the Lower Rio Grande Valley.* Menasha, Wis.: George Banta, 1917.

Ramsdell, Charles W. "Texas from the Fall of the Confederacy to the Beginning of Reconstruction." *Quarterly of the Texas State Historical Association* 11 (January 1908): 205–207.

———. "The Texas State Military Board, 1862–1865." *Southwestern Historical Quarterly* 26 (April 1924): 270.

Rankin, Melinda. *Twenty Years among the Mexicans.* Cincinnati: Chase and Hall, 1875.

Rayburn, John C., and Virginia K. Rayburn. *Century of Conflict, 1821–1913: Incidents in the Lives of William Neale and William A. Neale, Early Settlers in South Texas.* Waco: Texian Press, 1966.

Reed, Rowena. *Combined Operations in the Civil War.* Annapolis: Naval Institute Press, 1978.

Rippy, J. Fred. "Mexican Projects of the Confederates." *Southwestern Historical Quarterly* (April 1919): 298–99.

Rister, Carl C. *Border Command: General Phil Sheridan in the West.* Norman: University of Oklahoma Press, 1944.

Roberts, Col. Oran M. *Confederate Military History,* extended ed. Vol. 15, *Texas.* 1899. Reprint, Wilmington, N.C.: Broadfoot, 1989.

Robertson, Brian. *Wild Horse Desert: The Heritage of South Texas.* Edinburg, Tex.: New Santander Press, 1985.

Saldivar, Gabriel. *Historia compendia de Tamaulipas.* Mexico City, 1945.

Scott, Reuben A. *The History of the 67th Regiment, Indiana Infantry Volunteers.* Bedford, Ind.: Herald Book and Job Print, 1892.

Shearer, Silas I. *Dear Companion: The Civil War Letters of Silas I. Shearer,* ed. Harold D. Brinkman. Davenport, Iowa: Harold D. Brinkman, 1995.

Sheridan, Phillip H. *Personal Memoirs of P. H. Sheridan: General U.S. Army.* 2 vols. London: Chatto and Windus, Piccadilly, 1888.

Shorey, Henry A. *The Story of the Maine Fifteenth.* Bridgton, Maine: Press of the *Bridgton News,* 1890.

Silverthorne, Elizabeth. *Ashbel Smith of Texas: Pioneer, Patriot, Statesman, 1805–1806.* College Station: Texas A&M University Press, 1982.

Simpson, Brooks D. *Ulysses S. Grant: Triumph over Adversity, 1822–1865.* Boston: Houghton Mifflin, 2000.

Simpson, Harold B., ed., and Marcus J. Wright, comp. *Texas in the Civil War, 1861–1865.* Hillsboro, Tex.: Hill Junior College Press, 1965.

Smith, Ralph J. *Reminiscences of the Civil War and Other Sketches.* Waco, Tex.: W. M. Morrison, 1962.

Smith, Rebecca W., and Marion Mullins., eds. "The Diary of H. C. Medford, Confederate Soldier, 1864." *Southwestern Historical Quarterly* 34 (October 1930): 121–23.

Smyrl, Frank H. "Texans in the Union Army, 1861–1865." *Southwestern Historical Quarterly* 65 (October 1961): 240.

Spaw, Patsy M. *The Texas Senate: Civil War to the Eve of Reform, 1861–1889.* 2 vols. College Station: Texas A&M University Press, 1999.

Stambaugh, Lillian J., and J. Lee Stambaugh. *The Lower Rio Grande Valley of Texas.* San Antonio: Naylor, 1954.

Stillman, Chauncey D. *Charles Stillman, 1810–1875.* New York: Chauncey D. Stillman, 1956.

Supplement to the Official Records of the Union and Confederate Armies. 81 vols. Wilmington, N.C.: Broadfoot, 1994.

Swap, Andrew L. *A. L. Swap in the Civil War.* Izora DeWolf, 1914.

Sweet, A. E., and J. A. Knox. *On a Mexican Mustang through Texas from the Gulf of Mexico to the Rio Grande.* St. Louis and Houston: T. N. James, 1884.

Switzer, Jacob C. "Reminiscences of Jacob Switzer of the 22nd Iowa." *Iowa Journal of History* 56 (January 1958): 44–45.

Terrell, Alexander W. *From Texas to Mexico and the Court of Maximilian.* Dallas: Book Club of Texas, 1933.

Thomas, Emory. "Rebel Nationalism: E. H. Cushing and the Rebel Experience." *Southwestern Historical Quarterly* 73 (January 1970): 349.

Thompson, Jerry Don. *Juan Cortina and the Texas-Mexico Frontier, 1859–1877.* El Paso: Texas Western Press, 1994.

———. *Mexican-Texans in the Union Army.* El Paso: Texas Western Press, 1986.

———. "Mutiny and Desertion on the Rio Grande: The Strange Saga of Captain Adrian J. Vidal." *Military History of Texas and the Southwest* 12 (1975): 160–67.

———. *Sabers on the Rio Grande.* Austin: Presidial Press, 1974.

———. "Santos Benavides and the Battle for Laredo." *Civil War Times Illustrated* 19 (August 1980): 27–28.

———. *Vaqueros in Blue and Gray.* Austin: Presidial Press, 1976.

———. *A Wild and Vivid Land: An Illustrated History of the South Texas Border.* Austin: Texas State Historical Association, 1997.

Tilley, Nannie M., ed. *Federals on the Frontier: The Diary of Benjamin F. McIntyre, 1862–1864.* Austin: University of Texas Press, 1963.

Trudeau, Noah A. *Out of the Storm: The End of the Civil War, April–June 1865.* Boston: Little, Brown, 1994.

Tyler, Ronnie C. "Cotton on the Border, 1861–1865." *Southwestern Historical Quarterly* 73 (April 1970): 477.

Tyler, Ronnie C., Douglas E. Barnett, and Roy R. Barkley, eds. *The New Handbook of Texas.* 6 vols. Austin: Texas State Historical Association, 1996.

Vandiver, Frank E., ed. "Letters from the Confederate Medical Service, 1863–1865." *Southwestern Historical Quarterly* 55 (January 1952): 381–82.

Wallace, Lew. *Lew Wallace: An Autobiography.* New York: Harper and Brothers, 1906.

Waller, John L. *Colossal Hamilton of Texas: A Biography of Andrew Jackson Hamilton, Militant Unionist and Reconstruction Governor.* El Paso: Texas Western Press, 1968.

Warner, Ezra J. *Generals in Blue: Lives of the Union Commanders.* Baton Rouge: Louisiana State University Press, 1964.

———. *Generals in Gray: Lives of the Confederate Commanders.* Baton Rouge: Louisiana State University Press, 1959.

Watson, William. *Adventures of a Blockade Runner, or Trade in Time of War.* London: T. Fisher Unwin, Paternoster Square, 1898.

Webb, Walter Prescott., ed. *The Handbook of Texas.* 2 vols. Austin: Texas State Historical Association, 1952.

Welles, Gideon. *Diary,* ed. Howard K. Beale. 3 vols. New York: W. W. Norton, 1960.

Wiley, Bell I. *The Life of Billy Yank: The Common Soldier in the Civil War.* Baton Rouge: Louisiana State University Press, 1952.

Wilkinson, Joseph B. *Laredo and the Rio Grande Frontier.* Austin: Jenkins, 1975.

Windham, William T. "The Problem of Supply in the Trans-Mississippi Confederacy." *Journal of Southern History* 22 (May 1961): 160–68.

Winsor, Bill. *Texas in the Confederacy: Military Installations, Economy, and People.* Hillsboro, Tex.: Hill Junior College Press, 1978.

Woods, Joseph T. *Services of the 96th Ohio Volunteers.* Toledo: Blade Printing and Paper, 1874.

Wooster, Ralph A. *Lone Star Regiments in Gray.* Austin: Eakin Press, 2002.

———. *Texas and Texans in the Civil War.* Austin: Eakin Press, 1995.

Yearns, Buck W., ed. *Confederate Governors*. Athens: University of Georgia Press, 1985.

Young, Kevin R. *To the Tyrants Never Yield: A Texas Civil War Sampler*. Plano, Tex.: Wordware, 1992.

THESES AND DISSERTATIONS

Briscoe, Eugenia R. "A Narrative History of Corpus Christi, Texas, 1519–1875." Ph.D. diss., University of Denver, 1972.

Crews, James R. "Reconstruction in Brownsville." Master's thesis, Texas Tech University, 1969.

Dickeson, Sherrill L. "The Texas Cotton Trade during the Civil War." Master's thesis, North Texas State University, 1967.

Dillman, Charles D. "The Functions of Brownsville, Texas, and Matamoros, Tamaulipas: Twin Cities of the Lower Rio Grande." Ph.D. diss., University of Michigan, 1968.

Felgar, John P. "Texas in the War for Southern Independence." Ph.D. diss., University of Texas, 1935.

Graf, Leroy P. "The Economic History of the Lower Rio Grande Valley, 1820–1875." Ph.D. diss., Harvard University, 1942.

Gray, Ronald N. "Edmund J. Davis: Radical Republican and Reconstruction Governor of Texas." Ph.D. diss., Texas Tech University, 1976.

Hildebrand, Walter W. "The History of Cameron County, Texas." Master's thesis, North Texas State College, 1950.

Hoekstra, Robert. "A Historical Study of the Texas Ports in the Civil War." Master's thesis, Texas A&I University, 1951.

Irby, James A. "Line of the Rio Grande: War and Trade on the Confederate Frontier, 1861–1865." Ph.D. diss., University of Georgia, 1969.

Marcum, Richard T. "Fort Brown, Texas: The History of a Border Post." Ph.D. diss., Texas Technological College, 1964.

McGowen, Stanley S. "Horsesweat and Powdersmoke: The 1st Texas Cavalry in the Civil War." Ph.D. diss., Texas Christian University, 1997.

Petrovich, Margaret. "The Civil War Career of Colonel John Salmon 'RIP' Ford." Master's thesis, Stephen F. Austin College, 1961.

Thompson, James H. "A Nineteenth-century History of Cameron County, Texas." Master's thesis, University of Texas at Austin, 1965.

Townsend, Stephen A. "Steamboating on the Lower Rio Grande River." Master's thesis, Texas A&I University, 1989.

INDEX

Note: Photographs, maps and illustrations are noted in the index as **_italicized and bolded._** Newspapers are noted in _italics_. Union and Confederate regiments are listed at the start of the index, in numerical order.

body, 17; Granite City, 14, 36–37;
John F. Carr; 37, 62, 80; Mary Hill,
62; Matamoros, 26, 101, 112;
McClellan, 17, 26; Monongahela,
16, 26–27, 37; Mustang, 101;
Owasco, 16, 18; Penobscot, 37;
Planter, 64; U.S.S. Portsmouth, 4;
Sachem, 14, 74; Sciota, 36–38, 73,
74; Square Nose, 66; Virginia, 16,
26; Zephyr,80
Showalter, Daniel, 96, 99, 101, 105,
110
Shreveport, 12–13, 16, 46, 70, 76, 123
Slaughter, James E.: as commander of
Confederate forces at Brownsville,
102, 104, 118–21, 127–130, 134;
as commander of the Western Sub-
district, 114–16, 136–38
Smith, Ashbel, 61, 70, 75
Smith, Edmund Kirby: with the
Arkansas District, 114; as com-
mander of the Confederate Trans-
Mississippi Department, 45–48, 51,
54, 120–21, 123–25; with France,
116, 119; when surrendering Con-
federacy, 132–37; regarding Texas
coast, 58–61
Smith, Leon, 62
South Texas (Austin to the Rio
Grande), 11–12, 39, 48, 50–51, 107,
146–48
Southern Claims Commission, 65–66
Speed, James, 34–35
Sprague, John T., 124, 135–36
Stanton, Edwin M., 10, 42
Steele, Frederick, 43, 69, 85, 134, 139
Stillman, Charles, 4, 19, 148
Strong, James H., 16, 18
Swap, Andrew L., 33
Swisher, John M., 100

Taylor, Richard (Captain), 20, 35
Taylor, Richard (General), 15, 124
Taylor, Zachary, 18–19

Temple, Phillip E., 101–102
Ten Percent Plan, 70, 86.
See also Abraham Lincoln
(and administration).
Texas Marine Department, 61–62
Texas Overland Expedition, 146
Texas Unionists, 10
textile mills, 8, 70
Thompson, William G., 63–66, 74,
78–79
Trans-Mississippi Department: as led
by Kirby Smith, 45–46, 54, 56,
116–18; planned surrender of, 121,
123–24, 135–36

Union Trans-Mississippi Department,
92

Vera Cruz, Mexico, 9
Vermilionville (Lafayette), 15
Veron, A., 109, 111–13
vessels: *See* ships.
Vicksburg, 3, 9, 16, 26, 45
Victoria, Texas, 48
Vidal, Adrian, 83–84
Vidaurri, Santiago, 49

Walker, John G., 110, 114, 119–20
Wallace, Lew, 6, 116–21, 123, 131,
141, 146
Ware, A.J., 95
Ware, James A., 74, 78
Warren, Fitz Henry, 35–36, 76, 82,
101
Washburn, Cadwallader C., 28–31,
38, 40, 145
Watson, William, 6
Webber, John, 101
Western Sub-District of the Depart-
ment of Texas, 114, 136–37
White's Ranch, 110–11, 127–28
Woods, P.C., 51, 60, 63
Worthington, Charles, 85, 118